Plants for
Shade and Woodland

Plants for
Shade and Woodland

Allen Paterson

Fitzhenry & Whiteside

For Eve

Fitzhenry & Whiteside
195 Allstate Parkway
Markham, Ontario L3R 4T8

Photographs: Allen Paterson

Design: Ian Gillen

Jacket design: Darrell McCalla

Typesetting: ISIS Communications Limited

Printed and bound in Canada

Canadian Cataloguing in Publication Data

Paterson, Allen
  Plants for shade and woodland

ISBN 0-88902-917-2

1. Gardening in the shade.   2. Shade-tolerant
plants.   I. Title.

SB434.7.P37 1986   635.9′54   C86-093580-9

Introduction

In 1980 J. M. Dent & Sons published my *Plants for Shade*, a book that was designed to encourage, in the English garden scene a greater appreciation of the wealth of lovely plants that succeed in shady conditions (England is not a country renowned for blazing sun, anyway).

At that time I was curator of the historic Chelsea Physic Garden in London and had myself been gardening for thirty years; Chelsea had been cultivated for over three hundred. Chelsea is situated on the bank of the River Thames, which, until the Embankment was built in the last century, watered its southern side. The spot was chosen by members of the Worshipful Society of Apothecaries of London way back in the reign of Charles II as the site for their teaching garden for just the reasons that still make it one of the most favoured spots in Britain: it has light soil and an amazingly mild climate.

Established in 1673, the Physic Garden (or the *Giardino Botanico Chelseiano*, as a plaque dated 1674 on the wall still announces) is the second oldest botanical garden in England. Only Oxford predates it — by fifty years — and both were set up to support schools of medicine. Students regularly visited to learn to recognize the plants then considered of importance medicinally, and the gardens collected new species as, in that age of discovery, they flowed in from new worlds. From Chelsea, too, excursions were made into the surrounding countryside so that the apprentice apothecaries, who might well be obliged to make up the medicines they dispensed when in medical practice, could identify plants in the field. It was of no small importance to be able to distinguish woody nightshade from deadly nightshade, or foxglove from feverfew!

For teaching purposes the Chelsea Garden was laid out systematically rather like those of the Italian universities that initiated these early outdoor biological laboratories. The first were at Padua and Pisa in the

1540s, and the trend moved north with the extension of Renaissance learning. Soon botanical or physic (these were then synonymous terms) gardens flourished in Montpellier, Paris and Leiden. Like these other historic gardens that survive on their original sites, Chelsea is tiny in modern botanical garden terms — its surrounding countryside has been swallowed up by suburbia. But it is an inner-city oasis of extraordinary interest to anyone who loves plants.

An axiom of botanical gardens today is that they grow as wide a range of species as their conditions permit, to demonstrate to students the amazing diversity of the world of plants. On less than four acres it is hardly possible to grow representatives of all families, trees and shrubs, perennials and annuals from all over the world. But we tried. Not surprisingly, with five thousand or so different species things were a bit tight.

Yet that situation is the norm with most keen gardeners, however much or little space they have. There is never enough room, though sense would suggest the opposite (Who is going to look after it all, one might ask in a sober moment, as yet another bed is made?). To grow all one's favourite plants means using every speck of ground, every situation. With this philosophy, which clearly many people probably hold without ever really thinking about it, it is wonderful to see what effects are produced in small suburban plots and even smaller city courtyards.

Owners of those gardens have learned, as I did at Chelsea, that one must take a layered approach. Under trees there are shrubs; under shrubs there are herbaceous perennials, which in turn may grow out of a bed of low ground cover. Not all plants one admires will take this treatment: many must have full sun to survive, let alone flourish. But very many will, because they are evolutionarily programmed to succeed at these lower levels. These are the *Plants for Shade and Woodland*. Very few gardens can do without them if a fully furnished effect is to be obtained. No garden should be without them, because many are among the most beautiful plants we can grow.

Though North America was not entirely new to me, moving to Canada in 1981 emphasized, in a new gardening scene, that growing shade-tolerant plants was just as important here. Indeed, it is probably more so. Town and city gardens have similar needs wherever our Western life-style is followed, whether the gardens be in New Hampshire, New Brunswick or New Zealand: they are outdoor rooms that need furnishing. But here, in northeastern North America, we live in an area that until quite recently was entirely forested. Much of that forest still remains. Real estate agents, and presumably their clients, too, consider ravine lots especially desirable. Certainly such backyards offer the garden privacy that most lack today (but, then, of course, that is a quality that North Americans traditionally hold less dear than the British). And those lots are invariably wooded, as indeed are vast areas of flat land now being built upon. For intending gardeners, what is often unhelpfully called "the problem of shade" then raises its ominous head. What will grow in these naturally shaded sites or in those town yards bounded by high walls or in the lee of a high rise?

The answer is lots. Lots of the loveliest hardy plants known to man, or at least to keen gardeners. This is so true that many people go to great lengths to contrive the shade necessary to grow them. But if a shady site is seen as a problem, it will remain so forever; it will contain etiolated specimens of plants that the owner is determined to grow, or tries to, because he has not taken the trouble to look beyond the nearest garden centre for anything different. But those sun lovers will fail to flower properly and flop flat at the first summer storm. The situation must be turned around. The shade must be seen as encouragement, opportunity, *potential*. And there is no lack of good plants to fulfill it.

In my 1980 *Plants for Shade*, reference is made to "American plants." This was again using the term for a popular category of plants fashionable at the turn of the eighteenth and nineteenth centuries in Europe, especially in Britain. The botanical wonders of eastern North America were just becoming available to other than the few botanical gardens such as Chelsea and to private enthusiasts who had sponsored Mark Catesby and John and William Bartram, to name perhaps the most significant eighteenth-century plant collectors in America. My own famous Chelsea predecessor, Philip Miller (1700-1772) grew and wrote about these plants; his great *Dictionary of Gardening* helped to popularize them.

It must be remembered that until the accession of Britain's Queen Victoria in 1837, Europeans had seen little of the central parts of the vast North American continent. The Pilgrim fathers and their immediate successors merely scratched the maritime edge, and while the eighteenth century saw the development of a highly sophisticated and elegant Georgian life-style in both pre- and post-colonial cities, most settlers remained within the eastern forested belt. Opening the West remained the immigrants' dream, and this was only gradually achieved. One is still impressed by the immensity of the forested land, in spite of increasing depredations over three hundred and fifty years. At the time it must have appeared daunting in the extreme.

Drive hard for a full day due west from the New England coast. The Massachusetts Turnpike to Albany rushes you through unending forest; New York Route 90 takes you over to Buffalo and beyond. Along the southern shore of Lake Erie the forests continue, until at last, just beyond Cleveland, the first natural indications of the West occur: tiny precursors of the prairies. Trees are at last in the descendant, yet woodland, though of different types, continues for almost the same distance again.

The forest was king for hundreds of miles when the settlers arrived, and marvellously, it still is for much of the distance. Travel the same distance north of the line, cross into Canada at Niagara, or continue in America into Vermont or Maine, and the trees do or did march onward. To the south the same applies. Over this vast area, then, "majestic forests wave," to use Milton's phrase, varying in species type, but where latitude is little adulterated by altitude. This is the area scoured by those early collectors of "American plants."

They collected acorns from a dozen different oaks, all new to Western science, masses of maples (including one from whose sap it was seen that native people miraculously made sugar at the end of every winter), tulip trees, *Catalpa*, sweet gum; botanical treasurers seemed endless. And not just trees. Beneath them and in the forest clearings they found fine shrubs, and in spring were amazed by the sheets of trilliums and trout lilies, anemones and May-apples that covered the forest floor.

The extent of eastern woodlands can be mapped to show the differing areas of the major or dominant tree species. These in turn reflect not only climate, but also aspect and soil type to which different trees are particularly adapted. Similarly the understories of shrubs, herbaceous perennials and ferns will vary. One of the most diverse of the natural plant associations in this part of northeastern America is also the most productive of fine garden plants, especially plants for shade and woodland.

This is the Carolinian Forest flora. The forest's centre, as the name suggests, is in the Appalachian and Allegheny mountains of the Carolinas, but it spreads northward into Canada. Here in southern Ontario, of all Canadian natural floristic types it is most in danger of extinction, having been extensively cleared for agriculture over the past one hundred and fifty years. Though it once covered the north shore of Lake Erie and extended to a line drawn from London to Toronto, only vestiges now remain. Of Essex County, for instance, only a pathetic three percent of original forest still remains.

The point of this discussion is threefold. First, northeastern North America, the area for which this book is written, is or was almost fully forested. Beneath the trees has developed an extraordinarily beautiful ground flora made up of plants that, *faute de mieux*, are shade lovers. Thus we have all around us, for those willing to look and to think about what they see, a vast living textbook. This ground flora dismissed the problem of shade because it came to terms with it constructively over evolutionary time. Good North American gardeners do the same, but don't need to take so long.

Those early nineteenth-century European gardeners who sought American plants with such avidity were seeing an entirely new garden flora there. A clump of *Trillium grandiflorum* in full flower is still enough to invite the neighbours in for a Sunday prelunch drink to admire this exotic beauty. In North America, where it can be found by the acre, it is apt to be accepted rather casually as a pleasant wildflower. Even that complimentary title is restricted in its use: many marvellous plants fall over the edge into the category of weeds. Think how North Americans laugh when they see goldenrod carefully cultivated in an English stately home herbaceous border. There is something here about prophets not being without honour save in their own country. I shall employ this useful phrase again.

In Europe, to "American plants" in the "American border" were added forest and woodland edge plants from other areas of the temperate world as it began to be opened up to plant collectors. Suddenly, it seemed, European gardeners looked east instead of west. Products of Chinese and Japanese gardens, cultivated ceremonially for centuries, came by tea clipper. Chrysanthemums and camellias, peonies and azaleas, hitherto seen only as accompaniments to embroidered mandarins and dragons on screens and pots, became real.

And slowly the eastern Asiatic hinterland right up into the Himalayan peaks and beyond became grist to the plant collector's mill. The first half of our own century saw the high point of this activity. It must have seemed to Forrest and Kingdon-Ward, Farrer, Sargent and "Chinese" Wilson as if the very creation of the plant world had its epicentre in those Himalayan foothills. Unfortunately for gardens in our area, with the exception of Sargent and Ernest Wilson, who later became assistant director of Harvard's Arnold Arboretum, those epic journeys were made with Britain's gardens in mind. Many of the best shade-loving plants, especially among the rhododendrons, are not frost hardy with us. However, as those areas begin to be available again to travellers, another generation of collectors is even now gathering seeds and living material. Better forms of species at the highest limit of their range will surely provide further plants for our gardens. The future is not entirely in the hands of plant breeders; nature has still untold treasures to offer.

These riches are not all in the remote and mysterious Orient. From the moment the eyes of the colonialist world turned in that direction, creative collecting virtually ceased in eastern North America; apparently it had "been done." This is not to say that huge areas were not regularly depleted of trilliums and other well-known species and sold by mail order or over the shop counter in America and Europe. But only very recently is a systematic survey being done of other potentially valuable *garden* plants from the east of the country. Mount Cuba, near Philadelphia, is a great private estate now being turned into a research institution for just this role, under the leadership of Richard Lighty, latterly director of the Longwood educational program.

What becomes possible today with ever increasing sophistication of propagation methods is that a single new worthwhile form can be bulked up clonally by micropropagation in a tenth of the time it would take by conventional division. Rare *Hosta* and *Helleborus* hybrids are prime candidates for this. It is also now possible to keep ahead of virus debilitation and fungal-disease susceptibility.

Like any art form, gardens and gardening have always been subject to fashion. While the shade-loving plants, which are the subject of this book, have been admired and grown by the cognoscenti, we now seem to see them in the ascendant. There are several reasons. The room outside, regardless of its aspect, is today considered an essential adjunct to the house, and this room has to be furnished. Conventional labour saving, though obviously still very important, is beginning to be seen as having a stultifying effect: *Pachysandra* is a marvellous ground-cover plant, but by the acre it becomes more than a little dull. Herbaceous perennials, on the other hand, start to lose their image of grand country-house border plants, for their diversity makes it possible to find plants for all positions. And last, in North America there is a growing pride in the native wild plants that used to be taken so much for granted. In the more forward-looking states and counties, roadsides are encouraged to return from a dreary monoculture of grasses to a mixed community of brightly flowering wild perennials. Garden owners with large informal lawn areas are attempting the same. All find it ultimately more economical in maintenance — and more beautiful into the bargain.

Those species, of course, are generally prairie and meadow plants, but the attitude, in many ways a social one that encourages this trend — is the same as the one that sees shade in the garden as a potential for pleasure, not a problem or pain. *Plants for Shade and Woodland* is intended to be a part of that encouragement.

Part I

The Potential
of Shade

The Search for Shade

One of the great pleasures of gardening lies in that basic promise of a garden — that each is its owner's attempt at creating a personal paradise on earth. This may sound a pretty excessive claim; indeed, to suggest to some that man can himself "create" is little short of apostasy. Yet in the conceiving of what is loved and enjoyed as a whole, in the selection and arrangement of the parts and in the effective cultivation of the plants (itself an extraordinary combination of art and science) we most of us get as close to conscious creation as is ever likely.

The corollary to the fact of a *personal* paradise lies in the fact that every garden is different. The strips of land behind a 1950s subdivision, or the necessarily smaller plots behind those in a current development, may seem at first sight to possess a daunting similarity, but even before the choice or taste of the owners has been brought to bear, basic differences often exist. In the context of this book, the immediate difference between two otherwise identical pieces of ground each side of the dividing fence of a pair of conventional semidetached houses is highly significant. In bigger country gardens with a range of aspects, varying shade and even diversity of soil types, the possibilities of personal individuality are enormous.

It is, then, the effective use of a given site that in general makes a good garden. This consists of working with, rather than against, those given facts that exist and that cannot, without excessive expenditure of time or money — if at all — be easily altered. For it seems sensible, as with any other factor of life (and certainly of gardening) to behave positively, to work constructively and think optimistically about the situations that are to be confronted. Hence the *potential* of shade is here considered a more helpful phrase than that more usual one, the *problem* of shade.

It is to be emphasized at once that a garden without shade is a dull place indeed. The word *dull* is used advisedly; it may be brilliant with the unadulterated rays of the sun, but without their opposite, without chiaroscuro, much of their virtue is lost. Successful garden making, as with any art form, lies in the effective combination and juxtaposition of opposites or dissimilars. The slow movement of a symphony lies between two quick ones; the darkness on one side of a portrait emphasizes the light on the other cheek. The movement of dancing shadows on one side of the garden enlivens the clear sun on the other.

Unlike the sister arts, however, a garden is continually moving. The position of the sun, and therefore the lie of its light, varies from morning to evening and from winter to summer. The plants themselves possess different virtues in these ever changing conditions. The effect produced by tracery of bare branches through which a low winter sun shines is utterly different from that caused by a summer noonday blaze on the leaves or flowers of the very same plant. They could be separate species as far as their visual impressions are concerned. In woodland, the leaves of the tree canopy, quivering and blowing in the wind, permit sudden increased illumination at ground level, almost as if a light had been suddenly switched on and then, equally suddenly, dimmed. This sort of variation in light concentration is possible, of course, only under living shade (though it is significant that modern technology has produced sunglasses that react similarly to increasing or decreasing sun strengths). The shade of a building or a garden wall remains shade until the sun gets above it or moves, as the day progresses, around to the side.

Yet although shade of this type from a building may be complete, the actual light concentration at ground level can be relatively high, for unlike ground under the canopy of trees, the sky above is open, even if the sun cannot be seen. This is why many tiny town courtyards can be veritable oases of green and flower colour even though they seldom get a glimpse of the sun itself. White or pale colour washing of walls and the use of plants with glossy leaves help to capitalize on all the light there is, reflecting it back and forth. Rather as atomic fuel in a nuclear reactor is never used up, light is not a consumable commodity: it is always there to the maximum amount that is allowed in.

The phrase used here, "the potential of shade," suggests two particular aspects of garden planning. One refers to making the most of shaded areas that already exist. This offers a whole range of possibilities depending upon each individual site and its features, and is considered separately in Chapter 3. The other is, accepting that a shadeless area lacks much of what makes a garden beautiful, how can shade best be contrived?

It is generally agreed that the origins of our Western culture lie somewhere, ten thousand years ago or so, in the Fertile Crescent of

Mesopotamia. This was an area that even then held water at a premium — or why was the lush greenery of Babylon's Hanging Gardens so extraordinarily remarkable to the contemporary eye that the gardens became known as one of the Wonders of the ancient world?

There followed in other emergent civilizations of the Middle East and later around the Mediterranean littoral, as each people's security became more assured, the development of the arts. Of these the art of garden making proceeded from early food-producing techniques to highly sophisticated designs reflecting the ideals of the society concerned. Gardens have always embodied the concept of perfection, actual or anticipated ("and the Lord God planted a garden eastward in Eden . . . to grow every tree that is pleasant to the sight, and good for food"). Thus, in these areas, whether in Babylon, Egypt, Greece, Rome, Spain or the Riviera, emphasis in gardens was — and to a great extent still is — upon two main factors: water and shade. Both of these in the burning heat of a southern summer are always longed for, combining as they do to form the archetypal oasis, a paradise. But to make water flow where it has not flowed before or to cause trees to grow on inhospitable hillsides is not only paradisal but also an aspect of luxury exemplified; such gardens were (and are) not free from the mere wish to show off, to impress and both to lead and follow fashion.

As in our Christian era the focus of wealth moved from the Renaissance city-states of Italy to France and then to Britain, many aspects of the classical world became encapsulated in more northern cultures, as did so much of their languages.

During the mid-eighteenth century, architects throughout Europe and North America relied almost entirely upon classical precepts and models. So it was in other fields.

In garden design formality at first held sway, based upon the Italian and French garden practice of open parterres giving way to *allées*, *bosquets* and waterworks, the essence of the well-watered and shaded Elysian fields still catering, even in Britain's dull, northern climate, to a hot southern sun. But as is well-known (though the reasons continue to trouble scholars) Britain saw a dramatic change in taste leading to perhaps its one certain contribution to the development of art: *le jardin anglais*. It hardly matters whether Capability Brown's sweeping away formal layouts and bringing the park to the very doors of the house was a direct product of Joseph Addison's pieces in the *Spectator*. ("I cannot but fancy that an orchard in flower is not infinitely preferable . . . to the most finished parterre." This one from August, 1712); or William Kent, who soon after, according to Horace Walpole, "leapt the fence and saw all nature was a garden"; or that great mathematical schemes lost favor because they were French, foreign and frightfully expensive. What is significant within the context of this chapter is that although the climate of Britain in which the new landscaped grounds were being made had in no whit changed, the models were still classical, the attitudes still Mediterranean.

This time, however, they were based upon the idealized classical scenes of the Roman *campagna* as depicted by seventeenth-century painters Claude, Poussin and their followers. Examples of these works, brought back by the "grand tourists" of the day, soon began to grace the walls of new or classically refaced country houses. These took the place, in their own bits of British *campagna* as you walked through the park, of the distant temples seen through Claude's umbrageous views. Other art forms reflect these impressions, as well.

Remember that in Handel's opera *Serse* (in English, *Xerxes, King of Persia*) the king of the title is seen languishing, or about to languish, as the curtain rises, in a *"Belvedere a canto d'un bellissimo giardino, in mezzo di cui v'e un platano."* (That is, a beautiful garden shaded by a great plane tree.) In an opening recitative he addresses the "tender boughs" of the tree, then launches into Handel's "Largo." The subject of such deep emotion, however, would be a surprise to many music lovers. The line beginning *"Ombra mai fu,"* around which the noble tune is built, can be simply translated as follows: "Never was shade cast by any tree more dear." Only acceptance of the classical ideal of protection from a burning sun can give legitimate meaning to the piece. This extraordinary eulogy to shade (written in Italian and set to music by an expatriot German for an English audience) received its first public performance on April 15, 1738, in London. It is not at all fanciful to take it as a typical eighteenth-century expectation of the way in which classical figures in a landscape behaved and moved. As in those idealized landscapes of Claude and Poussin of the previous century, shade is seen and portrayed as an essential part of any perfect scene, as the obverse of the sunlit coin. Shade and sun complement each other, and each is necessary to civilized life.

We recall another of Handel's well-known settings, this time from Pope's *Pastorals*:

> Where'er you walk, cool gales shall fan the glade;
> Trees, where you sit, shall crowd into a shade;
> Where'er you tread, the blushing flow'rs shall rise,
> And all things flourish where you turn your eyes.

Here and throughout literature, the perfection of shade is shown. Such perfection is of course in a contrived landscape — or, in other words, a garden. Handel's French contemporary, Lully, produced what is now perhaps his best-known song, "*Bois Epais*":

> Lovely woods with paths dim and silent
> A haunt of peace for weary-hearted
> There's healing in your shade
> and in your stillness balm
> For all who seek repose

Shade as a necessary and expected part of the garden is maintained throughout the literature of the eighteenth century. Cowper's phrase "happy shades" in *The Shrubbery* indicates the way his and other poets' thoughts developed. In the next century, though to modern eyes horticulturally dull in the extreme, Victorian shrubbery provided just the necessary shade and visual protection for gentle dalliance between the heavily overdressed people of that period. Perhaps, as the classical images faded, shade in the garden became more associated with fashions of dress and appearance: for ladies, layers of cloth and a milk-white skin that needed protection when in the sun. The parasol could only be lowered where trees "crowd into a shade"; otherwise only expatriot Englishmen in the company, of course, of mad dogs, went out in the midday sun. As Noel Coward reminded us, even "The smallest Malay rabbit/deplores this foolish habit."

It is at this moment that it is possible to recognize, from a horticultural point of view, the spectre — as yet not more than the cloud over Vesuvius on a fine day — of that dread gardening topic "The Problem of Shade." The real problem, however — if there is any problem at all to worry about — is that of conventionally expected summer-flowering plants.

The eighteenth century saw no need for plants in great gardens to flower within the broad vistas seen from the house. They appeared in walled kitchen gardens and were available for indoor decoration, while unfashion-conscious cottage gardens possessed, no doubt, something of the happy miscellany that ordinary backyards still possess. The nineteenth century saw the introduction of numbers of exotic flowers that, with the rapid expanding technology of the time, could be grown under glass and planted out to produce the dazzling displays still to be seen in public parks and, to a lesser extent, everywhere else. People *like* petunias, and why not, indeed? The shrubbery kept to shrubs, while the open space was reserved for carpet bedding. Never, it might have seemed, would the twain have needed to meet. But horticultural innovators in the late 1800s such as William Robinson and Gertrude Jekyll recognized an ambiguity here. The shrubbery, with all its dark and gloomy Victorian connotations (so different from, for instance, eighteenth-century Sir Brooke Boothby's comfortably elegant "chequered shade," as his portrait by Joseph Wright of Derby amusingly shows) offered in fact great possibilities for the growing of many admirable plants that actually liked shade. This fact was emphasized by the artificiality of the carpet-bedding craze.

In many cases the plants were already to hand: the "American plants" (already mentioned, that became synonymous with calcifuge or lime-hating shrubby species regardless of their geographical origin) had already attracted some keen adherents, particularly at the beginning of the nineteenth century, and as the century progressed further, additional plants of this type from the Old and New World were brought in. Also, a mid-nineteenth-century enthusiasm for a diversity of hardy ferns brought some use to the shadier parts of the garden (consciously planted or naturally so).

Perhaps had society stayed static, the plantsmanship of Robinson and Jekyll and other early twentieth-century innovative plantsmen would have ensured that the traditional parts of the garden, open and shaded, would have remained equally necessary and equally used. But society and fashion do not remain static.

Several trends can be traced. As the twentieth century progressed, with the problems of obtaining and affording good paid help, gardens tended to become smaller. The once expected progression of terraces giving way to lawns, merging into woodland (natural or contrived), with separate gardens for specific groups of plants, ceased to be possible. Obviously many great gardens continued and, fortunately, still continue to be maintained. A few new gardens on the grand scale continue to be made. But the diminution is inevitable and inexorable, and no direct concern of this book. Except that with changes in garden styles has likewise come, a change in what people do in gardens. Decorous tea taken in formal dress under the necessary shade of the deodar on the lawn may still occur when the vicar comes to call (in England the association is inescapable; *Cedrus deodara* was, par excellence, a vicarage lawn tree — a Victorian ballad celebrates the fact). More commonly now, alfresco meals are taken in full sun beside a swimming pool, with a minimum of clothing.

It seems, then, that we have moved into a new age of Helios worshippers, whose acolytes are trained at various coeducational seminaries labelled "Clubs Méditerranées." So dominant has this "liberated" attitude become that it permeates a surprising number of aspects of contemporary life — not always to their benefit. Glass walls of office blocks and public buildings need immediate internal shading; "picture windows" (often with no picture in view but the opposite identical window across the road) in new subdivisions have to be draped immediately in a multiplicity of curtains for privacy and protection from the sun. For shade, it seems, is still necessary, and still enjoyed.

Most important, it is enjoyed by a large number of beautiful garden plants that succeed best, last longer and look best in the conditions for which they are particularly adapted. The ecological background to such development is considered in Chapter 2.

Shade Plants in the Wild

For any living organism, plant or animal, to succeed, it must be in some equilibrium with its surroundings. It is part of the food chain, or food web, by which numbers of highly dissimilar creatures are connected: it feeds; it is fed upon. To exist, to have developed, indicates that an organism has properties and adaptations that make it successful in its chosen habitat. But *chosen* is altogether too anthropomorphic a word: a mole has not chosen to live in a hole. Moles are organisms that, in response to pressures of competition and space, have managed to move into an otherwise underused ecological niche. To do so, over evolutionary time, they have made morphological adaptations that fit them ideally for such niches, just as they are unfit for anything else. Above ground, lack of effective sight would be highly disadvantageous to a mole, just as lack of strengthening tissue makes a high-and-dry water lily a poor thing indeed.

It is worthwhile keeping such general thoughts in mind when considering the broader aspects of the ways in which plants grow in the wild, because although our own garden palette may be almost entirely based upon man-bred cultivars, these are in fact still very close to their wild ancestors, and hence their needs do not differ markedly from what those forebears became adapted to and then could not manage without. This is significant when considering plants for shade and woodland situations.

First we should consider the basic facts of that branch of biology known as plant ecology. Ecology may be defined simply as the study of plants in the wild. It is not therefore primarily concerned with the cell structure of plant species (cytology) or formal relationship (taxonomy) or even with the way the plant works (physiology) — though it is bound to be concerned with the interaction of these and other branches of botany. For it is such interaction within individual plants that makes them interact with one another and makes possible, in response to the external factors of climate and soil, the typical aspects that we recognize when passing through any bit of countryside.

Even to the casual observer, that westward forest drive from the Atlantic Coast inland, starting in Maine, New Hampshire or Massachusetts, clearly moves through different zones. Pines seem to predominate at the start — especially on those Desert of Maine sands — and change gradually to deciduous oaks and maples. The whole feeling of the roadside changes.

Visitors to Britain are surprised at how a much shorter journey takes them through several distinct vegetative types. London to Bath is a splendid example as Surrey heathlands give onto chalk downlands (recent road cuttings help diagnosis no end) and later mixed woodland. Even to a casual observer — preferably not the driver, since botanizing at speed is not to be recommended — the vegetation, even if not identified, is different. The sparse yews and juniper, with traveller's joy clambering about, present a very different impression from the thicker canopy in the clay vale or the broad sweeps of purple heather on the moors.

Each of these areas has its own particular plant communities that make up clearly recognizable units of vegetation. Throughout the world such distinct communities, often highly diverse, can be found. The maquis of the Mediterranean or chaparral of Southern California is a community of tough thorny shrubs protecting an understory of early-flowering herbaceous plants. In the jungle of the Amazon headwaters, great trees, lianas, epiphytes and eventually terrestrial species combine to form an equally typical, though utterly different, layered community.

Within each community, however, there are usually smaller recognizable plant groups in which one type of plant is the most noticeable and has something of an overbearing effect upon its fellows. This is the dominant species or, if there are more than one, the co-dominants. Such a group is called a plant association, and any number of associations make up a plant community.

Since we are concerned here with shade-tolerant plants, it is suitable to choose mixed woodland to illustrate these ecological terms. In doing so something of the lives of woodland plants can be discovered.

Because it is in sight of my window as I write, I take a bit of the Niagara Escarpment, about fifty miles north of the falls. Sugar maple is the dominant tree, probably encouraged by landowners over the past two hundred years but still accompanied by white and red oaks, a few white pines (the best went years ago as masts for sailing ships) and so on. Mixed woodland. In the shade grows witch hazel, its branches tinged gold with flowers in November, and dogwood and brambles. Below these are herbaceous perennials, the lovely wildflowers of our spring, bloodroot and hepatica, trillium and trout lily.

Lower still, both in stature and evolutionary order, are ferns, mosses, a liverwort or two and algae. Such a community will not be constant, for where shade is less dense or availability of soil moisture or nutrient varies, clear associations develop. Herbaceous May-apple may be dominant in any one area over a number of less frequent species, and we could refer to this subunit as a May-apple association.

It is obvious that what is being described is the layered effect of natural vegetation or, as it is usually described, its stratification. Leave any area of soil free, even in the middle of the biggest town, and plants will take over, gradually building up to the community of plants that is natural to that area. (Or as near natural as is possible. In Toronto, for example, the availability of acorns to provide the eventual oak-tree layer that has been displaced by a hundred years of man's activities may be replaced by Manitoba maple, an immediate native colonizer, or the Asian tree of heaven, with subsequent differences in the lower layers because the humus formed by fallen leaves would be different.) Toronto without man would revert to woodland, however composed.

Hopefully such a contingency, except in the inflated imaginations of science-fiction writers is not likely to occur. But in the country it does. A marvellously documented example of this in Britain is at Rothamsted Agricultural Research Station, where small areas of land have been consciously left for over a hundred years naturally to regenerate from ploughland to Hertfordshire woodland. At our Royal Botanical Gardens, Hamilton, similar demonstrations on a once arable field now have two decades behind them, and already the effects are clear. The process is predictable and wonderful to observe.

First appear the small-seeded annual garden weeds, whose seeds may have been dormant for decades or recently blown in. Their rapid life cycle will soon be repeated, but by the end of the first year some plants are clearly going to overwinter. Such herbaceous perennials are soon joined by shrubs — dogwood or hawthorn — as birds coming to collect seeds leave the pips of fruits they have consumed earlier elsewhere. In the protection of these bushes tree seedlings grow into saplings and emerge above them, the speed of such regeneration depending on soil nutrients, weather and perhaps animals. Meanwhile, of course, the annuals have been crowded out, and no bare soil being available, further germination is impossible. Shortly, too, the earlier perennial colonizers will lack the space and full sun they initially enjoyed, and they will also have to move on. Eventually, then, a climax community fully adapted to the competition, the climate and the soil has developed and settles into the equilibrium mentioned at the beginning of this chapter. No doubt such apparent calm is only relative and this description is a gross oversimplification of what is in fact a highly complicated and sophisticated series of interactions. What is important, however, in the context of shade-tolerant plants for the garden is the realization that the best of these plants are those that, as products of such natural successions over millions of years, are programmed to succeed in just such a situation.

It is worthwhile examining the behaviour of woodland as it affects the plants in the lower levels, and also to consider the different types of natural woodland, because each encourages its own type of understory and, in a garden sense, permits a different range of introduced plants.

Entirely deciduous woodland as we know it is very much a western European speciality. The admixture of some coniferous evergreens in our area reflects the more extreme continental climate. This relatively temperate climatic zone with a marked but not excessively prolonged cold season is almost exclusively typical of the Northern Hemisphere, with the exception of certain mountainous districts in New Zealand and South America (these might well produce useful garden plants for us). In all areas with a marked winter, plants have to come to terms with low temperatures. In temperate zones most herbaceous plants go underground, and trees survive by dropping their leaves and becoming semidormant; the deciduous habit is obligatory − a product of evolutionary adaptation to habitat. Even if grown under glass, deciduous trees will colour and shed their leaves just as if they were outside.

What triggers this is still not fully explained, but day length must have some close effect, because each species goes through the process over a very short span regardless of where grown. The dramatic fall colours of Vermont and New England make an annual pageant that is splendidly predictable.

It should be noted in passing that many trees in tropical forests do become deciduous while not being typical deciduous trees. Their habit is a facultative leaf shedding that is less seasonal and not necessarily annual, but caused by the tree-soil-water balance being upset by drought. An emergency transpiration reduction becomes necessary, and how better to do this than by shedding those organs through which water loss occurs? Conversely there are very few evergreen broad-leaved plants of north temperate woodlands. In Britain they can be listed on fewer than the fingers of one hand: holly, ivy, box, Daphne laureola − and the last two are pretty uncommon at that. All must be seen as being on the northern limit on their range, and they get that far north only because of the modifying influence of the Gulf Stream Drift and of being on the western side of a great continental land mass.

In our area, though vastly bigger, there are fewer still. Mountain Laurel (*Kalmia latifolia*) is one, but as its name suggests, it is not really a woodland plant, though in cultivation it will take shade. The southern Appalachians impinge on an evergreen flora with Rhododendrons and other fine plants, but of course they do not enjoy winters farther north. Sending that famed Gulf Stream current across the Atlantic may be good for international relations, but it does reduce the numbers of good evergreens our gardens can grow.

The shorter summer (and longer winter) to the north and east and in montane regions of continental Europe and of North America encourages evergreen conifers. Their needlelike leaves are very resistant to winter cold and also to water loss (referred to as being xeromorphic). They are thus present to photosynthesize very early in spring and exploit the short summer to greatest effect. Larch, (tamarack), incidentally, though deciduous, manages to succeed with a high productivity made possible by the long days of a far northern summer.

But our broad-leaved deciduous trees, and the exotic deciduous species we grow from all over the temperate world, need a warm vegetative season of at least four to six months. Leaves that open anew each spring must have a photosynthetic season ahead long enough to build up extension growth, buds and flowers, as well as to set ripe fruit to reproduce the species. Adequate moisture during the growing season is also vital. In western and central Europe north of the Alps, moisture is pretty evenly distributed throughout the year; in eastern North America and eastern Asia the maximum rain comes in summer.

Because the tree species have become adapted to succeed in such conditions by becoming leafless for nearly half the year, other species have opportunely taken on the role of filling the time gap; indeed, there is otherwise little chance in dense woodland for them to do so. They must get on with their own life cycles while there is light enough to photosynthesize, for without light green plants cannot exist. While adequate moisture, nutrients, warmth, oxygen and carbon dioxide (four essentials for plant growth) are generally present, only the equally vital illumination rapidly decreases as spring gets into its stride. This is the season of woodland floor plants.

Obviously the amount of light reaching the forest floor, or the herbaceous plants growing there, depends not only on the species but on the general age of the species that is dominant. For example, beech forest in full leaf lets very little light down, and this is especially marked in European beechwoods. Here is a tree species that grows in unusually pure stands (it must be realized that there is very little truly wild woodland, entirely unmanaged, in Britain or indeed western Europe). A walk through such a wood in high summer is an almost eerie experience; the smooth elephant-grey trunks stretch up to an unbroken canopy of pale green. The analogy with a cathedral of Gothic cluster columns is not too fanciful when associated with the quiet and shut-in calm — even the wind seems a long way off — and at one's feet, almost like the strewing herbs of medieval times, a rustling carpet of dry, undecomposed leaves. This rather frightening, otherworldly atmosphere was recorded by the early explorers of the New England forests, where great trees, never logged, shut out the sky and seemed to go on forever.

In such woodland there are virtually no other plants. Only toward the edge or in glades caused by a forest giant crashing down, where light increases, is there any clear herbaceous layer. Here orchids such as bird nest (*Neottia nidus-avis*) and Indian pipes, saprophytes not dependent on their own photosynthetic powers, are apt to occur.

The dramatic drop in light availability at the beechwood floor has been measured: mid-May, 6 percent; one week later, 3 percent; 7 June, 1.5 percent. The diversity in herbaceous species is aided in oak woods or woods by one or more co-dominants. The more open canopy can give surprising bursts of light as branches move in the wind or as the sun travels across the sky; rays and flecks of light can raise the illumination on lower plants by ten to thirty percent, if only in short bursts. Even without such unpredictability a central European oak-hornbeam forest has given the following figures: 12 March, 52 percent; 15 April, 32 percent; 10 May, 6.4 percent; 4 June, 3.7 percent.

It should not be surprising therefore that woodland floor plants — even some of the woody ones — begin their seasonal growth very early, indeed. Yet surprised one always is. Every year, gathering holly in an English mixed wood for Christmas decoration, we are apt to remark on how the bluebells are sprouting and that the honeysuckle has fresh rosettes of leaves. And this on the shortest day, or near to it. But for those plants there is as much useful light as in high summer, and they have got to move ahead or perish. They come into flower in spring, the time of primroses, bluebells and Solomon's seal, and as the tree canopy develops, the herbaceous layer yellows and rests; its autumn starts in June.

In North America the situation is very similar. With a harder winter ahead, less appears above ground in fall — though the fleshy spears of skunk cabbage are an amazing exception. But the buds of all the other woodlanders, from anemone to trillium, are there under the leaf litter in a state of suspended animation, ready to burst when spring appears. They match its speed.

It is clear therefore that the microclimate on the woodland floor is vastly different from that in the open meadow beyond. Light is not the only difference. Temperature is more moderate, cooler in summer and milder in winter. Even though the tree canopy intercepts over ten percent of the rainfall, the humidity of the air at ground level, having protection from wind, is higher. The upper layers of the soil are quicker to warm up (the slow leafing of trees is to some extent explained by the coldness of the deeper levels of soil, where most of their roots lie). It is interesting to note that many woodland floor plants appear as open-ground species at higher altitudes, where similar humidity can be obtained.

But it is not all gain. In periods of drought, trees, with their higher cell-sap salt concentrations, have a greater "pull" on the available moisture, and with it, especially on shallow soils, take much of the available plant nutrients. In such cases the usual root-layer stratification, which may be seen as something of a mirror image of what is above ground, fails to occur. How wise, then, that the herbaceous layer goes to rest before the battle begins. The fact that so many forest floor plants have evolved storage organs is significant. Bulbs, corms and tubers are vital for surviving the inclement summer period, as well as for increasing the species by vegetative means. The production of seeds must always be seen as problematical, and the barren strawberry (*Potentilla sterilis*) is one woodlander that has quite given up the struggle. Most plants, however, maintain their fight; eventually in the wild even the noblest forest giant crashes to the ground, taking others with it and opening up a wide glade for regeneration to begin, from annual to oak tree, all over again.

Shade, Shade Plants and the Site

Effective gardening in a very specialized and sophisticated way does resemble the natural colonization of a site by plants just described. For it is concerned not simply with plants that are loved, admired or coveted, but more important with choosing the right plants for the right place and therefore, in the context of this book, to be using shade-loving or shade-tolerant plants effectively. There are two aspects to this. One, obviously, is to grow on north walls, in north-facing borders, in shady courtyards of whatever aspect, or under trees and shrubs those species that accept or enjoy the position because, as has already been explained, they are evolutionarily adapted to something similar in their natural habitat. The second is to find places for plants that, because of their inherent beauty (and, it must be realized, eyes of beholders are proverbially dissimilar) cannot be left out and that need shade. These may be, to mention but a few shade-loving herbaceous things, candelabra primulas, trilliums, *Smilacina racemosa* and meconopses. The list of exquisite plants could go on (and in subsequent chapters will).

In desiring to grow such plants the possibilities (or *Capabilities*, as the famous Mr. Lancelot Brown was apt to describe them in the eighteenth century) of each site must be discovered and exploited to the full. Actual lack of full exposure to the sun is not the only criterion. Growing plants are a product of their garden's soil, moisture availability, general climate, microclimate (which the plants themselves affect and help to make), as well as aspect.

In general the type of garden soil has two main facets that affect our choice of plants. These are moisture availability and acidity or alkalinity.

Soil water can be considered as being present in two ways. In addition to the water table, it is held as a film around every soil particle and thus its amount will be determined by the size of these particles. Soil particles, which are made by the weathering of rock forms and subsequently moved and laid down by the action of glaciation, water and so on, are of many types. Because of their quantity, the smallest, those of clays, hold around them a larger amount of water than the bigger sand particles. So much so, indeed, that clay soils are, to a gardener, wet and heavy to work and often with a completely saturated water table not far down. Paradoxically, in spite of much water being present, in periods of drought plants growing in very heavy clays often find it difficult to raise the water for their use.

Sandy soils, on the other hand, hold little moisture — though what exists is usually freely available — are easy to work and are quick to warm up in spring. Of course, what most of us have is something less extreme, with a mixture of sand and clay particles, the proportion of each causing the soil to tend toward one type or the other. Few unfortunately enjoy that fabled recommended desideratum of so many plants, "a deep, rich medium loam, well drained yet retentive of moisture."

What differences of soil moisture-holding capacity mean, in the context of this book, is the ability to grow woodland plants not only in soils ameliorated by centuries of leaf fall but in nonwoodland conditions, as well. In evolving to succeed in shade, most species have relatively large leaves to capitalize on what light they can catch. Little concern need be given to moisture retention because wind and exposure do not occur, so that water loss is not much of a problem. Out of this context woodlanders demand a consistently moist soil, and this, if its structure is improved by copious addition of humus (compost, leaf mould, spent hops, very well-rotted manure and so on) a clay soil can offer.

Even here, however, full southern exposure without midday shade, or a windy position, will be unacceptable — and anyway, to repeat the vital adage of "the right plant in the right place," such a spot calls for plants that actually enjoy the conditions. But it does mean that east or west aspects as well as the entirely shaded north-facing borders can offer highly acceptable homes to many lovely woodland plants. Not surprising, plants used to cool shade will have a shorter flowering season if they spend even half their day in sun, and petals of the most susceptible may bleach or burn.

Here northern gardeners have a great advantage: the high rainfall and more moderate sun make possible the use of many southern shade lovers as normal open-garden plants. The habitat range of the plants in a good Scottish herbaceous border is often a lesson in unlikely ecological associations.

While it is comforting to realize that the groans of the clay-soil gardener can be moderated by emphasizing clay's potential in this way, those of us on the lighter sands (smugly late-autumn digging with ease even after heavy rain) need also to search out the inherent potential in summer, as well, because the disadvantages are only too clear. Sunnier aspects will encourage all types of perennation form from ephemeral annuals to shrubs. But to vary the garden scene and capitalize on the site, shady borders under a north wall or against the house may be the only possible home not only for woodlanders, but moisture lovers, too, which would stand no chance in the open garden here.

The basic physical adaptations to habitat that woodland plants have to adopt have been mentioned already more than once. There is also a chemical aspect, which affects our choice of species and cannot be neglected. It is of course the fact of soil acidity or alkalinity (liminess) that cuts such a swathe through any hopeful, but uninformed, perusal of nurserymen's catalogues.

If the type of soil is not immediately apparent from what grows naturally on the site or in other nearby gardens — one really healthy rhododendron is a clear indicator of an acid soil — it is essential that the soil be tested. The answer is given on what is referred to as the pH scale. This runs from 1-14, with 7 as the mid and hence neutral point. Simple kits are available that by colour coding give a perfectly adequate guide.

Any reading above 7 indicates a concentration of lime that makes virtually impossible the growing of several large groups of highly desirable shade-loving or shade-tolerant plants, including particularly virtually all members of the Ericaceae family (rhododendrons, azaleas, heathers, etc.). Conversely, figures below pH 7 not only permit these groups, but do not militate against any lime-tolerant species — though the kitchen garden may have trouble with cabbages.

In practice, pH 4.5 is the lowest likely to be experienced in very acid conditions, and pH 8.5 above pure limestone. Ideally, were one able to choose the "deep rich loam," etc., it would also have a pH of 6.5 that will suit every plant one might wish to grow.

The determining factors of soil pH are several, but in brief, the origin of the soil's parent rock and subsequent plant deposition are most significant. Old igneous rocks and sandstone are most likely to give acid-reacting soils, and limestones and chalk soils have a high pH. Clays and sands, depending on their origin, can be of either type and, most important, can be varied by long periods of plant growth.

Centuries of leaf fall and accumulations of other plant remains have a naturally acid reaction. Acidity is extreme in situations of poor drainage, where anaerobic conditions produce peat. More normally bacteria and fungi break down the organic material almost at the rate at which it falls and the leaf mould in mature woodland indicates the sort of material, and its amount, that most develops. Although not very acidic by comparison with peat or moorland soils, such organic matter is likely to have a pH reading below 7 even when the woodland is growing over limestone or chalk.

In the wild this will be indicated by patches of calcifuge (lime-hating) species, which often appear at variance with the surrounding vegetation, and in woodland gardens especially by the presence of ericaceous plants. Attempts to artificially create acid woodland conditions unblessed by time are invariably doomed to failure — except on the smallest scale, though raised beds of imported lime-free soil in a courtyard situation can often be admirable. These will be discussed further.

What is obvious, therefore, from this discussion is that woodland plants, which make up so large a proportion of our garden shade lovers, shrubs, herbaceous flowering plants and ferns alike, are adapted to growing in organic soils with an acid reaction of greater or lesser concentration. Successful cultivation depends, as always, on reproducing as nearly as possible the conditions the chosen plants find ideal. This will differ with the site and the type of shade being afforded. Is it from buildings or from trees?

This last needs consideration. Anyone coming to a garden soon after the house has been built will soon discover that there seem to be almost as many bricks under the soil as above it. This is nowhere more true than in the borders under the walls of the house itself (it is to be hoped that such borders actually exist: what marvellous sites for growing plants of all types are wasted when the base of walls meet not soil but a sea of concrete). For shade-loving plants the obvious aspects will be used, and in an otherwise shadeless garden the opportunities for large-leaved, architectural things are invaluable. The bigger hostas, *Rheum palmatum* and rodgersias will contrast splendidly with vertical-leaved *Iris pseudacorus 'Variegata'* or *Yucca filamentosa*.

But for such garden pictures, shade must be complemented by a humus-rich soil, which is almost certainly not present. Building works bring to the surface subsoil, often virtually inert as a plant-growing medium — even though a thin layer of carefully spread top soil may initially obscure the dread fact. Lumps of impervious clay and other unpleasantness will have to be removed entirely and the whole border brought up to scratch, literally.

The initial alkaline reaction of both mortar and concrete should not be forgotten if calcifuge species are planned, so that peat and acid leaf mould will be necessary to maintain a below 7 pH reading even on soils that would have been naturally thus. Where this problem is thought to be considerable, a dressing of two to three ounces of flowers of sulphur or aluminum sulphate to each square yard of border, forked in at least a month before planting, will help. Naturally limy soil is of course accepted, but to increase the humus level is equally vital.

However, having been well prepared, house borders need cause little subsequent problems. A balance will need to be kept between the climbers and other wall plants and the low shrubs and herbaceous plants at their feet. But because of their very nature competition is unlikely to be a great problem.

Such, unfortunately, is not always the case when planting under trees. Established open woodland with a high canopy — the sort of perfect site that in any ideal world none of us would be without — needs little said about it. The shade-tolerant species will settle down in the leaf mould like a hen on her nest. Far more common is the situation where a garden tree or two call for underplanting, or where, it being the only place, shade plants are going to be grown, come hell or high water, as the saying goes. It is, however, not very apposite; low water would be nearer the mark.

Individual trees may well not be the ideal deep-rooted oaks, but have shallow and rapacious root systems that can seem to gobble up everything you put in for the herbaceous plants, like a flock of starlings on the bird table taking food meant for chickadees. Each site and each tree will need its own treatment, and it must be realized that under some trees little will grow unless much effort is put into the remedy.

Obviously if one feeds the soil under a tree (a single specimen seldom builds up much leaf mould underneath it) with organic material or inorganic fertilizers, and provides more water in times of drought, the tree will respond by increased growth both above and below ground. Neither is likely to help the shade lovers underneath. Thus a conscious program of branch thinning (not pollarding or irresponsible cutting back) should go hand in hand with root pruning to attempt to balance the situation — careful reduction of root or crown reduces growth in the other. In some cases it may be worthwhile to excavate the soil for a foot or so to where the tree roots are omnipresent and to lay a perforated plastic membrane and irrigation pipes before returning the (improved) soil. This certainly helps to retain moisture and prevent tree roots taking more than their share, but it is difficult to avoid a feeling of artificiality. Generally it is better to accept the possible and make the most of that, rather than fight a rearguard action every inch of the way. One could, as a last resort, always move.

Reference has already been made to shade from walls and buildings, where the situation is very different from that shade afforded by trees. It is at once more permanent, yet, through lack of an overhead canopy, less

dense. Close in the lee of high-rise buildings, as with the denser evergreen trees, sun may never penetrate at all. Yet this in no way means
that highly effective planting cannot succeed.

Every ordinary detached house — or garden shed, for that matter —
offers, in the simplest analysis, four basic aspects. Perhaps they may be
considered as the sun meets them, or fails to, as the seasons and the days
progress. The variation is considerable and becomes more marked as
one progresses to the poles from the equator. At the equator, of course,
there is no differentiation of season, with perpetual (and ultimately very
boring) summer being experienced at lowland levels, and in the mountains such extraordinary daily variation as to make the inhabitants of
Quito in Ecuador (at 9,000 ft. (3 km) one of the highest capital cities in
the world) assert that their climate progresses through the seasons each
day: in the morning it is like spring, noonday is high summer, autumn
comes by late afternoon and a wintry night follows. Permanent shade in
such conditions is particularly difficult to deal with.

In our north-temperate countries things are very different. Seasons are
marked, inexorable in their progressions — though of course weather, as
distinct from climate, produces records every year. Day length, too,
enormously significant to plant growth and flowering, is highly variable.
This may be of little significance to humans, who insist upon their eight
hours of nightly sleep, but it extends plants' photosynthetic time for as
long as illumination lasts.

The other side of the coin, inevitably, is extremely short winter days,
but to plants adapted to the regime that such a climate entails, this is of
remarkably little importance, as they are by then in winter dormancy.

The significance of such day length and seasonal variation to the shade
produced by an isolated building will be obvious. The farther north in
latitude one goes, the more of the northern sky is used by the sun, and
hence an even north-facing wall will get sunshine on it early in the
morning. Successionally, therefore, an east wall will be lit until noon; the
southern aspect enjoys full sun for toward half the day. At the end of the
western exposure the north wall again gets an hour or two of low sun.
Obviously all this must be kept in mind if each aspect is to be most
effectively used.

The Shade Providers
Trees for Small Gardens

In any new garden one naturally wishes to possess the ongoing beauty of trees. Their "weight" and height are essential to give scale to buildings, they enhance good architecture, both old and new, and ameliorate that which is mediocre or downright bad. They also create shade. From a specimen lawn tree the depth of shade may not be particularly important, as planting beneath it is unusual. For ourselves, on the hottest days, even though we are no longer dressed in Victorian black bombazine or serge, complete sun protection is still welcome. The wine stays cool at lunch and the butter does not run off the dish at tea. The old phrase "grateful shade" comes to mind.

In such a spot any tree that is considered beautiful, evergreen or deciduous, broad leaved or coniferous, is suitable. The grass beneath will not be particularly good; in winter it may almost disappear, but *Poa annua* or even crabgrass will bulk it up again in summer, when it is most wanted.

Unfortunately — in new gardens, especially — although the realtor's picture may have shown the property elegantly framed in leafy boughs like a picturesque engraving, the chances are that trees are not where they are wanted. Equally, there may be one or more where they are not wanted. In this case one should live with them for a while to make sure one's garden plan or style of living cannot accommodate these great organisms that predate oneself for a century or more. The chainsaw is very final.

Choice of trees to produce shade especially for growing the lovely woodland plants that a fully sunny garden finds impossible is, however, a different matter. The perfect species has not been invented, perhaps. But it is possible to list the desiderata and choose those that come nearest to the ideal.

First, of course, as the biggest plants around, the shade-giving trees must be beautiful in their own right. (As with the oft-quoted definition of equality, all trees are beautiful, but some are more beautiful than others. Much.) They should come into leaf late and drop their leaves relatively early to give the ground-level plants a maximum of illumination at times when they are (as evolved woodlanders) at the particularly important periods of their life cycles. Hence they will not be evergreen. And the higher the canopy, the better the understory develops.

The trees' habit should be open, with rather small leaves to permit a modicum of summer light for summer-growing woodland-edge plants to succeed. And, as underground parts of plants are likely to show a similar stratification of those above, deep-rooted trees leave the upper layers of soil free for the roots of shrubs and herbaceous plants. Last, they should not harbour pests or diseases that affect the species below.

Such requirements make certain lovely trees unsuitable for a mixed-green garden community. The woodland floor under naturally growing beechwoods is bare; their canopy is so utterly effective — for them. Anything left under common lindens in summer, whether a car or a baby in its pram, gets covered in sticky honeydew. Both those prized possessions can be washed, but plant leaves hold the honeydew long enough for subsequent growth of unsightly, sooty moulds to develop. The fallen leaves of sycamores (*Platanus occidentalis*) and horse chestnuts are of such a size as to damage semiresting herbaceous plants unless raked off quickly.

Of forest-sized trees (and it should be emphasized that small to medium-sized gardens can frequently benefit from bigger trees than are often permitted), the birches are in many ways ideal. It is sensible to use the plural, because lovely though our own 'Lady of the Woods' is (the common silver birch, *Betula papyrifera*,) there are several others that should be considered. The European *Betula pendula* 'Tristis' is taller, with delicate weeping branches. The Swedish birch is rather similar and equally beautiful.

From farther east come the lovely *Betula jacquemontii*, with brilliantly white trunks, and *Betula ermanii*, taller and with pinkish bark. *Betula* 'Whitespire' is a recent selection of the Japanese white birch that is relatively immune to borer, though the depredations of that wretched pest are always somewhat erratic. All these birches are splendid light-shade givers and their lovely trunks are enhanced by careful association of shade-tolerant plants beneath. Much of the beauty of birches in the wild lies in their frequently irregular growth. Gardeners are not foresters to whom gnarled and crossing trunks are understandably anathema. Thus the conventional straight standard tree is often best replaced by a multistemmed specimen. If this is not available from the nursery, three to five young plants — seedlings a couple of years or so old — can be carefully planted in one hole. Mutual competition will cause growth to lean outward and a beautiful "single" plant with several trunks will develop in a few years.

A similar growth pattern can be encouraged in other light-shade trees. If a deep moist soil is available *Cercidiphyllum japonicum*, the katsura tree, is a good choice — though not in areas subject to late-spring frosts. To fine shape and texture are added varying autumn colours as an annual, if unpredictable, bonus.

Other trees offer spring flowers, such as the small-leaved magnolias, for example *Magnolia kobus*, *Magnolia salicifolia* and *Magnolia x loebneri* (the latter is perfectly happy on very limy soils). So, too, do the more delicate crab apples and cherries. In almost all cases the wild species, if not so dramatic in their floral display, are more suitable for this particular garden role. They include *Malus toringoides* and *Malus transitoria* and *Prunus subhirtella* (the winter cherry is one of its forms and ideal above summer-flowering shade-lovers because its area thus offers interest for many months of the year). Closely related is the delicate *Amelanchier canadensis*. Much bigger but excellent for the job is our native *A. arborea*, which will get to forty or fifty feet high. *Amelanchier x grandiflora* is a hybrid of this, with finer flowers; pink-flushed selections are being offered under the names of 'Robin Hill' and 'Rubescens.' All have a fleeting flush of flowers, but summer fruit (delicious if you can beat the birds to it) and autumn colour add other seasons of value to these shadbushes.

Good, too, are the mountain ashes — species of *Sorbus* of the *Aucuparia* section. These have elegant ferny leaves, very distinct from the heavier foliage of the white-beam-type members of the genus. Young plants of mountain ash can be turned into multistemmed specimens as described for birches. Again the effect is so much more attractive than a straight nursery-stock standard standing to attention. All these cherries and mountain ashes, crabs and shadbushes are closely related (being in the rose family). The first pair prefer light sandy soils with good drainage, while the others can take heavy clay. However, in terms of most trees, none have a great life span; decades rather than centuries are the rule.

For small gardens other good shade trees are *Styrax japonica* — lime-free soil is essential — some of the maples such as *Acer negundo* 'Variegatum,' *Acer griseum* (rather slow growing, but the distinctive and attractive flaking bark shows from the very beginning); and the snake barks *Acer davidii* and *Acer pensylvanica*. The first-named of these acers is the only too common Manitoba Maple, often considered a weed tree. The variegated forms with green-and-white, pink-tinged leaves are much less robust, and male trees produce no seed, naturally. This lovely plant is underused in North America. While the Manitoba maple is happy in wet soil, European field maple (*Acer campestre*) takes the opposite. This, with its small, fall-gold leaves, is the best species for poor dry alkaline soils. Big plants will need branch thinning to avoid overheavy shade.

Although common, the not-to-be-despised stag's-horn sumach, *Rhus typhina*, is excellent. It is small, but of true trunk-and-branch tree shape, and very suitable for the smallest shade garden. Cut-leaved types are even more ornamental, but seldom get above shrub size. With sumach the female plant is to be preferred, with its furred, conelike fruiting heads. These hold on well into winter — a favourite food plant for the small woodpeckers. *Rhus copallina* has shinier leaves and is best chosen where the common staghorn is a local wildling.

Similar in habit but even more elegant is *Albizia julibrissin*, with fernlike leaves and pink mimosa flowers in late summer. It seems very happy in New York, and could well be tried a farther north in protected spots such as courtyards.

For the obvious reason of encouraging the early growth of the woodland floor species that are a part of this exercise in shade-garden picture making, all trees so far recommended are deciduous. Deep, dark evergreens would be out of place, but a very few are open enough in habit and light enough in shade production to be very acceptable. Several pines are excellent when mature — the Scots pine makes a marvellously architectural pattern after fifty years or so — but only *Pinus strobus*, our elegant white pine, is suitable in youth. Tiers of elegant branches hold sprays of blue-green needles to build up a beautiful tree.

While the white pine prefers acid soil, another possible native evergreen insists on it. This is *Rhododendron maximum*, which, extending right up into northern Vermont, is remarkably frost hardy. Mature plants can reach over thirty feet in height when the great heads of blush bells make a fine sight in late spring.

Where space permits the creation or development of a woodland garden proper, forest-sized trees will obviously be used. Birches and maples will still be valuable for their own particular virtues, but it is now possible to consider other species. As can be seen from an even cursory examination of natural woodland, oaks are ideal shade trees. They permit rich understories of shrubs and herbaceous plants; their fallen leaves make the best leaf mould; their roots are deep and thus compete less greedily than most other trees. But it must be admitted that many are slow to build up a crown. Hence they must no doubt be combined with other quicker yet more transient trees if a new wood or coppice is to be planted.

Fortunately several of our North American oaks are of more rapid growth than the classic European hardwood *Quercus robur*. Closest to this is white oak, *Q. alba*. This magnificent tree has large leaves (up to eight inches long and half as wide) that turn a fine deep purple in the fall. Trees of toward one hundred fifty feet tall have been recorded.

Even quicker is the red oak, *Q. borealis*. It can put on several feet in a season; its leaves open already yellow in spring and close the year with a brilliant autumn display in its best forms. The scarlet oak is apt to be confused with this, but is in general a less robust plant and apt to sulk badly for years after planting. On wet soils the pin oak grows well and makes a fine specimen; however, removing the low branches that almost sweep the ground like a wide crinoline to plant thickly underneath robs it of much of its beauty. Here, for instance, a simple carpet of blue *Scilla siberica* in early spring gives a spectacular display. No branch pruning is necessary.

Frequently in the garden situation only one full-sized tree is possible to produce shade. Many of the previously mentioned species are suitable (multistemmed again), but their number can be added to by plants that develop a distinctive outline when grown alone. Among the best is *Koelreuteria paniculata*, the willow pattern or goldenrain tree. The former vernacular name (although, of course, willow pattern plates are an English eighteenth-century confection in the Chinese taste and the romantic story that goes with them a nineteenth-century superimposition) admirably indicates its mature shape. Unlike many trees, however, it begins to assume it at a relatively early age.

Good, too — and very easy to grow — is a false acacia, *Robinia*, and its close relative the honey locust (*Gleditsia triacanthos*), both with typical ferny leaves. Other small-leaved trees for this role are *Celtis* (the hackberries) and *Zelkova*. These are relatively quick growing when young — a useful attribute in a new, bare garden — reminiscent of that now sadly almost historic tree, the American elm. *Zelkova* 'Village Green' is a highly recommended clone.

In a cold spot common ash is admirable, even on difficult heavy soil, and larch, a deciduous conifer, deserves to be considered much more often as a garden tree. Few plants have such refreshing spring leaves or such clear yellow autumn ones. Eventually, too, the shape of a mature larch grown as a specimen is magnificent. *Larix kaempferi* has a desirably more open habit, but cannot take such poor conditions.

The phenomenon of the deciduous habit is so common that we are apt to accept it as a part of the seasonal round without giving it sufficient conscious thought. Heavily shaded summer gardens paradoxically become light and open in winter, when, in fact, light concentrations are less. Views appear — sometimes to one's benefit, more often, just onto the neighbours' back door. This thought should help in placing of evergreens. The bigger the leaves of deciduous trees, the greater the change at their fall.

Of hardy trees, catalpa and paulownia have the biggest undivided leaves. Both are splendid flowering plants in their own right and, when adult, with their rather erratic branch pattern make admirable trees for underplanting with shade lovers, as well. They also have the advantage of late leafing in spring.

Other trees have long pinnate leaves made up of paired leaflets along a stalk. The despised, but often beautiful tree of heaven is the commonest (where would cities' waste lots be without it?).

Walnuts and hickories are similar, but less amenable to poor conditions. But they do offer a bonus of edible nuts (squirrels permitting) to their visual effect. Ultimately the English walnut makes the most picturesque specimen. Of the natives, the pecan has the most desirable fruit, with the hardier shagbark hickory coming second. It is often said that nothing will grow under black walnut, but I find that a carpet of lily of the valley is easily obtained. The effort required to obtain the meat from the nuts is just not justified, however, by the little heap of shattered fragments one has amassed hours later.

Though not related, *Phellodendron amurense* rather resembles the walnuts, but with a wider branching pattern that offers an extensive and quick-forming shade canopy. *Euodia daniellii* is another similar tree, also from northern China; this with high-summer plates of white flowers and shiny black seeds emerging from the capsules in autumn is worthwhile in its own right.

The pinnate leaf pattern and its fall contrast is most distinctive with *Gymnocladus*, the Kentucky coffee tree — not, in spite of the name, to be recommended as a beverage, or to be considered merely a Southern plant. It is wild into the Niagara region of Ontario. Here the blue-green leaves are up to a couple of feet in length and the bare winter branches appear strangely stubby without their clothes on. It makes a striking architectural pattern against the winter sky.

Finally, in the discussion of trees to provide light shade we come to a group that is usually considered only from the point of view of their flowering qualities. "Flowering trees" is a strange phrase. It is the most obvious truism, because if a tree species did not flower it would cease to exist, asexual reproduction being ultimately a dead end. What is meant of course is "pretty" or "eye-catching." Horse chestnuts are certainly this, but their shade is too dense for our particular need. Thus we can turn to several lovely North American woodland edge plants that flower spectacularly (and less fleetingly than the amelanchiers already discussed) while offering an open canopy to encourage underplanting.

Where it succeeds, the flowering dogwood is a nonpareil. But to obtain that exquisite layered effect and small-tree height, it needs adequate moisture and its own shade from forest trees above. The pink form, though frequently sought out, is dangerously close to sugar icing and less easy to use in association with other flowering plants out at the same time. The white is exquisite. In northern areas it is important to obtain stock from clones that are known to be winter bud hardy. There is nothing sadder than the wizened, half-open bracts of those that have been badly frosted. It is unfortunate that the Oriental alternative, *Cornus kousa chinensis*, which is certainly more tolerant of winter cold, lacks the gracious habit of the American.

At almost the same time come the redbuds. *Cercis canadensis* in both the regular and the fine white form ("white redbud" is such a contradiction that it is a name better avoided) does not easily make a tree to sit under. Indeed, the wide low form, often seeming to prop itself up on its elbows, is so typical also of the almost identical Mediterranean *Cercis siliquastrum* that it has the name of Judas tree. It is said that by its shape the plant still shows the indignity of being chosen by Judas as his gallows.) However, less morbidly, the thin round leaves, well spaced, give ideal shade for underplanting. Here is the perfect occasion for felicitous plant associations: under the bright pink form, lily of the valley, *Smilacina*, trilliums and ferns; under the white, forget-me-nots, *Mertensia* and trout lilies. The permutations are endless.

Two other natives flower a little later; both are admirable. *Chionanthus virginicus* is the fringe tree; its masses of narrow-petalled flowers perfectly justify the name. It needs to reach a decent size before the rather coarse foliage seems to become in proportion. The lovely snowbell, *Halesia monticola*, has no such problem and always looks well. Here is a small tree that one must be able to look up into when it hangs out its thousands of little white bells. The form 'Rosea' has nothing of the stridency of redbud or dogwood, but leans almost toward palest apricot.

Other plants could well be included in this discussion, and some will be found in the lists that follow. Few of us have the space or inclination to grow all of them, and here, as in other areas of the garden conscious, individual choice makes the final decision.

Part II

The Plants for Shaded Situations

In order to avoid a dauntingly long alphabetical list of shade-loving and shade-tolerant plants, it seems best to divide them into groups with similar needs or groups of similar habit. This also avoids the necessity of a large number of symbols. We begin with shrubby calcifuges, those plants that insist on a lime-free soil. Thus readers who garden on lime have a splendid opportunity to skip a whole chapter. Or nearly.

It has already been remarked more than once that successful gardening depends upon working with, not against, those natural factors of climate and soil each of us is blessed or cursed with. (And it is psychologically sensible to presume the former.) This is nowhere more true than when trying to grow members of the Ericaceae on chalk. One of the most depressing garden sights I have ever had the misfortune to see was in a little valley in the English South Downs where the sides, lining a little (artificial) stream, had been extravagantly planted with mature rhododendrons. Tons of peat had been imported, but still the plants were dying, chlorotically and in obvious pain. Not only did they resent the omnipresent lime in the soil and the soil water, but also the lack of shade, which, combined with the naturally free drainage, kept the plants in a state of near drought.

This horticultural horror story (sadly true) is equally unpleasant ecologically. We do not all go about consciously thinking of the positioned rightness of plants, but any keen gardener develops an instinct for what looks innately right or wrong. And ericaceous woodlanders in an open limestone landscape is among the most blatant "wrongs." But if the "I'm on lime" school is still with me, there is a logical and possible way to use some of the plants in this chapter.

To attempt to integrate the ecologically impossible into the natural landscape or informal parts of the garden must be accepted as (to say the least) unwise. If such plants are to be grown, they must be brought to the obviously and acceptedly *made* areas close to the house or its associated buildings. The inevitable shady borders exist and can happily take what would not grow — and look wrong if it did — in the open.

There is still the problem of providing the right growing medium, but this is not difficult. Highly desirable are beds raised above the general soil level. Against a shady wall, a yard-wide bed might be supported by a foot-high retaining wall in front. The existing soil is removed to a depth of a foot (300 mm) and the hole filled with a leafy lime-free medium.

This does not mean that limy water will not seep in or that roots of the bigger plants will not eventually extend into the limy substrate, but in courtyard shade, with its relatively high humidity, quite remarkable plants will flourish. I know one little courtyard, not far from the horrendous garden described above, where *Lapageria rosea* scrambles about fifteen-feet-high (4-5 m) camellias planted in two feet (500 mm) of pre-pared border.

It must be emphasized, of course, that against any type of wall with a damp course the surface of the raised bed must either be below or the bed must stand free of the building, with both front and back walls of its own.

Equally, in our harder winters it is important that roots of plants in raised beds are not more vulnerable to frost. In a recent development at Royal Botanical Gardens with a range of such timber-framed beds, those that are above grade have a polystyrene lining to the insides. This also helps to keep the soil cool in the summer, an equally necessary step for shade-loving woodland plants.

In such a situation — either in shady courtyard of a large garden or a small-town yard consisting of nothing else — a marvellous range of plants can be grown: dwarf Himalayan rhododendrons or native decidu-ous species, woodland floor beauties of our own or from the Orient, the smaller bulbs and perhaps a Japanese maple as a focal point. These exquisite shrubs are the first in the calcifuge list that follows.

But before beginning on the list, a final note must be made about plant hardiness. In such a vast area as North America, stretching from latitude 25° N (Florida almost touches the Tropic of Cancer) to 70° N (not that anyone gardens much up there) and with 65° of longitude, it is hardly surprising that efforts have been made to help gardeners by di-viding the country into zones of plant hardiness.

While this is a great help in deciding what to plant in our gardens, it is also apt to act as a strait-jacket. Every garden is different and every garden has its own areas of microclimate both warmer and cooler than the norm. Thus, within broad bands one has to make one's own deci-sions. In general it pays to be intelligently optimistic, especially with herbaceous plants. Usually the texts err on the pessimistic side (not this one) so that authors are subsequently safe from readers' complaints that they have been led astray.

Thus, here I have taken the United States Department of Agriculture map and zone numbering. This lists my own area as 6a, which sounds so much more heartening than the Arnold Arboretum's map, which puts us at a depressing Zone 5. But this is all something of a nonsense. There are marvellous gardens way up beyond Quebec City, just as there are dreadful ones where apparently every prospect pleases.

The book, however, centres on 6a, give or take a zone which happens to include the most populous areas of northeastern North America; in general, this is north of Virginia and east of the Great Lakes. Here a climate exists that enables a vast range of lovely plants from all over the world to be successfully grown.

	Zone 1	below −46°C
	Zone 2	−46 to −40°C
	Zone 3	−40 to −34°C
	Zone 4	−34 to −29°C
	Zone 5	−29 to −23°C
	Zone 6	−23 to −18°C
	Zone 7	−18 to −12°C
	Zone 8	−12 to −7°C
	Zone 9	−7 to −1°C
	Zone 10	−1 to 4°C

Shrubs for Shade
The Lime-haters

Acer. The maples are usually more shade-providing than shade-accepting trees and the beautiful snake-barks, such as A. *pensylvanicum* and A. *davidii*, have already been recommended to that end. But the Japanese maples, especially in their delicately cut leaves or golden forms, are so apt to scorch in full sun that they are best included here.

japonicum 30 x 20 ft. (10 x 6 m) While this, like the next species, can make a considerable and very lovely tree — the sort of individual specimen that would be ideal in a small garden — it takes many years to get beyond the scale of a medium-sized shrub. Listing Japanese maples as lime-haters is not entirely correct. A pH higher than the neutral pH of 7.00 is not in itself a problem; what they really resent is dry lime alkaline soils. Here the leaves are thin and often become brown at the edges. This is also what is apt to occur in exposure to winds. Thus what they require is a deep moist, "woodsy" soil, or one that has been made so, in a sheltered spot.

Maples are not renowned as flowering plants, but A. *japonicum* has bunches of purple-tinged flowers that hang down from the branches just before the leaves unfold, and make quite a show. The leaves, however, are its chief glory. These usually are seven lobed, and a clear soft green throughout summer, colouring dramatically in fall. Even the bare-branch pattern is attractive throughout winter. There are several variants commonly offered.

'Aconitifolium'. The fernlike leaves are deeply lobed and turn a clear dark red in fall. Deep shade will reduce but not kill this effect.

'Aureum'. lobed leaves, circular in outline, open and remain a soft buttercup yellow throughout the season. This is a very slow-growing form, ideal for a focal point in front of dark conifers.

'Vitifolium'. The vine-leaved Japanese maple is one of the joys of autumn wherever it is grown. Unlike many fall- colourers that are constant in their chosen shade, this marvellous maple varies from plant to plant and even between branches on the same tree, scarlet, orange and purple.

palmatum 20 x 20 ft. (6 x 6 m) This is generally a smaller plant than the above-mentioned, and often wider than high. Having been cultivated for centuries in Japan before being introduced to the West in the early 1800s, it exists in a wide range of forms. Not a shrub for deep shade, however.

'Atropurpureum'. One of the best-known of all purple-leaved shrubs. Like all of them, it is splendid as the young leaves open in spring and again in autumn, but can look heavy in high summer. 'Bloodgood' is a newer and perhaps superior selection.

'Dissectum'. A group of small-growing Japanese maples in which the leaves are divided into the thinnest of fingers to present a finely cut, ferny effect — a sort of animated origami. Mature plants, even a hundred years old, seldom exceed ten feet in height. They have marvellous mounds of green or purple foliage. Half shade and considerable patience are required.

'Ozakazuki' is one of the *heptalobum* group, with relatively large leaves. In Britain, even with its softer climate, this plant is dramatic in fall; here it almost seems to be set on fire.

'Senkaki' is of relatively recent introduction, but has become — and rightly so — very popular. The branch pattern, unlike most of this group, is upright and soft green. Summer foliage turns pale gold in fall, and then suddenly it seems to light up in the low winter sun: every young shoot is bright shrimp pink or, to be more exact, the coral colour of cooked crayfish.

Arctostaphylos. A group of ericaceous evergreens native mainly to open coniferous forests of western North America: California and Oregon are their main home, where they are known as manzanitas. They make distinctively architectural bushes, with smooth mahogany bark matter like that of their big coastal relation, *Arbutus menziesii*. Sadly only one species is hardy with us.

uva-ursi 6 in. x 5 ft. (150 mm x 1.5 m) This is the ubiquitous bearberry, occurring right around the Northern Hemisphere at high latitudes. Doing well, it is one of the best of all ground covers — a dense green carpet above which the heads of nodding pink and white heather-bells make quite a show in spring; scarlet pea-sized fruit follows in late summer.

This is classically considered a lime-hater, more, perhaps, through its relationships than real observation. It will in fact take a higher than neutral pH so long as drainage is good and the ground well prepared with plenty of organic matter and sand. Then it will succeed happily in dry half shade.

A fine new selection is being distributed from the University of British Columbia Botanical Garden, Vancouver, under the name of 'Emerald Carpet.' It is well worth searching out.

Andromeda. A couple of little peat-bog plants of which the following is the better known and hence is more likely to be available.

polifolia 1½ x 1½ ft. (450 x 450 mm) This is bog rosemary. Unfortunately, unlike bog myrtle, the resemblance is not olfactory, merely visual. But the plant is not therefore to be discounted. The margins of the narrow, leathery leaves are recurved, as in true rosemary, though with a more distinctive milk white reverse. Flowers are typically heatherlike, waxy, pink and white bells.

This charming little shrub is not for the general border but for peat walls or the lime-free rock garden with a northern aspect.

Calluna 1-2 x 2 ft. (300-600 x 600 mm) This is the well-known Ling or Scots heather that covers so many miles of open moorland in northwestern Europe, dramatic in late summer effect. It is also often seen on the poor "Bagshot sands" area of Surrey, south of London. There in half shade with silver birch and wild rhododendron it gets taller, flowers less, but still makes a very satisfactory association of long season interest. Out of flower the tiny, tightly packed little leaves give the impression of a dwarf conifer. There are no ornamental fruits, but the dried flower corollas often remain on the plant, silvery in effect in winter.

Scots heather is happy in moist and dry positions so long as peaty, acid conditions can be assured at the root. When clipped over with a pair of shears in spring, tighter mounds of foliage can be maintained, and planted in groups of differing heights, marvellously billowing swathes can be obtained.

vulgaris is the only species, but it has given rise to vast numbers of forms that have been collected both in the wild and from gardens. The typical September-flowering soft-purple type can now be supplemented by others with colours ranging from white to pink and all shades of mauve and flowering times from July to November. Many are double, and foliage can be golden, grey or bronze. Where possible, specialist nurseries or named collections should be visited. From this plethora among the best are:

'Blazeaway.' Flowers not spectacular, but foliage turns red in winter, though less dramatically in shade than in the open.

'C. W. Nix' has long feathery spikes of dark crimson flowers.

'Gold Haze.' Here the white flowers are held against a background of bright golden foliage that is maintained throughout the year.

'H. E. Beale.' This is deservedly one of the most popular heathers, with its long spikes of rose-pink double flowers. 'Peter Sparkes' is similar; darker flowering later and thus good for a succession of bloom.

'Serlei' is perhaps the tallest *Calluna*, sometimes attaining three feet in height, with masses of white flowers. It has produced forms with golden leaves ('Serlei Aurea') and dark red-purple flowers ('Serlei Rubra').

'Tib' is among the first to come into bloom in July, with good double rosy-red spikes.

It should be added that North America has a long way to go in the use of this range of plants. Their foliage diversity especially is liable to be something of an aesthetic snare, and great care is needed in using some of the brighter colours if a decidedly garish effect is to be avoided.

Chamaedaphne. Another small native ericaceous shrub for peaty soils, where it associates happily with its close relations such as *Pieris* and *Leucothöe.*

claviculata 3 x 3 ft. (1 x 1 m) In May this is a pretty little shrub, with the last two or three inches of each shoot crowded with typically urn-shaped, white heather flowers. After this it remains distinctive in summer with its tidy green habit, and as colder weather begins, its leaves take up an almost vertical position to display their rusty reverse.

Clethra. There are species of sweet-pepper bushes disjointedly spread from eastern North America to China and Japan (what *Clethra arborea* is doing in Madeira is anyone's guess). Those we can grow have spikes of scented flowers in late summer and the pattern is maintained by the dry seed capsules throughout the following winter.

alnifolia 8 x 6 ft. (2.5 x 2 in.) The best form of our native sweet-pepper bush is 'Paniculata,' with much bigger flower spikes than that normally seen. 'Rosea' is pink in bud, and 'PinkSpire' keeps its colour throughout the flowering period. The forms look well, planted together. Almost any condition other than ill-drained clay soil, in sun or shade, seems to suit. This is a greatly underrated plant, and perhaps it is yet another horticultural example of a "prophet not being without honour save in his own country," etc. In which case a fine Japanese species is an alternative. This is *barbinervis.* A taller plant with bigger flowers on longer spikes, this Japanese pepper bush has the potential for much greater use. Mature specimens have the virtue of a striking bark colour, grey to warm brown, and so polished that the passer-by cannot fail to reach out to shine it further.

Comptonia peregrina, 3 x 3 ft. (1 x 1 m), is the sweet fern of our eastern coast, a typical pineland edge plant in areas such as the Desert of Maine, where it flourishes on those dry acid sands.

Sweet fern is, of course, not a true fern at all, but a close relation of bayberry and bog myrtle, and like them has deliciously aromatic leaves. It is also attractive in its strange saw-edge pattern. It has no floral display worth the name, just burlike greenish clusters. It is almost ironic that this reticent little plant should have been chosen by Linnaeaus to commemorate the great plantsman-prelate Bishop Compton, whose seventeenth-century garden at Fulham Palace in London held one of the first extensive European collections of North American trees and shrubs.

Cornus. This big genus needs to be listed here as well as in the section of lime-tolerant shrubs. Fortunately it divides easily from a visual point of view, as well as cultivationally. Here, for organic soils (where a certain amount of liminess is acceptable) are the lovely flowering dogwoods, whose buttonlike clusters of tiny flowers are surrounded by big petallike bracts, the whole appearing to be one large open flower.

florida 20-30 x 30 ft. (6-10 x 10 m) In our eastern woodlands, from Florida (how apt) in the south to the Niagara Peninsula in the north, flowering dogwood lights up the woods with its snowy flowers before the leaf canopy above unfolds. It must be one of our best-loved plants, and deservedly so. Little general description is necessary other than to commend the tiered habit that is typical of several dogwoods. It is the ideal plant around which, and under the canopy of high forest trees, to build one's woodland garden.

While the late-April or May floral fortnight is the peak of the dogwood's year, it offers beauty throughout the full twelve months. Pale leaves darken to a strong green and change to a glowing purple in autumn; when they fall, the crimson fruit is all the more noticeable. If missed by the robins this last display may persist into December. Then the habit becomes the feature, with the tight buttons of next spring's flowers on the end of every shoot as if to offer comfort that winter will again give way to that blissful season.

This last attribute does present something of a snare: with such a wide natural distribution it is obvious that one must obtain stock that originates in a climatic zone close to one's own; otherwise in the north brought-in plants may not be winter bud hardy.

With such a lovely and popular plant it is not surprising that numbers of varieties have been selected for size of and colour of bracts, foliage habit, even of fall colour effect. Dr. Dirr in his *Manual of Woody Landscape Plants* lists over thirty, and his recommendations should be consulted. Personally I prefer plants close to the white species, so long as flower quality is good. The pinks are apt to be rather sugar icing in effect, and the variegated forms just unbelievable.

There is concern for the health of many East Coast dogwoods since many have a die-back of branches and spotting of bracts. Many suggestions have been put forward for reasons and cure. In general, to give good growing conditions making robust plants is the best one can do.

kousa 15-20 x 15 ft. (4.5-6 x 4.5 m) Here is the Oriental flowering dogwood, usually seen under its varietal name *chinensis*. It is without doubt bud hardier than our own species and can therefore be tried where the latter fails. The display begins later, at the end of May or early June. "Flowers" have the typical button eye, but the bracts are narrower and pointed. Beginning green, they change to white and often end pale pink a good month later. Autumn colour is also more protracted. By fall the long pedicels, which have held the flowers above the tiers branches like an immensely involved *épergne*, are no match for the weight of the spherical scarlet fruit, which now hang down for the final display of the year.

Again an organic woodsy soil is enjoyed. While it grows well enough with us in Hamilton on stiff alkaline clay, it never seems quite at ease and fails to flower with complete abandon. Investment at the root pays dividends above ground. An essential woodland edge plant.

Corylopsis. Although related to the witch hazels and to *Parottia*, this lovely genus much more resembles, as its name suggests, the true hazels (*Corylus*). But the resemblance is superficial in that the soft-yellow spikes, though hanging down like hazels' lambstails, are complete, insect-pollinated flowers, not the anemophilous male catkins they seem. The delicate yet penetrating perfume of cowslips is there to attract pollinating insects (and gardeners), something that plants depending upon the wind for this function do not need.

The half-dozen or so species, all from the Orient, flower before the leaves in April. They need protection from excess exposure, whether it be sun, wind or frost, and hence are ideal woodlander or for enclosed north-facing shrub borders.

As a sophisticated alternative to forsythia, with its often hard-yellow flower, the primrose yellow corylopsis is to be highly recommended. It is inevitably more difficult to obtain and correspondingly expensive. Even a single plant, however, is a lovely sight.

glabrescens 15 x 15 ft. (4.5 m x 4.5 m) This can be taken as typical of several Orientals, including *platypetala* and *veitchiana* (West China), *sinensis*, of which the preceeding may be a variety, and *spicata* (Japan). All are elegant in flower and foliage.

pauciflora 3-5 x 4 ft. (1.2-1.5 x 1.5 m) As this lovely little shrub has the largest flowers (though fewer to a spike) of any other species we grow, it illustrates to perfection the occasional — and heartening — fallibility of botanical nomenclature. It enjoys moist shade and the company of other choice woodland plants, in perhaps a shady courtyard with daphnes and dog's-tooth violets. Young leaves open pink throughout the summer as growth proceeds.

willmottiae 12 x 8 ft. (4 x 2.5 m) Distinctive with its purplish opening leaves, for which a name and clone 'Spring Purple' has been selected. Flowers are palest green-yellow, as if corolla and calyx of primroses had been mixed on an artist's palette, watercolours, not oils.

Dirca. There are just two species in this genus closely related to *Daphne*. One is from California and thus of no concern to this list; the other has an East Coast spread, in moist leafy ravines, from New Brunswick down to Florida.

palustris, 3 x 5 ft. (1 x 1.5 m), is a quiet little shrub with small pale-yellow flowers in April before the leaves open. Summer leaf pattern, on a plant often wider than high, is distinctive, and often a clear gold fall colour follows. The extreme strength and flexibility of the branches give rise to its local names: leatherwood and ropebark (used thus and for bow strings by the native peoples). The other names are less obvious. The significance of "moosewood" can be guessed at, but "wicopy" has a marvellous country mystery sound about it. What can it mean?

Disanthus cercidifolius 10 x 10 ft. (3 x 3 m) Probably unobtainable, this rare Japanese woodlander has insignificant purplish flowers in autumn rather like those of *Hamamelis*, to which it is related. But the redbudlike leaves, bluish in summer, colour magnificently in fall. The show begins with individual leaves in late August that may go orange or red or purple, and gradually the whole shrub seems to catch fire. The plant resembles rather a small *Cercidiphyllum*, which must be sufficient recommendation for anything, and likes similar conditions.

Enkianthus. This genus of Japanese rhododendron relations, though never common, can be one of the joys of acid soils in half shade. Growth is open and tiered, and the strings of bell-shaped flowers hang down in May like red or white currants. All species have brilliant if unpredictable leaf colour in fall.

campanulatus 8-10 x 6 ft. (2.5-3 x 2 m) Perhaps the easiest to please in conditions that suit flowering dogwood. In good years bushes become draped with dark yellow to bronze red-veined flowers.

cernuus rubens 6-8 x 6 ft. (2-2.5 x 2 m) This is the brightest in flower colour, especially if the bells can be admired with the light behind them, when they appear to have switched on their own internal illumination like myriad Tiffany lamps.

perulatus 6-8 x 6 ft. (2-2.5 x 2 m) The only white *Enkianthus*, it is also one of the most beautiful when hung with almost translucent bells. It can be compared to snowbell (*Halesia*), but it is much smaller and more elegant in habit. Well worth every effort to obtain for that special spot.

Erica. The heathers are not plants for deep shade, but they enjoy the thin shade of open woodland right up to the boles of forest trees, where, if looked after in the first year or two, they seem able to withstand tree-induced drought remarkably well. The genus is a huge one, with hundreds of species native to South Africa (one or two are grown here as florists' pot plants) and a few from Mediterranean Europe and its northwest. Obviously only the latter have any hope of success with us.

They are all low-growing heathland shrubs, visually and botanically close to *Calluna* as well as being the type-genus of *Ericaceae*, that vast calcifuge family that includes rhododendron and azalea. The heather season begins with this first named species.

carnea (syn. *herbacea* 1-2 x 2 ft. (300-600 x 600 mm) In British gardens there is no more valuable winter and early-spring flowering plant for providing swatches of colour in sun and the half shade of woodland edges. With the right selection of cultivars one can expect to have flowers from this one species from November through to April. In northeastern America this is a vain hope; nonetheless the "winter heathers" are too valuable a plant for the shade gardener to neglect.

Where plants are happily protected throughout winter under snow, flowers can be expected as soon as spring arrives and a couple of months of colour can therefore be expected. Of the cultivars likely to be available, the following are among the best — but all are worth trying:

'King George' ('Winter Beauty'), bright rose-pink; 'Springwood Pink' is paler and 'Springwood White' the best white. Both 'Springwoods' have distinctive trailing growth that rapidly colonizes bare ground. 'Vivellii' is a tighter plant, with deep carmine-red flowers set off against the winter-bronzed foliage.

These heathers and those that follow are best planted as ground covers, eighteen inches (450 mm) apart, among and in front of their ericaceous relations. An organic soil encouraged with peat or leaf mould and, at the highest, a neutral pH (7.00) reading are required. Marvellous effects are obtained with, for example, *Rhododendron* P.J.M. in full flower growing out of a pink or white carpet of *Erica carnea*.

By July, although in fact there are some lovely things to come, there is apt to be the feeling that the woodland garden has passed its floral prime and that we can now only look to the herbaceous border, the bedding and the roses. Fortunately this is not true, especially for those gardening on thin acid soils than are often unkind to those lush summer beauties. With such soils, as always it is best to search out those plants that are evolutionarily programmed to succeed in them. Which brings us to the summer heathers flowering from June to October.

cinerea 21 x 1½ ft. (300-450 mm) This is the common bell heather that covers untold miles of moorland in Britain, from Cornwall to northern Scotland. Pink, red, purple and white forms have been selected from mutants in the wild and from garden seedlings. There are others that provide interesting foliage effects: 'Golden Drop' is well suited in name to summer, but with cooler fall temperatures its leaves turn red, until lost into snow.

tetralix 1 x 1½ ft. (300 x 450 mm) The grey to nearly silver foliage of the best forms of the cross-leaved heather is a good foil to the hotter colours of bell heather. Again there is a range of flower colours: 'Alba Mollis' and 'Con Underwood' are respectively white and crimson. Any others available should be tried. It might be mentioned that nurseries in Oregon and British Columbia are more likely to offer these plants, and a small outlay and initial care will prove how well they can do in the East.

Fothergilla. Two or three shrubs from our eastern woodlands related to witch hazels (*Hamamelis*), they enjoy conditions similar to azaleas and *Enkianthus*. Open woodland or association with taller shrubs is ideal, though too much shade reduces the brilliance of the autumn colour.

gardenii 2-3 x 3 ft. (600 mm-1 x 1 m) This charming little shrub commemorates two significant eighteenth-century plantsmen, one on either side of the Atlantic. Dr. John Garden of Charleston discovered this — to him, local — species, and it was introduced in 1765, to Britain, where, in his garden at Stratford-le-Bowe, north of London, Dr. John Fothergill cultivated it in one of the most comprehensive collections of American plants then known in Europe.

Dr. Garden's, or dwarf *Fothergilla*, flowers in April before the leaves open — two-inch-high spikes of creamy stamens, deliciously honey scented. It looks particularly well sitting in a sea of species *Crocus tomasinianus* or *C. chrysanthus*, a combination that will excite newly emerged honey bees to a frenzy of spring joy.

major 6 x 6 ft. (2 x 2 m) A more robust plant, and one that is probably easier to grow. But the same conditions apply: a cool acidic root run in half shade. It flowers a little later, as the leaves emerge: creamy-green bottlebrushes with a hint of underlying pink.

If the floral display of fothergillas is not extravagant, no such reticence is maintained in fall. Then the witch-hazellike leaves blaze into red, orange and yellow, all on the same plant. A northwest exposure so that they are lit up by the low afternoon sun provides added pleasure.

Franklinia. This noble plant is one of the treasures of East Coast gardens and a part of the heritage of plant discovery on this continent. It was first found by John Bartram on the banks of Georgia's Altamaha River, and son William returned in 1778 to gather ripe seed. From this one collection, it is believed, all existing plants descend, for *Franklinia* has not been positively identified in the wild since 1790, the year in which Benjamin Franklin, whose name it carries, coincidentally died.

alatamaha 10-20 x 10 ft. (3-6 x 3 m) One can do no better than to quote from William Bartram's own description: "It is a flowering tree, of the first order for beauty and fragrance of blossoms. . . . The flowers are very large, expand themselves perfectly, are of a snow-white colour and ornamented with a crown or tassel of gold-coloured refulgent staminae in their centre. . . ."

In fact, "very large" can mean three inches across, rather like a cup-shaped camellia blossom. August is their month, but flowers frequently continue to open throughout September, when the last flowers of the season become framed in the orange and red of the fall foliage. Though still uncommon in gardens, it is not difficult to grow. It succeeds wonderfully in Cleveland in half shade in the typical cool acid, leafy soil that suits all the plants in this section. The beauty and aristocratic antecedents of *Franklinia* should not put off those of us who cannot personally compete with such grandeur.

Gaultheria. There are over two hundred species, usually small evergreens, strewn around the world in the Americas, the Himalayas, montane Southeast Asia and even subtropical Australia. They are typically

ericaceous, needing moist acid soil. Urn-shaped flowers are followed by
fleshy berries.

procumbens 6 in. x 3 ft. (150 mm x 1 m) Checkerberry, creeping wintergreen, partridgeberry, boxberry — all the local names help in the description of this valuable evergreen ground cover. It enjoys the shade of
other shrubs, but some sun helps to redden the foliage at the onset of
colder weather in late fall. The charming flowers and scarlet fruits are
apt to be hidden in the leaves. All parts produce wintergreen oil, once of
considerable use in medicines and flavouring. (Sweet birch, *Betula lenta*,
is now the natural commercial source of this.)

shallon 2-4 x 3 ft. (600 mm-1.2 x 1 m) This is a valuable evergreen from
the West Coast, first collected by David Douglas in 1826. Stems of leathery leaves are topped by *Pieris*-like spikes of pinkish flowers on pinker
stems in early summer. Purple berries follow, which are edible (just).
Salal or shallon seems not to be grown in the East, but as it comes from
areas similar to that of the highly successful Oregon grape (*Mahonia
aquifolium*), it should be tried. Holiday makers should be encouraged to
collect propagating material from as high up the Rocky Mountains as
they can find it and try it in the East.

Gaylussacia is the box huckleberry, another small eastern ericaceous un-
dershrub needing similar conditions to wintergreen and offering similar
pleasures. Well worth planting if it can be obtained in the typical moist
peaty soil it comes from.

Hamamelis. Without doubt the witch hazels are the first of winter-
flowering shrubs. In mild areas they begin to open in early January. With
us, late February and throughout March comprise the witch-hazel weeks.
A season to anticipate with the greatest pleasure.

   While accepting lime, they are best given some summer shade in a cool
leafy soil. Their open habit of growth makes them ideal "stratification
plants" to give further protection to small ericaceous shrubs or woodland
herbaceous layers below. Leaves are obviously hazel (*Corylus*)-like, distinctively ribbed. Clear gold fall colour can be expected from most witch
hazels, but some are vastly more dramatic than others.

x *intermedia* 10-20 x 10 ft. (3-6 x 3 m) This is a hybrid group of witch
hazels that combine much of the beauty of *H. mollis* with the vigour and
hardiness of *H. japonica*. All have the typical *Hamamelis* flower clusters
with each little cup-shaped calyx carrying four spidery, twisted petals.

   'Arnold Promise' is, with us in southern Ontario, the best for all-round
effect. A vigorous vase-shaped bush, it is covered, as I write in December,

in little furry buds. Though a mild week in February will bring out a few flowers, by March it will be aglint with gold. When these flowers are over, the reddish calyces remain long enough to give interest until the leaves take over. Fall colour is superb, with each leaf taking on bands of red, orange and gold., As they drop next year's flowers, buds are there, the whole a miracle of seasonal display and seasonal anticipation.

Other recent cultivars include 'Jelena,' a lovely growing copper-flowered form from Mr. de Belder's Kalmthout Arboretum in Belgium, and 'Ruby Glow,' which is rather darker. I do not know 'Moonlight,' but hope to obtain it, because not only is it described as a clear soft primrose yellow, but also as being fragrant. Both these are attributes of my own favourite witch hazel, *Hamamelis mollis* 'Pallida' (one of x *intermedia*'s parents). Sadly the Chinese *H. mollis* is the least hardy with us, but this lovely form should be tried in any protected spot.

The other parent, *H. japonica*, is not so fine in flower, but eventually makes a marvellously architectural small tree, with long forty-five-degree branches arising from a short trunk. The Orient has no monopoly on witch hazels, as two are our own natives. They are useful but less spectacular plants.

vernalis 6-10 x 10 ft. (2-3 x 3 m) From Missouri and other central states, this is an extremely hardy plant, with fragrant flowers that usually open in February. The petals have the convenient ability to close and unfurl again as the weather permits. Happy even on heavy clay, it is the easiest of its genus.

virginiana 15 x 20 ft. (5 x 7 m) This is an understory shrub in our northern Carolinian woodlands and spreads south throughout that floristic region. As a late-fall flower, it has an as yet unrealized potential for extending floral interest in areas where it is traditional (if unnecessary) to tuck up the garden for winter in October, not to emerge until May.

A difficulty is that many forms of this plant combine their gentle flowering display with the similarity coloured leaf fall so that the former is utterly lost. Both Kalmthout and our Royal Botanical Gardens are making selections that flower late. We are also propagating selections with distinctive flesh-coloured flowers found wild on our own properties that might one day offer useful garden plants. Even now unselected plants are worth their space, offering good autumn colour, fragrant flowers and the possibility of distilling one's own witch-hazel liniment to sooth muscles sore from an excess of gardening.

Ilex. As one travels south on the East Coast, the increasing proportion of nonconiferous evergreen plants in gardens, roadside plantings and parks marks the real transition to warmer climes. Of these broad leaves, the hollies provide a strong basis, adding foliage strength throughout the year and dramatic fruiting effects of several fall and winter months. We Zone-Sixers, around whom the selection of plants in this book is arranged, are in a very dangerous position: our zone might be considered the zone of temptation as far as hollies are concerned. And, as Oscar Wilde pointed out a century ago, that is the only thing one cannot resist. What follows, however, is a very restrained list: it resists tempting with mouth-watering accounts of Chinese *cornutas*, or English *aquifoliums* and even native (Massachusetts southward) *opacas*. Except, of course, to suggest ever so quickly — get thee behind me, plantsman — that sheltered half-shady spots might well offer a home to plants otherwise considered impossible. Extending the range is what much adventurous and enjoyable gardening is about. Professor Dirr should be consulted for a list. However, even without foolhardiness there are some very useful plants for general use.

crenata 5-8 x 6 ft. (1.5-2.5 x 2m) Japanese holly, to the uninitiated, is very much like boxwood, but rather more boring. There are many of the hundreds of named forms — synonomy seems endemic with this plant — which do not even need clipping to keep them as bland little evergreens. Thus they are ideal for foundation plants around the dwellings of nongardeners. Flowers are small and whitish, fruits small and black, insignificant in each case. It is unfortunate that gold-leaved forms lose this one desirable attribute in shade. Our native inkberry, *Ilex glabra*, from Nova Scotia southward, is rather similar, but acceptance of wet acid soils give it a specific use.

x *meservae* 8-10 x 8 ft. (2.5-3 x 2.5 m) Here is a group of real hollies, hardy hollies, for which we have Mrs. Leighton Meserve of St. James, New York, to thank. The Meserve hollies combine *Ilex rugosa* with the desirable attributes of the English holly. 'Blue Princess' and 'Blue Prince' are the two clones most likely to be available. They are slow-growing bushes, but begin when still only a foot or so high, as they mean to go on, to make a strong statement. They have tight dark green spiky foliage with an almost indigo cast and brilliant sealing-wax red berries.

Both sexes, of course, are necessary for fruiting, and one prince among a whole harem of princesses is sufficient. They will light up the darkest of courtyard corners with their light-reflecting leaves and showy berries.

More recent Meserve hollies are *Ilex cornuta* x *rugosa* hybrids. 'China Boy' and 'China Girl' are robust plants, faster growing, that promise to be much bigger when mature. Clearly they are to be sought out.

pedunculosa 15-20 x 10 ft. (5-6 x 3 m) Sometimes called the Longstalk holly, this is a very lovely tall evergreen from China and Japan. Both the branch pattern and the hanging fruits give a softer feel different from the rather stiff twigginess of most hollies. Leaves are unarmed, waved at the edges, always attractive. This is a splendid woodland edge plant for half shade. Dirr refers to its indefatigability at (−18°F) and happiness in heavy clay. Why do we not see it more? It is superb at Swarthmore.

verticillata 8-10 x 6 ft. (2.5-3 x 2 m) Coralberry, winterberry, Michigan holly: this could hardly be more different with its deciduous habit and berries tightly packed along the branches. But although failing to fulfill our expectations of "holliness," it is an excellent plant in its own right for fall fruiting effect.

The species is native to much of the Northeast in wet acidic soils. This fact deals with cultural requirements, and half shade is entirely acceptable, as is some lime in the soil. Over the years many fine selections have been made to add fall colour ('Autumn Glow'), particularly good and lasting fruiting ('Sparkleberry' and 'Winter Red'). 'Nana' is half the size of the type, and orange and yellow-fruited forms are also available. Again a male plant must be made available if fruiting is to occur.

Kalmia. While Linnaeus commemorated himself with the tiny little twinflower (*Linnaea*), to his pupil Peter Kalm he gave this spectacular shrub. Though there are a half-dozen species of *Kalmia*, to most of us the name evolves just one plant: mountain laurel, surely one of North America's most beautiful plants. This is, of course,

latifolia 8 x 8 ft. (2.5 x 2.5) A broad-leaved evergreen, rather rhododendronlike in out-of-flower appearance and, as a relation, associating very well with that genus in the garden. Florally it is wonderfully distinct.

Mountain laurel is native from Quebec down to Florida, often on open hillsides, where old plants develop a handsome shape with fine bark. In gardens it seems to take on a suitably demure aspect, very tidy and compact, whether grown in sun or shade. Something between the two is perhaps ideal in acid, peaty soil.

Flowers open in early June or a little sooner, and the bud pattern itself is charming. Each is like one of those sugar-icing whirls used for decorating cakes. They open to inch-wide cups, holding ten stamens bent back to await explosive triggering by a visiting insect, the target and recipient of the pollen.

Even in the wild there is a wide range of colour forms, from pure white to deep rose-pink with darker bands. Horticultural selection has added to this and some named clones such as 'Ostbo Red' and 'Pink Charm.' Kalmias are notoriously difficult to root from cuttings, and micropropagation techniques are now being employed with success. This will help both the availability of good forms and eventually their price to the backyard gardener.

angustifolia 2-4 x 3 ft. (600 mm-1.2 m x 1 m) Names such as lambkill Kalmia or sheep laurel indicate the potential toxicity of this pretty little shrub to browsing animals — not, fortunately, a problem in the garden. It is a front-row shrub for peaty soil in semishade. Heads of typical *Kalmia* flowers, less than half the size of K. *latifolia*, open rather later in the season.

Ledum. A small group of native *Kalmia* relations needing similar conditions of most acid soil and enjoying half shade.

groenlandicum 2 x 2 ft. (600 x 600 mm) This is Labrador tea, a high latitude evergreen shrublet that in June has attractive heads of white flowers rather in the manner of some of the more esoteric Himalayan dwarf rhododendrons. The related species L. *palustre* is virtually identical from a garden point of view. Either should be snapped up if seen at a local nursery so long as the usual ericaceous conditions for success can be met. A nearby genus both alphabetically and botanically is *Leiophythum buxifolium.*

It comes from the pine barrens of New Jersey, as well — in a rather different form — from the Piedmonts. The little bush is described as covering itself with white flowers, pink in bud, and certainly looks charming in illustrations. Sadly this is a plant I have neither grown nor seen; an omission to be remedied at the earliest opportunity.

Leucothöe. Another group of native ericoids of considerable value under trees, on banks and in the front-line of shrub plantings. Acid, leafy soil is required; like Ericas they seem able to accept dry shade well enough if looked after until well established. Searing winds, however, are anathema.

fontanesiana 5 x 5 ft. (1.5 x 1.5 m) Lovely arching wands of the fetter-bush, carry long, narrow leaves with, in June, tassels of white pieris-shaped flowers in their axils. Although evergreen the foliage often takes on a burnished purple sheen in winter.

There are forms with variegated foliage, splashed pink and cream, that seem to me better in the lists than in the garden, where the type, doing well, needs no mirror. *Leucothöe axillaris* is reputedly less susceptible to the leaf spot diseases that can plague its cousin, but it is a stiffer, less elegant plant.

Linnaea. This little honeysuckle relation is the one that commemorates the great Swedish botanist Linnaeus. With undeserved modesty both on his own part and that of the plant, he described it in 1737 as "a plant of Lapland, lowly, insignificant, disregarded, flowering but for a brief space — from Linnaeus, who resembles it."

borealis. 6 in. x 3 ft. (150 mm x 1 m) Though Linnaeus indeed found it in Lapland, twinflower grows in high latitudes around the Northern Hemisphere. North America forms are said to be the easiest in cultivation.

From its trailing, evergreen growth, delicate stems emerge with the paired white flowers opening in early summer. It needs shade, a leafy soil and moisture. Doing well it makes excellent ground cover.

Magnolia. It would be easy to devote a whole chapter to this marvellous genus, not only because of its range of type — tree and shrub, spring and summer flowers — but also because it bridges the cultivational divide of calcifuge and calcicole. Hence it is not restricted to this particular lime-hating section.

Generally magnolias do not *need* shade, yet their early flowers are wisely protected from the early-morning sun, and, as with many rhododendrons, woodland association, where this can be contrived, gives a far more satisfying effect. In the context of this list they fall into two main groups.

Spring-flowering magnolias

kobus 20-30 x 20 ft. (6.5-10 x 6.5 m) Like many people who plant it, this lovely tree is slim in youth but fills out in middle age; the analogy with *Homo sapiens* might be combined where some forms mature young, while for others life only "begins at forty." I possess each of these: one flowered at the first year of planting, the other, now four metres high, looks as though waiting to celebrate my own dotage. Thus vegetatively propagated clones known to flower early are a better bet than seedlings.

Doing well, *Magnolia kobus* makes an elegant little tree in effect, which from a distance is transformed into a shimmering cloud of white. Individual flowers are made up of up to nine narrow petals surrounding a mass of fleshy stamens and stigmata, pink flushed. The flowers are fragrant, as are the crushed leaves and young twigs; this attribute is especially marked in the similar *Magnolia salicifolia*, a species worth searching out.

stellata 12-15 x 15 ft. (4-5 x 5 m) The star magnolia is often considered to be a tight shrubby variant of the above species. It seldom exceeds a dozen feet and can take twice that number of years to attain it. For this reason it is frequently recommended as the magnolia for small gardens. Certainly the size is right, but it seems to need the moral support and protection of other plants around it: not a plant for isolation, where its early April flowers scorch in sun and wind.

Flowers have twice the petals of M. *kobus*, reflexing with age like a snowy sea anemone opening in slow motion. Lovely variants include 'Centennial,' palest pink flushed; 'Pink Star,' opening pink and paling to white. 'Royal Star,' perhaps suitably, makes the best show with us at Royal Botanical Gardens; pure white, in a good year not a branch can be seen for the cloud of flowers.

x *loebneri* 20-25 x 25 ft. (6.5-8 x 8 m) This combines the virtues of the two previous species in a miraculous way. It has the early floriferousness of the sometimes rather costive *stellata*, which is combined with the free open growth of *kobus*. The type is white, while 'Leonard Messel' is a lovely gentle pink. 'Merrill' is a fine white tinged pink. All these lovely plants are lime tolerant but, like all magnolias, repay some soil preparation at planting time; good drainage and lots of organic matter.

x *soulangeana* 20-30 x 30 ft. (6.5-10 x 10 m) There is no doubt that this is the most popular of its genus with its vertically held vase-shaped flowers, varying in colour from white to deep purple-pink. Though resenting the thinnest limy soils, it accepts clays with relative equanimity.

Eventually it makes a huge wide-spreading shrub. It flowers when very young — although the blooms ridiculously dwarf the branches. Many clones have been named since M. Soulange-Bodin's first cross was made in the early nineteenth century.

'Alexandrina' (white), 'Lennei' (cream and mulberry shaded) and 'Rustica Rubra' are but three, all lovely, with great scented waxy-petalled flowers open in April. It is best to visit an arboretum or botanical garden with a representative collection before choosing the single specimen one has room for.

Obviously pruning can keep the plants from becoming impossibly large; this is best done at flowering time for magnificent arrangements indoors. It is also the moment to volunteer to do the altar flowers at church. For real extravagance one can also cut magnolia during winter. Buds of M. Kobus force very satisfactorily. It does not matter if the bigger forms do not come out, as the buds are as attractive as pussy willow, which they closely resemble, furry and silver.

The parents of M. x *soulangeana* are both very worthwhile plants in their own right. M. *denudata* (*heptapeta*) is the yulan, eventually a big plant with pure white flowers; earlier than its children, it has great presence. M. *liliiflora* (*quinquepeta*) gave the diversity of colour to M. *Soulange*-Boudin's famous hybrid.

Typically the rather narrower flowers are purple outside and white within; 'Nigra' is even darker. May is usually their month, but flowers occur sporadically throughout the summer. M. *liliiflora* has been used in recent years to produce a range of hybrids for small gardens that are valuable where M. *stellata* flowers too early and gets frosted. They have girls' names, from Ann to Susan with half a dozen in between. Again they need to be seen to enable one to choose the right colour for one's own taste and garden scheme.

Later-flowering Magnolias

A final group within this marvellous genus takes over from the *liliiflora* hybrids just described. They make tall, sparse shrubs with particularly lovely pendulous flowers of translucent white, each with a purple or crimson "eye" of stamens.

sinensis 10 x 10 ft. (3 x 3 m) The June display, against the fresh young pale-backed leaves, is spectacular but brief.

M. *wilsonii* is marginally more striking but possibly less hardy. A putative hybrid between these two Chinese species occurred at Highdown, the famous garden in a chalk pit on the south coast of England; from such a spot M. x *highdownensis* is naturally very lime tolerant.

sieboldii 10 x 10 ft. (3 x 3 m) My favourite in this group, which extends the season from late-May into August, a few flowers opening each day. The perfume is of gardenias washed down with lemon juice. If like its cousin it can be planted in an elevated spot where a woodland walk passes beneath, the full beauty of the nodding flowers can be enjoyed.

virginiana 10-15 x 15 ft. (3-4.5 x 4.5 m) A final magnoliaceous thought. Anyone with a bit of moist, even boggy acid woodland should plant the swamp bay. The narrow leaves — some stay on all winter — are brilliant white underneath and flash in the wind. The flowers are the size shape and colour of pale pheasants eggs, with an utterly unique and delicious scent — a perfect table centre for a summer evening, possible from June to September. This is something of a southern plant, but hardier forms are being selected. Do try it; we are doing so.

Menziesia. Another little group of ericaceous shrubs of which one in particular is useful to extend the range of interest in a peaty, half-shady spot. The name commemorates Archibald Menzies, who was botanist cum ship's surgeon on Vancouver's great expedition of discovery, 1790-5.

Enonymus alatus

Tulipa saxetilis

Helleboras orientalis

Sanguinaria canadensis

Crocus tomasinianus Whitwell Purple

Aescubus parviflora

Vinca major, 'variegata'

Cyprepetinus parviflorum

Primula viallii

Hydrangea, Astolbe R. rubrifolia

Magnolia stellata

Azalea

Sambucus canadensis laciniata

Lythrum salicaria, Lysimachia punctaba

Golden Philadelphus, polargonium

Iris cristata 'alba' in shade

ciliicalyx 3 x 1 ft. (1 m x 500 mm) This species is from Japan. It is both the hardiest and that most likely to be available. Soft, downy deciduous leaves and dangling clusters of flowers in May, cream, pale pink or near purple. A charming plant.

Mitchella. Some resemblance to *Linnaea* is not borne out by botany. Known also as partridgeberry, twinberry (*not* twinflower) or squawberry, this is a rather surprising relation of coffee and gardenia.

repens 3 in. x 3 ft. (150 mm x 1 m) Creeping evergreen ground cover, rooting as it goes in moist peaty soil. Pairs of leaves and little pinkish flowers are followed by bead-sized scarlet fruits. This is another good native plant, sometimes sold in sods taken from the woodland floor.

Myrica. Interesting associates for heathers, but in no more than half shade. Plants with such aromatic leaves, to touch as one passes, are always a delight — another of the senses to be used in the enjoyment of gardens.

pennsylvanica 8-9 x 12 ft. (2-3 x 4 m) Northern bayberry or wax myrtle, this must have been among the first plants to have been noticed by Europeans landing here, as it grows on the seaside sands of the New England coast. In spite of this it will take heavy clay, some lime and even shade with impunity. Visually unimpressive in leaf and insignificant in flower, compensation comes in fall and throughout winter, when the bare branches (or some of them — the effect is erratic) become crowded with distinctive berries. These are pea sized and covered with the waxy blue-white bloom that is still collected and used in the fabrication (manufacture is too commercial a word!) of candles. They are expensive but deliciously perfumed by the scent, which penetrates the entire plant.

gale. 3 x 3 ft. (1 x 1 m) Bog myrtle from the far north carries tiny flowers in catkinlike heads, the sexes on separate plants. It accepts the moist acid and boggy situations where little else will grow, looking well under silver birch. The aromatic foliage is a joy, but there is no fruiting display worth the name.

Oxydendrum. Here is a monospecific genus, split off from the now much reduced *Andromeda*. Certainly this plant could hardly be more different from those that remain.

arborea 25-35 x 20 ft. (8.5-12 x 7 m) Like a vast deciduous *Pieris*, this superb plant could well belong to the shade-tree section. But it flowers and fruits when young and in a way, unlike the bigger Magnolias, that does not appear out of scale. Thus it is not a plant to be avoided even in small gardens, where it may be the one tree-sized plant to reach maturity.

Commonly known as sourwood (a direct translation from its Latin name — or perhaps the other way round) and as sorrel tree, this name refers to the pleasant acid-tasting leaves. Lily of the valley tree is more usually suitable a title when in late-June it is draped in scented white flower sprays. Fall colour can be dramatic — red, orange and purple — after which the dry seed clusters and attractive bark combine to give definite winter interest.

This lovely plant grows slowly even in perfect conditions of acid well-drained leafy soils. A position in half shade on the edge of woodland is probably ideal. Certainly every effort should be given to make it happy; there will be an equal and reciprocal effect on the planter.

Pachysandra. A couple of extremely valuable ground-cover plants without which modern gardens can hardly manage. They turn the dullest, darkest, shadiest spots into deep pile carpets of gorgeous green. If laid with care, these will wear as well as broadloom Wilton. But perhaps Aubusson, if the analogy is to be worked to death, is better; to be looked at, not walked on.

procumbens 9 in. x infinity (250 mm x oc) A lovely native from the mountains of Virginia and Kentucky, it needs cool acid leafy soil to do well in full, but not deepest shade. Occasionally gleams of sun are desirable to enjoy a strange luminescence on the bluish-green leaves. Fuzzy flowers spikes, white and pink flushed, appear at above the foliage in April or May.

Although its Oriental relation (below) has become a cliché, this plant should be given a trial — though it is without doubt more demanding, and deservedly so.

terminalis 1 ft. x infinity (300 mm x ∞) Japanese spurge (actually a relation of boxwood) will take deepest shade, even under shallow-rooted trees, so long as initial preparation is good. Adding plenty of organic matter makes even a limy soil acceptable, and rapid extension form will cause small rooted plants to join up for complete evergreen form and cover. The white flower spikes in spring make a decent show after a mild winter; black fruit may follow.

One must add a couple of caveats. *Pachysandra* should not be allowed to dominate the scene to the exclusion of other plants simply because it is easy; it must be a part of the considered scene, a horizontal dimension. Shrubs planted in it add vertical lines but may need wire netting wrapped around stems at ground level, as the evergreen *Pachysandra* ground cover gives perfect protection for little rodents to take up winter quarters and feed on the bark of the other, more delicious things.

'Green Carpet' is a lighter-coloured more desirable cultivar, to be preferred if it can be found, and variegation with silver-edged leaves is excellent where the robustness of the typical form would be out of place.

Pieris. A gem of a genus for shade and acid soils with, typically, white urn-shaped flowers in crowded spikes. Apparently carelessly, the buds are fully formed in fall and held throughout winter before opening in April. But they come to no harm in normal years.

floribunda 5 x 5 ft. (1.5 x 1.5 m) A lovely native from the mountains of Georgia, making a tidy evergreen hummock with distinctive upright flower spikes arranged in a shuttlecock position. It is sometimes known as fetterbush, a name shared with other plants.

japonica 8-10 x 8 ft. (2.5-3 x 2.5 m) A splendidly distinctive evergreen with glossy-waxed leaves that set off to perfection the little white urn-flowers. Here they are carried in copious drooping panicles, like bunches of lily of the valley worn as a corsage. In 'White Cascade' they are much longer.

Recent forms brought into cultivation have a decided pink flush to pedicel, calyx and even into the corolla, offering a new colour range to the genus; 'Christmas Cheer' and 'Flamingo' are two such, which are lovely in close detail but less effective at a distance in the garden scene. There is also an attractive form with variegated leaves; slower to growth and less floriferous, it is good for brightening a dark corner throughout the year. Its young growth is pale yellow.

Rhododendron. This is the biggest genus — and most diverse in appearance — that we need to consider. There are some eight hundred wild species from all over the world (except Africa and South America) utilizing every habitat from exposed mountainside at great altitudes to deep subtropical jungles, where humidity seldom falls below one hundred percent. Some of the high alpines never exceed a foot in height (though their flowers may be hugely out of all proportion to their bodies), while lowland species can reach full forest-tree proportions and are among the showiest plants in the world. Their colour range almost spans the spectrum, with flowering times from January to August (a few make a second autumn flush as if the genus cannot bear not to offer something to every month of the year). They may be evergreen or deciduous — separating deciduous azaleas from evergreen rhododendrons is convenient but has no botanical validity — with leaf-colour variation rivalling that of conifers and size and texture brooking no comparison in diversity.

In addition to all this, hybridization and selection ever since the first Himalayan species were brought into cultivation in the early decades of the nineteenth century have added very many hundreds of more or less distinct plants. More appear every year.

Following now is a short list of some of the most beautiful (a highly subjective selection) members of the genus, species and hybrids. This may act as something of an aide-mémoire, but the only way to choose rhododendrons for one's own garden is to visit others to see what does well in one's own area, to see how they are used and to pick out the personally irresistible.

Virtually all rhododendrons insist upon an acid, leafy soil; they have shallow fibrous root systems that make them easy to transplant (huge plants at show exhibits in full flower can be back in their home gardens the next week without having hardly noticed the journey), but very vulnerable to drying out and winter freezing. Thus they must be protected from seering winds and winter sun and are best placed with north or eastern exposures. Flowers of sulphur and iron sulphate can be applied to soil to lower pH values, but this is a vain exercise if adequate moisture and organic content in a suitable site are not maintained. Raised beds help to reduce uptake of limy water where soil is not naturally acid, but they must be big enough for a decent-sized planting of calcifuge plants or they become even more vulnerable spots for winter freezing.

There are many specialist books on rhododendrons, and keen growers will turn to these. In general it is true to say that magnificent though evergreen rhododendrons are in flower, year-round garden effect comes from healthy leaves. If these are ratty the plants are not worth their space. For convenience here it is simplest to divide the genus into the two most obvious visually different groups.

Evergreen rhododendrons. It must be repeated that while every opportunity should be taken to experiment and take risks with plant hardiness (the definitive book will never be written) the tried, hardy forms must be the backbone of any rhododendron planting, especially in the Northeast. Thus hybrids based upon our native R. *catawbiense* the lovely mountain rosebay of Virginia — are a good start. So too are those with the Caucasian R. *smirnowii* in them, especially where the distinctive white undersides to the leaves remain a dominant and attractive characteristic.

One of the very best of these is the comparatively recent 'King Tut,' bred by A. M. Shamarello, who has concentrated on plants for the Cleveland, Great Lakes, area. In turn he has crossed 'King Tut' with R. *yakusimanum*, a species from one of the Japanese off-islands that is clearly destined to be a part of many new rhododendrons. Even selections from wild plants are splendid enough. They make low mushrooms of relatively large leaves and carry compact heads of pink buds that turn gradually to white on opening. The new growths are bright silver and this indumentum is retained on the leaf reverses as it turns into dark brown suede.

The hybrids have names obsessed with hierarchical nobility, or perhaps a pack of cards: 'Yaku-King,' 'Yaku-Queen,' etc. 'Yaku-Prince' is the raiser's favourite.

Other breeders have concentrated upon other species, and hence different races of hybrids have been produced. These include the Gable hybrids, Glen Dale hybrids, Dexter hybrids, Nearing hybrids and so on. We can only be grateful to men who devote their lives to this task.

Earlier in this list a number of small ericaceous plants were recommended. Lots of the rhododendrons are similarly sized and are worth searching out. Rr. impeditum, racemosum and russatum and their hybrids are examples. Taller, but still light in effect, are species such as Rr. dauricum (its child P.J.M. is one of the simplest of all to grow), hippophaeoides and mucronulatum. This last is a deciduous species, exquisite in flower.

Deciduous Rhododendrons

Azaleas. It is usual to expect azaleas to be deciduous and rhododendrons to be evergreen, but such apparent simplicity is not fully maintained. Nonetheless the biggest, most typical groups of azaleas do lose their leaves in winter and therefore often offer splendid autumn colour as an addition to their early summer effect.

The archetypal azalea is *Rhododendron luteum*, a lovely yellow, sweetly scented bush, six to eight feet (2 x 2.5 m), from the Caucasus. It is so much at home here that it has become naturalized in several places in open woodland. Its gentle colour and open habit, fragrance and later autumn colour make it an invaluable acid-soil shrub. With other, mainly American species, it produced the Ghent hybrid azaleas, beginning in the 1830s. Most of these are in shades of yellow and soft orange. Delicate cream, pinks and pale apricots occur in the Occidental hybrids. These too are deliciously scented.

General lack of scent is a sad omission in the biggest groups, Knap Hill, Exbury and Mollis azaleas. Their superb heads of flowers in amazing shades of scarlet, vermilion, fiery reds and salmon pinks make them inevitably highly considered. The display is truly remarkable, but it is not precious to state that careless juxtaposition of brilliant azalea colours with the bluish reds of evergreen rhododendrons produces an effect that must at the kindest be described as decidedly restless. Here is the great danger of the acid-soil shade-garden, just as it is its great potential. Success in garden terms is not how kaleidoscopic an effect can be obtained — that is easier than falling off the proverbial log with these plants — but how satisfactory garden pictures can be built up to provide interest and beauty throughout the year. Hot colours, if they are to be used, must be separated and "cooled" by the use of foliage plants or the palest shades. Hostas, Solomon's seal, *Alchemilla*, *Smilacina* and other predominantly green plants are ideal as members of an herbaceous layer to grow with these shrubs.

We are particularly fortunate in that eastern North America is the native home to a number of exquisite wild azaleas. Often referred to as "swamp honeysuckles," they have both the grace and scent of true honeysuckle flowers. One, among the latest of its genus, *Rhododendron prunifolium*, can offer flowers into August, and anyone with a bit of thin woodland on acid soil should try to succeed with them. The best species include *Rr. arborescens*, *atlanticum*, *canescens* and *calendulaceum*.

No paragraph on deciduous azaleas could be complete without mention of one of the loveliest of all. An Oriental, *R. schlippenbachii* will flower, in perfect proportion to its size when only a couple of feet high, though huge plants ten feet through are known. The wide saucerlike flowers are a soft and clear pink and precede the foliage. In fall it, in company with most deciduous rhododendrons, turns yellow or flame. This lovely group of plants enjoys shade. We should see them more.

Skimmia. In mild areas this little group of Orientals is among the best of deep shade-bearing evergreens.

reevesiana 2 x 3 ft. (600 mm-1 m) This is the hardiest of the genus. It does well at, for instance, Swarthmore College near Philadelphia, and the Scott Horticultural Foundation there may offer it in their plant sale on occasion. Certainly for the heads of summer-scented white flowers and sealing-wax red berries throughout winter it should be tried. A group must be planted for cross-pollination.

Stewartia. A lovely group of deciduous camellia-relations, enjoying edge-of-wood conditions. All have white flowers on large shrubs or small cherry-sized trees. As summer flowers they are invaluable for giving late interest to the acid shrub garden. A courtyard with shade and shelter could well use a stewartia as a single specimen tree where habit, flower, autumn colour and ornamental flaking bark combine and succeed each other, enlivening season after season.

pseudocamellia 25 x 15 ft. (7.5 x 4.5 m) This is perhaps the best for general use — and probably the only one commercially available. Its flowers are individually fleeting, but repeat over a long period. *S. koreana* is similar, with wider opening flowers around the boss of golden stamens. *S. sinensis* is also highly covetable, as is our native *S. ovata*. This, however, is a southern plant and may be less hardy than the Orientals.

Styrax. The snowbells are valuable summer-flowering large shrubs or small trees enjoying the same conditions as stewartias. They can be used in the same way, as specimens in significant spots.

japonica 20 x 15 ft. (6 x 4.5 m) The most generally available and fortunately the most satisfactory for cultivation. It needs a position in semishade where there is room for its elegantly tiered branch pattern to develop fully and be appreciated from, say, the living-room window. The myriad flowers need closer inspection, and as they hang from the branches, the plant is ideally placed where a path can run underneath and one can look up in June into layers of whiteness.

Other species, all lovely, include *S. americana*, a native ten-footer and *S. obassia*, also shrubby with fragrant flowers and large lindenlike leaves.

Vaccinium. An invaluable genus for the heather garden and associating with rhododendrons, beneath which many are happy as an understory. Cowberry, *V. vitis-idaea*, is one that makes good shade ground cover, as does low-bush blueberry. Half shade is acceptable, but any more reduces both flower (and hence the delicious fruit) and fall colour. Acid soil, however dry, will support this plant.

Slightly better conditions will encourage the highbush blueberry; this is *corymbosum* 6-8 x 6 ft. (2-2.5 x 2 m) An East Coast native from Maine southward, it can reach ten feet or more. So valuable as a fruit, many forms have been selected and local conditions will suit one or another particularly. The pink-and-white flower display is visually worthwhile, too, as are the white-bloomed purple fruits in August. Acidic peaty soil, natural or artificial contrived, is essential; without it plants are chlorotic and obviously miserable.

Xanthorhiza. Yellowroot is the most unlikely of buttercup relations, with spikes of tiny purplish flowers before the leaves in spring.

simplicissima 2 x 4 ft. (600 x 1 m) A thicket of twiggy stems develops handsome, ferny foliage that colours well, yellow and orange and purple, in fall. This makes splendid ground cover under trees spreading gradually by suckers but never becoming a nuisance. Dwarf bulbs such as scilla will succeed among the stems and flower before yellowroot's leaves appear. A bit of lime, so long as the soil is rich in organic matter, does no harm.

Zenobia pulverulenta 3 x 3 ft. (1 m x 1 m) A charming little ericaceous shrub thriving in the semishade of bigger calcifuges — rhododendrons and the like. It has spikes of lily of the valley flowers in June and conspicuously white-dusted leaves. It comes from North Carolina southward but seems hardy enough farther north.

Shrubs for Shade on Limy Soil

As has already been discussed, generations of deciduous leaf fall in woodland gradually build up a soil with a high humus content that, because of its organic origin, is almost bound to have an acid reaction, even above a limy substrate. It follows that plants directly associated with such conditions in the wild are evolutionarily adapted to succeed not only in shade, but also on acid soils. Some groups must be described as obligate calcifuges; the rhododendrons and heathers, indeed the vast majority of their family, the Ericaceae, are examples: they cannot take lime. For them we must provide a soil high in organic content and low in pH readings, helping this by adding flowers of sulphur or aluminium sulphate.

There seems to be no such group of shrubs on the other side of the fence; "calcicole" must be taken as *lime accepting* rather than the often used phrase "lime loving." The significance of this is that the following shrubs offering a wide range of splendid effects for shady gardens on limy soils can without exception also be grown in a lower than 7 pH. They may, however, look thin and starved on dry acid sands and some feeding and irrigation will be necessary. In general this is the easiest group of plants to grow, for they earn their keep with a minimum of effort from the gardener. Even pruning is less of a chore than often suggested. In general, plants that flower on wood made in the previous year can have a few of these branches cut out *at* (for house decoration) or *immediately after* flowering time. Those late-flowering shrubs with flowers on current year's growth can have crossing or ugly branches cut out in spring. But *never* should flowering shrubs be clipped over with shears, unless they are to make a hedge when formality of aspect is more important than flowering or well-being of the individual. Evergreens need very little pruning indeed. For all shrubs pruning is to be

73

considered a way of maintaining vigour, of encouraging a natural, balanced plant. It is seldom right to use it as a way of keeping plants small; if this is necessary, then the wrong plant has been chosen for the site and it might be better to start anew with a plant that will be in proportion to needs.

Finally, when in doubt whether to prune or not, DON'T.

Here now are shade-tolerant shrubs for all soils, including those with lime.

Acanthopanax. There are several of these garden-useful ivy-relations from the Orient. Only one, however, is really hardy and at all available.

sieboldianus 6 x 8 ft. (2 x 2.5 m) This Japanese species can take almost all conditions, even dry shade, one of the most difficult situations for plants. It will build up a strong thicket of spiny stems carrying distinctive five-lobed leaves, a dark glossy green until late fall. White flowers, more interesting in detail than decorative in the mass, appear in golf-ball-sized heads in high summer.

A variegated form, its leaves elegantly banded with white, does exist and is well worth searching out. As with all plants whose photosynthetic areas are thus reduced, it is much less vigorous than the type.

Aesculus. The buckeyes or horse chestnuts are among our most spectacular flowering trees. One, however, is a tall suckering shrub that can be included here.

parviflora 10 x 15 ft. (3 x 4.5 m) Those of us who boast "small Latin and less Greek" (probably the only time we can compare ourselves to Shakespeare) may discount this plant from the specific description. This would be a great mistake. Individual flowers may be small by comparison with some of the others, but the general effect can rival any. Indeed, the bottlebrush buckeye is one of the very best of summer-flowering shrubs, a favourite plant.

The pleasures began as the elegant fingered foliage opens in May, pink flushed. The foot-long flower spikes begin to appear in late June, looking strangely thin and abortive, but in the ensuing month the buds swell. The display is dramatic and lasts for at least three weeks, each white spike a fuzz of projecting stamens and styles. Little conker fruits follow to ripen with the clear yellow fall colours.

The bottlebrush buckeye is best sited on the edge of lawn where it is happy in full sun or considerably less. In complete shade it grows well, suckering about, but naturally does not flower as freely. Even then, however, it is an eye-catching plant. Any soil suits.

Amelanchier. Shadbush, shadblow, serviceberry or more evocative of spring floral effect, snowy mespilus. The bigger species have already been discussed under *Trees for Shade.* The smaller ones offer their own value to the shade gardener. They are naturally woodland edge plants and hence are best in dappled shade, where they offer something for every season. All have white flowers and purplish fruit.

alnifolia 8 x 6 ft. (3 x 2 m) is the Saskatoon serviceberry now being offered in selections with bigger and better fruit. 'Regent' and 'Success' are recommended.

stolonifera, as its name suggests, is a suckering shrub. Only three or four feet high, it spreads outward to make a miniature copse of upright twiggy growth. Again, fleeting white flowers before the flowers and agreeably flavoured midsummer fruit, to which migratory robins are apt to beat the resident gardener.

Aralia. A genus of strange ivy relations with enormous divided leaves as if angelica had taken to the air.

spinosa 15-20 ft. (4.5-6 m) Devil's walking stick and Hercules club are names that refer to this native plant when it is in its winter, leafless state, a spiny skeleton of its summer self. Then the sparsely branched plant carrying its great green fronds is a splendid sight. A froth of white flowers is added to this in late summer. The black berries are soon dispersed, but the pattern of the flower-fruit sprays continues to be ornamental until everything falls.

This *Aralia* is often described in pejorative terms as "coarse" and "gaunt"; "architectural" is an equally valid word. Used in situations with strong man-made forms Hercules club can look magnificent. There is a fine plant outside the O'Keefe Centre (not the most elegant of theatres) in Toronto; this indicates both its hardiness and ability to take inner-city conditions. High wall shade is entirely acceptable.

elata is its Oriental counterpart, even hardier and possibly taller. Otherwise it is almost identical. A couple of fine variegated forms exist, but they have to be grafted, are difficult to obtain and slow to establish. If the top dies off one is left with a stock that will produce the green leaves of the type — a very expensive way to buy it.

Berberis. A huge genus of generally prickly growth offering both spring flower and autumn berry. The best flowers, however, usually produce the more inconspicuous fruit and vice versa. Barberries have received an unfortunately bad press through a few of their number being the winter alternate host of wheat rust; obviously any of these should be avoided, literally, like the plague. *Berberis vulgaris* and *B. canadensis* are the culprits and any hybrids with either as a parent are best avoided, as well. Apart from these there are some fine plants that will take half shade happily.

calliantha 3-4 x 3 ft. (1-1.2 x 1 m) A charming tidy dome of a bush with a definite "presence." Young stems are at first pink and the leaves beautifully white bloomed beneath. The hanging flowers are among the largest in the genus; pale primrose-yellow bells followed by dark purple fruit. This is a Tibetan plant. A related species from China, also evergreen, is *B. candidula*, similar but rather bigger.

thunbergii 4 x 4 ft. (1.2 x 1.2 m) The yellow flowers make little show, but the autumn display of flame-coloured deciduous foliage and scarlet berries is magnificent. 'Superba' is a bigger form, while 'Atropurpurea' is its invaluable purple-leaved form, excellent in mixed shrub plantings and as a hedge. Not for heavy shade, however.

wilsonae 3 x 4 ft. (1 x 1.2 m) Like other deciduous barberries from the Orient, this is only suitable for half shade. It makes low mounds of blue-green leaves that colour well in autumn as the fruits ripen to shades of coral and crimson. Several fine hybrids have been named, larger in size and even more prodigal in fruit. These include 'Barbarossa,' 'Bountiful' and x *rubrostilla*.

Buxus. One needs to visit old gardens in the Tidewater or in Britain to see what common box or boxwood can do. The great billowing evergreen heaps, like thunderclouds settled down on earth, develop even in the shade of European beech, one of the densest canopied trees. Box has a distinctive scent that is particularly evident after rain and is loved by some, hated by others.

japonica 3-4 x 3-4 ft. (1-1.1 x 1-1.2 m) Japanese box is smaller in size and usually in leaf. Some of its forms (especially var. *koreana*) are even hardier and hence are valuable in foundation plantings and for low formal hedges. However, because it is so tolerant to shears and secateurs, many people seem to believe garden box-bashing to be an essential ritual of the year, like grouse shooting in Scotland. Left alone the taller types make upright five-footers with sprays of attractive foliage throughout the year, especially valuable in winter for decoration indoors and out enlivened by fuzzes of horn-yellow flowers in April. Its fragrance is a fact of spring.

sempervirens 15-20 x 20 ft. (5-6 x 6 m) While this, the common box, lacks hardiness, forms have been selected with this attribute. They are generally small, however. Half a dozen feet is about the limit. 'Green Velvet' is one of a series of Canadian hybrids with Korean box that maintain a bright green-leaf effect in winter. 'Vardar Valley' is a low-growing variant of the species collected in the Balkans. This is the one to choose if winter conditions are particularly fierce, as it succeeds even in Zone 4.

Ceanothus. Again one must go to the West Coast to see this genus really showing off, perhaps the best of blue-flowered shrubs. Our one eastern species is less spectacular, but a useful, dry-shade shrublet.

americanus 3 x 4 ft. (1 x 1.2 m) New Jersey tea suggests one use, happily superseded, but other names such as mountain sweet and wild snowball offer other, visual, pleasures. As a midsummer flowerer in sandy soil even under pines, it is not to be neglected. Mountain sweet has been used with C. *coeruleus*, from Mexico, to produce the bispecific hybrid, C. x *delilianus*. Selections have brought together a deciduous group that is worth trying in sheltered half shade and treated like buddleia, that is, pruned down hard in spring. 'Marie Simon' and 'Gloire de Versailles,' pink and powder blue respectively, are distinctive.

Cephalanthus occidentalis 6-8 x 4 ft. (2 x 2.5 x 2 m) The buttonbush of moist woodland stream sides seems unfairly unconsidered in gardens. The floral display is exquisite in detail, each cluster an inch-wide snowy sphere with projecting stamens like an exploding firework. They are followed by purplish seed heads that look well throughout fall on forms that fully cast off their dead flowers.

One snare in cultivation is that the long glossy leaves appear so late in spring that every year one is convinced the shrub has succumbed to winter. However, to get light to a herbaceous layer beneath this is a definite plus.

Chaenomeles. On limy soils in cold areas these take on something of the place of camellias in the red range of early flower colour. Semidouble as well as single forms exist, carried (apple-blossom-like) on tight spurs against the branches. Most give a bonus of golf-ball-sized yellow quinces in autumn from which a distinctive preserve can be made.

japonica 2-3 x 2 ft. (600-900 x 600 mm) A small twiggy bush with brilliant flame-coloured flowers in May. This must be kept clear from anything pink flowered at this time, but associates well with the smaller yellow daffodils and tulips.

speciosa 3-4 x 4 x 4-5 ft. (1-1.2 x 1.2-1.5 m) It is this group that is commonly and confusingly referred to as "japonica." Here is another plant that, having been in cultivation for centuries in the Orient before it came to the West, has a wide range of colour forms from white ('Nivalis') through pink ('Cameo') to dark red ('Simonii'), with most intermediate shades occurring, as well. The last named is a low-growing plant, good under a window where taller things would be inappropriate.

Crosses between the two species listed are known as C. x *superba* and also come in a range of fine cultivars; some pick up the orange tinge of C. *japonica*. Among the best are 'Knap Hill Scarlet' and 'Romance,' a fine blood-red.

Because of their spur-flowering habit, Japanese quinces are admirable for formal espalier training against walls or on wires to make a narrow hedge division. As free-standing bushes they also can be used to form impenetrable hedges. Often slow to settle down to flower well, they do eventually earn their keep well. Summer shade is acceptable.

Conifers. It is convenient to list together those conifers happiest in shade conditions. Because of their generally dark demeanour, soaking up light as sponges soak water, their use in shady spots is limited. The effect is too sombre, yet to give evergreen bulk and shelter to the base of an otherwise tall copse of deciduous trees is often desirable, for within such shelter more exciting things can grow. And as focal points at the side of steps or as ground cover on banks, several of the prostrate junipers are as useful in shade as in sun.

Many conifers grow in almost pure stands in their native habitats, and hence, to ensure regeneration, their saplings are adapted to tolerate shade to a remarkable degree. Thus the white fir, *Abies concolor*, can be considered for this very use as an evergreen nurse, although it may have to be removed later — if space is limited — when its charges ceased to be children and its job is done. Similarly the elegant eastern hemlock (*Tusga canadensis*) has much to offer to the shade gardener. It is surprising that such an ornamental plant has remained almost entirely the possession of the forester, who finds it ideal for bearing shade under the mature trees that it will one day succeed. Of the pines the lovely white pine is the best (*P. strobus,*) very elegant in youth. More generally, however, the garden value of conifers is as specimen plants, where their distinctive shape and texture can be individually appreciated here. Therefore only those most proved are described, although many conifers could be tentatively listed for woodland use.

Cephalotaxus. There are relatively fewer evergreen shrubs that are happier in shade than deciduous ones and proportionately even fewer conifers; their role is usually to provide the shade-*giving* layer. But the plum yews, a small group from eastern Asia, are exceptions to the rule. All are yewlike shrubs or small trees with rather bigger leaves than yew held in elegant fronds and purplish fruits that resemble ripe olives in size and colour. The two species available are visually pretty close. *C. fortuni* is from China, while the hardier *C. harringtonia* is Japanese. (Incidentally, a chemical extract from the latter, Harringtonine, is currently being tested as an anticancer agent.) In the garden these are admirable shade-tolerant evergreens, greatly underused. Brooklyn Botanical Garden grows a splendid flat form of Harrington's plum yew.

Junipers. The prostrate junipers (the tree-sized species have little to offer us here) are plants of open moors, downs and shorelines. They are thus not plants for undertree shade, understandably being intolerant of drip. As already mentioned, however, courtyard shade open to the sky is acceptable to several useful plants.

These are the species and forms of *J. conferta*, green and prickly, *J. horizontalis*, especially eye-catching in blue-green types such as 'Bar Harbor,' and *J. sabina*, whose *tamariscifolia* is particularly good. *J. x media* has produced the most useful juniper of all in 'Pfitzerana.' As the invaluable Hillier's *Manual* so rightly states, it "is a friend of the landscape gardener, it never lets him down, it marries the formal into the informal, it embellishes his layout and hides his errors." The strong forty-five-degree branches with pendulous tips make a fine pattern, and though commonly seen, do not become a cliché if sensibly sited. There are several other *J. x media* forms, all worth consideration. A relatively new conifer to cultivation is *Microbiota decussata*. Like a low, rounded juniper, it seems to accept building or wall shade very well.

Taxus baccata, European yew, has innumerable garden uses from classic hedging to formal sentinels and effective ground cover. The fleshy red or yellow fruits are often carried, on pollinated female trees, in sufficient quantity to make quite a show, but the birds seldom permit it to last for long. The fleshy outside aril is pleasantly edible, the hard seed inside highly poisonous. Birds, of course, pass it through; humans spit it out.

In its normal form the effect of yew is so dark as to be almost black, especially in shade, where light is already scarce. Here the golden 'Elegantissima' is admirable, and though in deepest shade much colour is lost, the ultimate effect is not as dark as the type. The Irish yew is the one that maintains an upright habit, while 'Cavendishii' and 'Repandens' make splendid horizontal ground cover. In heavy shade these are much more successful than the prostrate junipers. It should be added that yews well cared for do not deserve their reputation for slowness of growth.

In cold positions the Japanese yew, *Taxus cuspidata* and its equally varied forms, is to be preferred. There are also crosses between the two species known botanically as *T.* x *media* and sometimes called the Anglo-jap yew — which sounds less like a plant than a rather doubtful political treaty.

The cultivar 'Hicksii' has the columnar habit of Irish yew and hence is desirable for formal effects in cold areas. Where snowfall is heavy, it will need wiring to prevent branches breaking out and ruining the desired symmetry.

Cornus. Many of the calcicole dogwoods are grown especially for the bright winter bark of their young growth. Unfortunately, though they will do well enough, this colour is so reduced in shade as to be of little use for that purpose. However, the variegated forms of *Cornus alba*, up to eight feet (2.5 m) tall and as much across are admirable as foliage plants. 'Elegantissima' and 'Spaethii,' white striped and yellow striped respectively, make a bright splash throughout summer, and their leaf sprays are admirable for indoor arrangements. *C. stolonifera* and *C. sanguinea* are similar in bark effect.

alternifolia 20 x 20 ft. (6 x 6 m). Though without much to offer in flower or fruit — both rather fleeting — the horizontal branch pattern of this native woodlander is sufficiently distinctive for it to deserve a focal spot in the half wild garden. The name pagoda dogwood refers to the tiered branches, not to any Oriental origin. It will take the lime and heavy clay that flowering dogwood resents. A smaller variegated form is splendid but extremely difficult to obtain. Sadly this must also be said of the magnificent *Cornus controversa* from Japan and China. The branch pattern is even more distinct and the plant can reach forty feet (12 m) or so. The variegated form is truly ravishing.

mas 15 x 20 ft. (4.5 x 6 m) This is the cornelian cherry, noted especially for its welcome early flowers opening in March. Pale yellow, they make a fine effect in the garden for several weeks. It would seem to be ideal cut material to bring indoors, but warmth accentuates the pervading smell of old fish boxes. A plant under a big English beech in my garden (in southern Ontario) flowers well but fails to produce the brilliant red, oval, cherry-sized fruits in fall. Thus perhaps the yellow fruited forms are also not for shade. A variegated type, slow growing and smaller, is admirable. *Cornus officinalis* is very similar and equally valuable for early flower in cold spots.

Corylus. Coppiced (that is, cut to the ground on a ten-year cycle for hurdle making, etc.) hazel is the classic crop plant grown under developing standard oak trees in European woodlands. Its myriad catkins waving in a February breeze is one of the most heartening signs of incipient spring.

avellana 10 x 15 ft. (3 x 4.5 m) Here it grows within similar woodland conditions, and if there is space, a few plants will well earn their keep both visually, in March, and economically to provide beanpoles or tree stakes. Squirrels will probably get to the nuts first, so little can be expected on that score.

For a small garden or courtyard (in a dominant position) the corkscrew hazel ('Contorta') can be used as a specimen plant, with its twisted stems and puckered leaves. A mature plant in flower is a splendid if rather bizarre sight. Winter branches are always in demand by flower arrangers. Day and night guards are often necessary before an important show.

maxima 10 x 15 ft. (3 x 4.5 m) The filbert, bigger than all its parts but just as attractive. The purple-leaved form adds a sombre yet luscious note to any planting of foliage shrubs. It is good with golden elder or variegated cornus, but one must beware of the dangerously heavy late-summer effect that most purple leaves impart.

Cotoneaster. One of our most valuable genera, offering shade-accepting evergreens varying from low carpeters to small trees. Most have white- or pink-flushed flowers in early summer followed by prodigious crops of usually red fruit in autumn. Often this holds on for several months.

Low-growing cotoneasters, less than three feet (1 m)

apiculatus. The cranberry cotoneaster is well named for the fine large fruits that make a good autumn show. Individual plants can reach six feet (2 m) across, twice their height.

dammeri. A lovely ground hugging shrub that follows exactly the contours beneath it, rooting as it goes. Dark evergreen leaves studded with red fruit. An amusing use is to plant it by steps, where shoots will grow across the angle of the risers to etch each step with green.

horizontalis. Rockspray is the commonest and still the best, with its dramatic herringbone pattern branches. This species is deciduous and its leaves colour as brightly as its berries. Against a wall it can get quite high. An admirable dark courtyard or north-wall plant. There is a pretty variegated form, though slow growing and mean in fruit. The flowers are very attractive to queen wasps. *C. adpressus* is similar but more compact.

microphyllus. Equally good as ground cover or to plant at the top of a retaining wall. Curtains of foliage will then descent to the ground, pink and white with flowers in June, scarlet with fruit in November, glossy green for the rest of the year.

salicifolius repens. A low-growing form of a much bigger plant (see below) that differs greatly in effect from the other carpeters. The strong arching growths have large leaves two to three inches (50-70 mm) and carry heavy bunches of fruit.

Medium cotoneasters, 5 — 8 ft. (1.5 — 2.5 m)

conspicuus 'Decorus.' Although often described as a dwarf, this plant gradually builds up a high mound of arching branches. It is particularly free with both flower and fruit.

harrovianus. Another lovely arching shrub that would be worth growing for its flower even if no fruit followed. In fact, the second display is particularly good and admirably late.

Large cotoneasters, 8 — 12 ft. + (2.5 — 4 m +)

lacteus. A strong "weighty" plant. The leathery leaves are white-felted beneath and set off huge heads of fruit.

salicifolius. The narrow willowlike leaves are carried on elegant arching branches that bend farther with the weight of its fruits. A most graceful plant at all times, it can act as the shrub layer in an open woodland stratification or be trained up to near tree size itself. It has been used as a parent in many hybrids that are given the group name of

x *watereri*. Of the named clones, good ones with red fruit include 'John Waterer' and 'Cornubia.' In gardens where birds are more than usually greedy and leave little time for visual enjoyment of berries, 'Pink Champagne' and 'Exburiensis' are admirable; our feathered friends wait around for them to ripen to edible red, which, happily, they never do. Both gradually change from yellow to pink. These fine cotoneasters, though typically evergreen, may behave as deciduous plants in the north without necessarily coming to harm.

Daphne. Some of the most desirable shrubs belong here. Tidy growth, earliness of flower and intense fragrance are hallmarks. However, the small mountainside species are not for shade and a couple of other beauties lack hardiness.

burkwoodii 4 x 4 ft. (1.2 x 1.2 m) A lovely semi evergreen for half shade. It likes a leafy soil but has no objection to lime, and carries heads of pink scented flowers nestling among the leaves at the top of each twig. It can begin in May and flowers may still occur at the end of November. Leaves stay green even longer. Named clones include 'Somerset' and 'Carol Mackie,' the latter with white-edged leaves to add to the pleasure.

mezereum 3-4 x 3 ft. (1-1-2 x 1 m) The well-known deciduous mezereon is a plant of northern Europe woodlands. It does best in cool spots on moisture-retentive soil but is always erratic in length of life; sometimes an apparently healthy plant will flower well and then quietly subside. Perhaps it is naturally not long lived. Certainly it is a martyr to a debilitating virus and should be regularly sprayed against insect vectors that can spread the virus.

The usual type has strong purple, fragrant flowers, carried bottle-brushlike up the bare stems. The white form ('Alba') is more upright growing and has yellow berries as distinct from the red ones of the type. Both are highly poisonous to man but irresistible to birds. A branch should be netted and seeds sown as soon as ripe to keep good young plants growing. Self-sown seedlings sometimes occur and often make the best plants.

Deutzia. Foaming white or pink flowers in June and July are the characteristic of this easily grown group. Not for deep tree shade, but they succeed happily on the north side of buildings, lighting up their spot. Some of the flowering growth should be cut out each year to keep an open bush and one must be careful not to snap off the emerging new growth when so doing.

Among the best of the bigger deutzias, attaining six feet (2 m) or eighty are x *elegantissima* and x *kalmiiflora* (the individual flowers really are like *Kalmia*, impossible on a limy soil). Both are white, pink flushed. For small gardens or narrow borders the *gracilis* and x *rosea* types are best, making tidy hummocks of growth.

Euonymus. Here is a group of widely differing shrubs. Seeing them only in leaf, relationship would seldom be guessed, but in the fall, or as long as they hang on, the fruits of euonymus proclaim the fact. The typical hanging bunches of lobed capsules split to display vivid seeds inside. They could only belong to the spindle bushes.

alatus 10-15 x 15 ft. (3 x 4.5 x 4.5 m) The Winged Spindle Bush is one of the most valuable of shade-tolerant shrubs. While it may even reach 20 feet (6 m) in height its leaf pattern and small but brilliant fruits are in scale even when the plant is tiny. As with others of its genus, the greenish flowers make little show. Autumn is the time to wait for when the foliage turns a clear rose-red dotted by points of light, which on closer examination are seen to be the orange seeds hanging out of the capsules. One of the best colourers for shade.

Dwarfish compact forms are occasionally offered but this is a plant whose lightness of effect makes its adult size compatible with all but the smallest gardens. It could make the one specimen "tree," suitably pruned, in a town courtyard.

europaeus 10-20 x 10 ft. (3 x 6 x 3 m) The European Spindle Bush is there a common hedgerow plant of chalk and limestone hills. With us it accepts half shade without fuss and fruits well — fine hanging clusters of pink capsules opening to display the orange seeds. But it is rather a coarse plant and can be a martyr to scale insects. 'Red Cascade' is a cultivar highly recommended on both sides of the Atlantic.

fortunei If Robert Fortune were associated with no other plant from his Oriental travels in the middle of the last century, gardeners in the Northeast would have reason to remember him gratefully for winter-creeper. We have no more adaptable broad leaved evergreen. Its forms and uses, if not quite legion in the Biblical sense, are very considerable. Groundcover, self-clinging climber, bush, fruiting ornamental, foliage plant; all are here. It would be ungrateful to ask for more than the little green stars as floral display.

Like English Ivy there are creeping or climbing stems incapable of flowering until adulthood is reached. Selection has produced named types that remain immature or, alternatively are fully mature, flowering and fruiting at an early age. See also the 'climbers' section.

Of the named forms 'Coloratus' is the biggest, climbing to twenty feet, its leaves turn wine-purple in winter. 'Vegetus' is more compact but will still climb. I have this scrambling through a huge old *Viburnum x carlecephalum* bush to which it gives a marvellously furnished winter appearance holding its fruit throughout January and beyond. 'Gracilis', 'Silver Pillar', 'Silver Queen', 'Golden Prince' are admirable little variegated shrubs, superb alike for winter garden and cut-foliage decoration indoors. Perhaps their most valuable contribution is at those weeks of pseudo-spring when almost nothing seems to be moving, then, as foil for the earliest spring bulbs (snowdrops, aconites, crocus, which can look so naked and vulnerable alone), they produce the first fresh garden pictures of the year.

nanus 3 in. x 2 ft. (80 x 600 mm) A tiny semievergreen creeper for ground cover for heavy shade. Small leaves bulbs such as scilla or chionodoxa will come through it happily.

Forsythia. This brilliant spring effect is one that everyone, even the most non-gardening, knows and welcomes. The fact that Forsythia has not even had to have a 'common' name invented for it indicates its ubiquity; though the use of the short y for Mr. Forsyth's name-shrub aproaches one.

There is little doubt that the brassy yellow forms are over-planted and can look unpleasantly fierce in the gentle spring scene. However, in shade bud development is less solid and the growth more open, creating a more elegant effect.

x intermedia 8-10 x 10 ft. (2.5-3 x 3 m) This hybrid group, based around the well-known form 'Spectabilis' is *the* forsythia in most places. Huge mounds of growth and usually of flower, but there is a problem of bud hardiness in cold areas. This has been worked upon by, among others on this continent, Dr. Felicitas Svejda at the Dominion Arboretum in Ottawa. 'Northern Gold' is the form so far most distributed, but others in a range of sizes are still on trial.

Meanwhile other cultivars are available of various origin. 'Lynwood' is a fine form, slightly paler than 'Spectabilis,' while 'Spring Glory' is sulphur yellow and more compact.

ovata 4 x 4 ft. (1.2 x 1.2 m) This little bush is one of the first to flower and is ideal to add its soft yellow to plantings of spring heathers if the position is too exposed for *Corylopsis pauciflora.* 'Ottawa' is a form renowned for its bud hardiness. 'Sunrise' should also be sought out.

suspensa 10 x 10 ft. (3 x 3 m) In the open, with unlimited space, this makes a great fountain, like a golden Roman candle firework. It is one of the best shrubs to train on a shaded wall; prune after flowering. I have seen it tumbling through an old yew tree, the pale golden yellow admirably set off against the dark of the yew. It is also splendid on banks: planted at the top it will cascade down.

Hydrangea. In addition to the well-known mop-head hydrangeas, so much a feature of potted arrangements at summer celebrations, the genus contains several other excellent shade-needing and shade-tolerant plants. It might be mentioned here that the mop-heads are garden forms in which many of the fertile flowers in the centre of a naturally flat head have become sterile, developing the extravagant sepals normally possessed only by the outer ring.

arborescens 4-5 x 5 ft. (1-1.2 x 1.2 m) An unsatisfactory name (i.e. "treeish") for what can be treated as an herbaceous plant without any permanent wood at all. In spite of Dr. Dirr's strictures, I find it is a valuable and most beautiful plant in southern Ontario. The shoots of soft green leaves carry spherical heads of mainly infertile flowers that exhibit a parade of gentle colour over several months. They begin lime green, pass through cream to white, become green again and eventually brown and papery. They remain in this condition throughout winter, adding texture and colour. Holding a handful of soft snow, each head returns to its summer whiteness, if briefly.

'Annabelle' is the superior form usually grown. Whichever is chosen, it is important not to prune hard for size of inflorescence. They become too heavy for the stems to support and flop about most unaesthetically.

Another lovely native, grown in Britain as *H. cinerea*, has a similar habit but grey-dusted leaves. *Hortus III* refers to it as *H. arborescens discolor*, but I have not seen it here in cultivation. It is worth searching out.

These white summer subshrubs look particularly well as a foil and backing to orange lilies.

paniculata 5-10 x 10 ft. (1.5-3 x 3 m) As the name suggests, the flower heads have triangular rather than the typical round or flat head of other hydrangeas. Well fed and hard pruned (after a framework has been built up), in spring this produces heads of monumental size. (But then they need support; for normal garden decoration a gentle thinning of growth is sufficient). They are white and darken gently to pink. For windy, cold gardens the smaller 'Praecox' is a wiser choice.

One sees enormous plants of this against porches of old houses in Vermont and Maine, looking splendid in their season, a cascade of white. In deep shade they flower less but still usefully; 'Grandiflora' does so late into September and beyond, and hence is very valuable. Colchicums underneath look splendid in half sun.

quercifolia 6-8 x 5 ft. (2-2.5 x 1.5 m) A shrub layer plant of the tulip-tree woodland of the southeastern United States. Though not exciting in flower, it comes into its own with dramatic autumn leaf colour of foliage that has great visual presence through summer. Cultivars such as 'Harmony' and 'Snowflake' have better, whiter flower heads. Again they can be overheavy for the strength of stems.

The common garden hydrangeas are based around two Japanese species, H. *macrophylla* and the smaller H. *serrata* (which in fact may be just a geographical variant, smaller in all its parts). It is the former that has given us the splendid florists' 'Hortensia' mop-head hydrangeas.

In most areas they are definitely better in shade, under taller shrubs or north walls, and they are especially valuable on acid soils to extend the season of interest when a predominance of planting has been given to the earlier Ericaceae. Here many of the hortensias take on shades of brilliant blue, while these same cultivars on limy soils are pink. Where soil is near neutral, blueness can be artificially maintained by the frequent use of an aluminum-sulphate-based "bluing powder." But it is a mistake to try this with a high soil pH; the resultant miserable purplish tints are seldom of much virtue. Better to enjoy the pink and the white.

In mild and humid areas these plants can make huge bushes ten feet high and as much through. Half that size is more common. It should be mentioned that their habit of making next year's flower buds in the previous autumn and being tempted into growth by false springs causes the loss of these buds in areas susceptible to late frosts. Avoid especially an eastern exposure.

While one may have success with a hydrangea bought for house decoration and subsequently put out, it should be realized that different cultivars have been developed for the two jobs. Among the best for outside in southern Ontario are the following. They should perform equally well throughout the Northeast.

Mop-heads. 'All Summer Beauty,' pink or blue; 'Bouquet Rose'; 'French Blue.'

Lacecaps. Closer to the wild species are forms with only an outside ring of big infertile flowers. The flat heads can be very striking. 'Blue Wave,' central fertile flowers blue, with the outside flowers pink or blue. 'Mariesii,' mid pink or clear medium blue.

'Maculata' and 'Tricolor' are both blue-flowered variegated-leaved forms. They are probably less hardy.

'Preziosa' is a cross between *H. macrophylla* and *H. serrata.* The influence of the latter keeps it small — to four feet (1.2 m) or so — while the former provides the ball-like heads of flowers that open pale and darken to purple as autumn approaches (such a colour change is common with hydrangeas) and many remain ornamental throughout winter, especially under hoarfrost, maintaining inflorescence structure although the flowers have become papery and brown.

'Pink Beauty' is similar, and on neutral soil keeps that colour without going mauve.

There are several lovely Himalayan species that should be tried wherever they can be obtained. *H. villosa (aspera)* is the finest, with hairy leaves and stems and fine purple lace caps on an eight-foot (2.5 m) plant. Of similar size and of undoubted hardiness is *H. heteromalla*, with flat and rather sparse flower heads up to ten inches across that gradually turn rose purple. A gawky but distinctive shrub for shade.

Hypericum. The St. John's worts make up a bright, happy group of shrubs untainted by any hint of guile; their open full-faced cups of gold are centred with a conspicuous fuzz of stamens. All take half shade, some much more.

androsaemum 2-3 x 2 ft. (600-900 x 600 mm) The northern European tutsan is one of the best small shrubs for under tree (or indeed any) heavy shade. The heads of small yellow flowers are succeeded by red fleshy capsules, soon turning dry and black. In this state they hold on for months. A child of this (with *H. hircinum*) is *H.* x *inodorum*. Its form 'Elstead' is an altogether brighter and more desirable plant, especially as the fruits remain brilliantly pink. A succession of flowers and fruit occur together and provide a very gay combination of colours. "Tutsan," incidentally, is a reduction of the old optimistic herbal name *toute-saine* (cure-all: sadly it doesn't).

calycinum 1 ft. x infinity. This has the finest flowers of any hardy hypericum. Three-inch wide cups, each with a great brush of stamens, stud the little creeping plant; even on a shady dry bank it becomes a carpet of gold in high summer. But so invasive is the plant that it must be used with some care. Under trees and mature shrubs it can be happily introduced, but newly planted things will not enjoy such boisterous competition. Extensive plantings can be mown in the spring to promote clean young growth.

patulum. Around this name are grouped some splendid garden shrubs from China that make symmetrical domes of shining leaves and bright gold flowers. They vary in height from two feet (600 mm) in *H.* x *moseranum* (which has *H. calycinum* as a parent but does not inherit its rampageousness) to 'Hidcote,' attaining six feet (2 m) or so in a mild spot. *H. forrestii* and 'Gold Cup' are intermediate in size. All are as wide as they are high.

The Orientals may be cut to the ground or to snow level in hard winters, but usually return to put on a respectable show the following summer. They should be used more in half shade or sun.

prolificum 4-5 x 4 ft. (1.2-1.5 x 1.2 m) This is one of a group of Americans with a montane-southeast States distribution. *Hh. buckleyi, frondosum* and *kalmeianum* are others. All make twiggy bushes with masses of yellow flowers and distinctive stamen fuzzes for several summer weeks. Evergreen or near so, the fall and winter combination of beaked capsules and blue-green leaves continues to give visual interest.

Itea virginica. 4-5 x 4 ft (1.2-2 x 1.2 m) The Virginia sweetspire is the only North American member of a group of otherwise eastern Asiatic shrubs (sadly they do not like our winters). But our native flies the flag bravely, with midsummer spikes of scented white flowers and long-lasting fall colour. In half shade it forms a suckering shrub that will offer divisions to extend its group or to make friends with those who admire it.

Kerria japonica. The bright butter-yellow, rather ragged double flowers of this old cottage-garden shrub always make a good spring show. It is the double form we usually see, often eight feet (2.5 m) up a shady wall.

But the type with single flowers, like a tiny 'Harison's Yellow' rose, is a more elegant plant only half the height. The variegated-leaved forms are rather delicate but worth the effort in a small garden. With plenty of space *Kerria* will make fine thickets of green shoots as bright as any evergreen in winter.

Laburnum. The lovely golden rain tree is common in European gardens as a specimen standard, but it is in fact an edge-of-woodland plant and hence does well under taller things. In our climate it enjoys the protection. Multistemmed plants against the dark of conifers make a marvellous show of long, yellow, wisterialike tassels.

alpinum 20 x 15 ft. (6 x 5 m) From the mountains of southern Europe this is perhaps the hardiest of the long-tasselled types, and as a true species it can be grown from imported seed if plants of those so often recommended, such as *L. x watereri, L. x vossii,* are unobtainable. Flowering takes five years or so. One warning: the small pea pods and their seeds are very poisonous and babies in prams should not be parked underneath. They look edible enough to the unsuspecting infant.

Ligustrum. Ordinary Amur privet is one of the dullest plants, a reputation gained because of its ability to put up with everything. It thus gets the dullest sites.

ovalifolium 8-10 x 8 ft. (2.5-3 x 2.5 m) The green form is no great improvement, but the golden 'Aureum' is as bright from a distance as *Forsythia* (if you would like *Forsythia* in flower for over half the year). 'Argenteum' is silver privet with white-edged, green leaves. Both provide excellent cut foliage and are excellent as open free-standing bushes in half shade.

Lindera. Of the eighty or so species that are strewn around Asia (with a few in North America) only our locally native spicebush is at all often grown.

benzoin 6-8 x 6 ft. (2-2.5 x 6 m) The fuzz of little yellow flowers in early spring makes little show at a distance, but is attractive in detail.

On female bushes they are followed in fall by brilliant scarlet fruits, like small elongated cherries. They make their show after the leaves have fallen in a blaze of golden glory. These and the bark, as one might expect from the Laurel family, are strongly aromatic. Spicebush is happy in half shade and, as has been emphasized for several other plants, can do well in shade if initial soil preparation is done with care and the first couple of years given attention to adequate watering. This always pays off. A more spectacular species from China, Japan and Korea is *Lindera obtusiloba*; bigger, with black fruits, its autumn colours spectacular.

Lonicera. The twining honeysuckles have been described in the appropriate section in this book, but of the one hundred eighty or so species in the genus (as well as many garden selections) the majority are in fact free-standing shrubs. They offer clusters of often scented flowers and usually a good fruiting display beginning as early as July. The three that follow encompassed their qualities, but many more may be chosen from.

fragrantissima 8-10 x 8 ft. (2.5-3 x 2.5 m) This rather inelegant shrub fully lives up to the Latin superlative in its name when in flower in early spring. Mild spells in winter may bring a few out earlier and certainly twigs should be cut as with forsythia, for forcing indoors. They will scent a whole room. Though the leaves do not colour much in autumn, they do hold on into late November or even beyond and extend the plant's interest.

korolkowii 8-10 x 8 ft. (2.5-3 x 2.5 m) This can be taken as typical of the summer flowerers, but its pale bluish-grey foliage, almost ruelike in colour, picks it out from the throng. Flowers in June are normally pink, but there are named colour variants such as 'Aurora.' Fruit is a bright red-currant shade. This is a plant worth searching out.

pileata. 2-3 x 5 ft. (600-900 x 1.5 m) A semievergreen of almost *Cotoneaster horizontalis* shape, and it is excellent in similar positions — for shady banks or under light trees. It offers several particular moments of quiet attraction, in summer when a whiff of typically honeysuckle fragrance comes from a source that seemingly could not possibly produce it. (Even when the plant is identified the little creamy flowers have to be searched out under the leaves.) Then in autumn it is worth picking a few sprays of the translucent purple berries, and in spring there is pleasure when the fresh leaves start to replace the dark ones.

Mahonia. This genus used to be included in *Berberis*, but though closely related (closely enough for hybridization to occur between the two genera) they are visually very distinct. Mahonias are all splendid ever-greens with long pinnate leaves and sprays of yellow flowers in spring.

With a Pacific-rim distribution from Mexico northward to British Columbia then Japan, Formosa and into Nepal, it is hardly surprising that few can take our continental climate. But the two best ones can if placed with care.

aquifolium 6 x 6 ft. (2 x 2 m). The typical form of Oregon grape makes a tight thicket of stems whose side shoots produce whorls of glossy leaves. They are roughly toothed but not as prickly as the name *aquifolium* (holly-leaved) would suggest. In the centre a mass of short yellow flower sprays emerges in spring. This is a good bird shrub. To my specimen just by a dining-room window come the first hummingbirds in April, and in late summer when the grape-bloomed fruit is ripe the cedar waxwings seek it out.

At all times of the year Oregon grape earns its keep in the garden. The foliage is also invaluable in cut arrangements indoors; green in summer and bronze in winter.

Dwarf forms exist; spreading by underground suckers, they make splendid evergreen ground cover under trees. Various names occur on the list, such as M. *aquifolium* 'Heterophylla' and M. *repens*. All should be considered.

japonica 6 x 8 ft. (2 x 2.5 m) This superb species only wants the addition of delicious-tasting fruit to make it the ultimate desirable plant. Apart from this it really does have everything: magnificent evergreen leaves in great whorls, long sprays of scented flowers — pale yellow and lily of the valley scented — in early spring and a strikingly handsome architectural habit. It looks equally well in the informality of woodland as in a sophis-ticated courtyard.

But how hardy? In an open position at Swathmore College it looks very happy, and we are trying it at Royal Botanical Gardens in southern Ontario. It is worth every effort to grow a good plant as the dominant individual in a carefully composed association.

Try it, but avoid M. *bealei*, with which it is confused. This is a gawkier, coarser plant with upright flower spikes, hardly scented at all.

Malus. This is not the place for a discourse on the hundreds of ornamen-tal crab apples; many indeed are big enough to be shade providers rather than taking on the subordinate role of being plants for shade. Yet it is worth remembering that the wild crabs are hedgerow and wood-land plants and thus they succeed admirably in the light shade of bigger trees. This encourages rather more open growth and less flower, giving a lighter and in many ways a more beautiful effect than the solid lumps of unadulterated colour, however magnificent, of specimen lawn trees. One needs to visit a mature collection both in spring and in the fall and add together the attributes to choose the couple one has room for.

My personal choice — if it had to stop at two — would be Sargent's crab, a low, wide bush, white flowered and red fruited, and *Malus toringoides*. This is a full-sized apple tree with creamy, white flowers and in fall a dramatic display of yellow, pink-flushed fruit (or in more sun pink, yellow flushed). It comes from Szechuan and has the elegance of Chinese calligraphic brush strokes.

Paxistima canbyi. A dreary little Virginian evergreen, often recommended but clearly the last resort of those who go in for some desultory foundation planting before moving with evident relief into an apartment. *Paxistima* will take shade or, indeed, anything else.

Philadelphus. The lovely mock oranges are not for deepest shade (although *P. coronarius* will grow even under conifers, it flowers there so poorly as to be not much point), but, like the deutzias to which they are related, half shade from above and north-facing borders are perfectly acceptable. In such positions the sadly short flowering season is extended somewhat. They should be planted where the drifts of perfume can be appreciated on early summer evenings.

coronarius 8-10 x 8 ft. (2.5-3 x 2.5 m) However common, this is a beautiful plant when bowed down by its creamy fragrant flowers. It has a good variegated form and a superlative gold-leaved one that flowers as well as the type. This plant really does need shade and succeeds admirably here in southern Ontario.

Hybridization has produced some excellent garden plants. Several are really small, such as 'Manteau d'Hermine' and 'Avalanche'; bigger are 'Conquête' and 'Norma.' The double-flowered forms, though splendid at a distance, lack the virginal perfection of the singles, as well, it seems, actual strength of petal texture.

Potentilla. The shrubby cinquefoils flower best in full sun, but in a north-facing border they still put on a sufficient show to make themselves worthwhile. They are so late to come into leaf (one is always convinced that new plantings are dead) that they make a good shrub layer above early bulbs in a small stratified association. They take dry, very alkaline soils with apparent relish. Dozens of cultivars and several species are on offer such as:

arbuscula 1½ x 3 in. (450 x 900 mm) Big, (for a potentilla, one and a half inches across) yellow flowers for a long period — July to October on a dwarf bush. This is an admirable front of border plant.

fruticosa 3-4 x 4 ft. (1-1.2 x 1.2 m) This has a vast natural range around cold parts of the Northern Hemisphere that its forms, first from the wild and then from gardens, are legion. I like the pale-coloured forms with grey leaves, such as 'Vilmoriniana' and 'Primrose Beauty,' and also 'Elizabeth,' a hybrid of the two species listed above.

The new, much vaunted red shrubby cinquefoils are something of a disappointment, but 'Tangerine' is good, as well as being self-descriptive.

Prunus. Of the flowering cherries much the same can be said as of the Malus though they are less happy in heavy clay soils and resent wet feet. Similarly, top-grafted plants get beaten up in cold areas — and show it. Thus, of course, woodland-edge protection is a great aid.

laurocerasus is the cherry laurel from the eastern Mediterranean, a great evergreen with leaves like those of *Magnolia grandiflora*. Not a plant for the north. But there are a couple of dwarf forms, of which 'Otto Luyken' is usually available. Keeping to a metre high but getting twice that across, it is a marvelous broad-leaved evergreen for shade. In cold areas it may only survive below the snow. With us it flowers surprisingly late in summer, which probably relates to the previous sentence.

Ptelea trifoliata. Hop-tree is a tall native shrub that in its Canadian manifestation grows in the sands of Point Pelee on the north shore of Lake Erie. Here it takes full shade and makes an attractive plant. Trilobed leaves and fragrant greenish flowers give way to clusters of papery fruits that were used, it seems, in times of dire emergency to flavour beer. Hence the name; they do not particularly resemble the conelike clusters of real hops. Golden and glaucous-leaved forms are listed, which add a bonus to this quiet shrub.

Pyracantha. There are few plants that put on such a double show as the firethorns. The narrow evergreen leaves disappear once in June under clouds of hawthornlike flower and again in good years under berries in autumn. As with *Cotoneaster*, (near relations) the scarlet-fruited forms can be stripped by birds in a few days. Where this is likely, orange and yellow types maintain their display much longer. All make admirable north-wall plants and trained espalier-fashion can create a fine formal effect. Among the best are:

atalantioides 10-15 x 10 ft. (3-4.5 x 3 m) A fine Chinese species whose red berries usually last well. 'Aurea' has yellow fruit.

coccinea 'Lalandei' 10-15 ft. (3-4.5 m) A vigorous shrub with relatively broad leaves and masses of orange-red fruits. 'Orange Glow' is a hybrid, making an impenetrable mass of thorny shoots and carrying long-lasting crops of fruit.

Unfortunately scab disease seems to be on the increase, which makes the fruits and leaves look as if they had first been dunked in treacle and then in soot. Cultivars recommended locally as resistant should be sought out.

Rhodotypos scandens. When this unobtrusive shrub had its alternative name, *R. kerrioides*, one got an immediate mental picture: much like *Kerria*, but white flowered. In addition it has shining black fruits, like four little nuts on a saucer. The common name describes this admirably, though with some redundancy: black jetbead. It makes a pleasant fountain of stems, interesting even out of flower.

Ribes. There are few more spectacular north-wall plants than well-fruited, trained red and white currants. Unfortunately, to satisfy the stomach one has to deprive the eye. But even if the former temptation is unresisted there is still pleasure in the formal branch pattern and the jars of red currant jelly in the larder.

alpinum 3-5 x 5 ft. (1-1.5 x 1.5 m) An undistinguished plant useful for hedging in shade. There are dwarf forms.

odoratum 5 x 4 ft. (1.5 x 1.2 m) Good golden spikes of flower with the fragrance of cloves. It associates splendidly with scented spring flowering bulbs such as blue and white hyacinths.

Rosa. Although some rose species grow well enough in shade, their flowering and fruiting are restricted. Obviously therefore no strong recommendation can be given. But there are at least two exceptions. The lovely little Scotch Burnet roses (*R. spinosissima*) will make their low thickets in dry shade and still offer their early flowers. With the second any reduction of flowers and hips is not important; *Rosa glauca* (*rubrifolia*) is still invaluable. Its elegant shape and six-foot-high grey-purple stems and leaves combine perfectly with martagon lilies, or later with pink Japanese anemones. This is one of the best shrub roses in any position. Modern bush roses grown in shade become etiolated and weak. But a few climbers are admirable north-wall plants.

Rubus. Our own black raspberry (*R. occidentalis*) demonstrates perfectly the process succession in woodland regeneration. It quickly moves in to an open glade to take over from herbaceous things, but is eventually shaded out by the trees to which it gave protection while they were still seedlings. With its pink-finished, whitened arching canes it does make something of a winter eye-catcher in rough places and the fruit is always welcome in June and July.

cockburnianus 6-8 x 8 ft. (2-2.5 x 2.5 m) For a dark spot, though not in a tree drip, this fierce Himalayan "whitewash bramble" is even more striking with its fountain of vivid white stems. Flowers and apricot-coloured raspberry fruits (though edible) are pretty undistinguished and the old stems are best cut out in early summer to allow full development of the new. *Rubus biflorus* is similar.

odoratus 6 x 3 ft. (2 x 1 m) Our wild thimbleberry makes a fine clump in open woodland or in a big north-facing border. Unlike most brambles, it is not prickly and has soft green vinelike leaves and pink or white flowers resembling small roses (the relationship is close) in summer. The flat pink fruit are dry and bland to the taste.

calycinoides 5 in. x 5 ft. (150 mm x 1.2 m) A new introduction from the mountains of Formosa, this makes marvellous ground cover of round, two-inch-across hairy leaves. Though seared by very low temperatures, it is perfectly safe under snow and most of us have enough to cover this almost horizontal plant.

Sambucus. The elders are undervalued shrubs: accepting almost any conditions they are ideal woodland-edge plants.

canadensis 8 x 8 ft. (2.5 x 2.5 m) The American elder is best in its 'Maxima' form, pruned in spring like buddleia. Splendid divided foliage and huge flat flower heads result, followed by black berries.

nigra 10-15 x 10 ft. (3-4.5 x 3 m) The most spectacular wilding of European limestone hedgerows is eminently suitable for bringing into all but the most sophisticated gardens. The fragrant flower heads make wine (as do the purple berries) and that most delectable of country brews, elderflower champagne, which, fit to be drunk in a fortnight, is ideal for the impatient. The shrub exists in various forms with variegated, cut leaved and golden leaves.

racemosa 8-10 x 8 ft. (2.5-3 x 2.5 m) Here the greenish flower heads precede the foliage and are succeeded by bright-red fruits ripening in summer at the same time as the rowan (one sometimes sees them together in open Scottish woodland). Its form 'Plumosa Aurea,' with golden fernlike foliage, is one of the best of foliage shrubs.
    A relation, *S. pubens*, is our native North American red elder with similar attributes. The big swelling buds on bare stems in earliest spring

is an annual encouraging sign that winter is at an end. These are valuable plants for cold gardens. If the coloured-leaved forms are cut back hard in spring the foliage is bigger and brighter, but at the expense of flowers and fruit.

Sarcococca. Low boxlike evergreens with highly scented petal-less flowers in earliest spring, followed by black berries. Happy under trees, although rather slow growing.

hookerana digyna 2 x 2 ft. (600 x 600 mm) Narrow leaves make this a more elegant plant than the true box but equally useful as evergreen hummocks to associate with the earliest spring bulbs in any sheltered northern exposure. There are other sarcococcas that need trial in up-country areas. They could well replace the dwarf boxwoods or *Ilex crenata* in town courtyards.

Spiraea. A highly diverse genus with many good garden shrubs for spring and summer display. One or two of the commoner sorts, such as *S. salicifolia*, accept undertree shade and make pleasant thickets in a wild place. Others are suitable for north-facing borders but resent tree drip. The smaller *bumalda* types associate well with herbaceous plants.

x *bumalda* 'Anthony Waterer' 3 x 2 ft. (900 x 600 mm) One of the best-loved front-of-border shrubs, it can be left shrubby or cut to the ground every spring. The current year's shoots carry flat heads of deep pink. 'Gold Flame' is a fine new selection, with developing foliage of soft pinkish orange that pales as the midsummer pink flowers open. A gentle clipping over when they are done encourages further leaf colour.

x *vanhouttei* 5 x 5 ft. (1.5 x 1.5 m) An elegant shrub making a fountain of branches that foam with white flowers in their season. Common, easy and good.

Staphylea. The bladder-nuts are tall pale shrubs. The name refers to the inflated, irresistibly poppable seed capsules.

colchica 'Coulombieri' 10-12 x 10 ft. (3-4 x 3 m) As the soft green leaves unfold a raceme of white, gently scented flowers develops from the end of every twig. This is a perfect plant for a half-shaded corner in a white garden. *S. trifolia* is our native species, very similar in effect; a charming plant.

holocarpa 'Rosea' 8-10 x 10 ft. (2.5-3 x 3 m) A most distinct bladder-nut with pale-pink flower heads strung from the branches, whose unfolding foliage is a complementary soft bronze. It would be nice to know this were offered in the trade.

Symphoricarpus. The snowberries make pleasant thickets of twiggy growth, unexciting in flower but with pleasant grey-green leaves and grape-sized berries making a long-lasting autumn show.

rivularis 5 x 5 ft. (1.5 x 1.5 m) This is the commonest snowberry, often planted as game covert in Europe and hence perfectly happy under trees. S. *albus* is similar but smaller. Hybrids now include 'Magic Berry' and 'Mother of Pearl,' with rose-pink berries in such quantity that the branches are bowed with their weight. 'White Hedge' and 'Erect' are more upright and can be used as small internal hedges in shade; the latter has pink fruit. Birds generally leave them alone.

Syringa. As everyone knows, the big hybrid lilacs are not for shade; they etiolate, fail to flower and get mildew. But shade gardeners who feel deprived without a whiff of lilac scent each year can take heart.

meyeri 4-6 x 6 ft. (1.2-2 x 2 m) A dwarf lilac, fragrant though not quite typically so that covers itself, even facing north, with spikes of pale purple flowers — it is often listed as 'Palabin' or S. *palibiniana*. The cut-leaf lilac L. *laciniata* is able to take similar conditions and has interesting foliage in the bargain.

x *chinensis* 10-12 x 10 ft. (3-4 x 3 m) This is one of the loveliest lilacs by any standard, except that of flower-spike size. It makes a huge heap of lilac purple, smelling like a lilac ought and doing it well in at least half shade. White and pink forms exist.

reflexa 8-10 x 10 ft. (2.5-3 x 3 m) More like a buddleia in effect, with arching growth and long narrow flower spikes, this is not a plant to assuage any atavistic longing for lilacs. But it is most distinctive with its pink-flushed white flowers and elegant showering habit.

Viburnum. Without doubt one of the most valuable shrubby genera that we have for garden decoration in shady spots. Viburnums offer good foliage, flower and fruit, though seldom admittedly all three on the same plant. Perhaps that would be too much to expect. While viburnums are generally happy on limy soils, being mostly natural woodlanders they appreciate a leafy, organic soil at least to start them off. As with most organisms, plants or animals, the nursery years are vital. The best species (of the two hundred plus existing as well as their garden selections) can be listed against their major feature.

For Foliage

rhytidophyllum 12 x 10 ft. (4 x 3 m) Although quite striking in flower, with flat plates of off-white (a rare pink form is worth seeking out) and in a good year fruit (needing some friends around to help with pollination), it is as a foliage plant that the leatherleaf viburnum is grown.

It seems to raise strong feelings in those that know it (an unfortunately small percentage of the population), being loved or loathed with little in between. Long narrow corrugated leaves are dramatic in effect, but in towns they pick up and hold dust and give early an air of summer exhaustion. In a clean and moist country site, planted with other strong foliaged plants such as *Ligularia* or *Petasites*, they look splendidly architectural. Leatherleaf is not for cold gardens, but if cut down it usually recovers without much fuss. Hardier, however, is the following, one of its hybrids.

x *rhytidophylloides* 10 x 8 ft. (3 x 2.5 m) This has as its other parent the European wayfaring tree, V. *lantana*, from which it gains the ability to go deciduous if necessary without coming to harm. Leaves are less elongated and flowers rather whiter than the leatherleaf. The fruiting is more pronounced so long as others not of the same clone are about. Cross-pollination seems very necessary to viburnums, which is why the show is seemingly so much better in a botanical garden collection, where the choice of partner is wider. 'Alleghany' and 'Willowwood' are recommended selections of this useful plant.

For Flower

carlesii 4-5 x 5 ft. (1.2-1.5 x 1.5 m) This lovely plant is well-known, perhaps through the well-contrived name Korean spice. It appreciates shade from the east to reduce flower damage from late-spring frosts to which it is sadly subject, and the half shade extends the rather short flowering season. While it lasts, however, all is joy: rounded heads of pink-flushed white flowers with a delicious spicy fragrance.

This attribute is maintained to a greater or lesser degree in its hybrid offspring, all of which are valuable plants. They include V. x *burkwoodii*, which is much taller and thinner in growth; it can be semievergreen and has a long, though less dramatic flowering period. A good northern plant. 'Anne Russell' and 'Mohawk' hark back more to V. *carlesii*, as does V. x *juddii*, which combines the Korean spice with another Oriental species.

The Chinese snowball, V. *macrocephalum*, is like a vast V. *carlesii*, with similar attributes plus the advantage of flowering both later and longer when all danger of frost is past. However, it lacks hardiness. A cross between the two is V. x *carlecephalum*, fully intermediate. A huge plant in my garden is a joy through May. Growing through it is some *Euonymus fortunei*, which adds a winter evergreen and fruiting effect. They seem to live together quite amicably.

plicatum 6-8 x 8 ft. (2-2.5 x 2.5 m) Like *Staphylea*, in flower the Japanese snowball or doublefile is a marvellously "cool" plant. Round heads of sterile flowers are brightly green to begin with and gradually turn through cream to white, as does *Hydrangea arborescens*. The bigger 'Grandiflorum' is the one to grow.

These were popular garden plants in the Orient long before they were introduced to Britain by Robert Fortune in the 1840s. The wild type that flowers later, like the lacecap hydrangeas, has flat flower heads with just an outside ring of big sterile flowers.

Its garden effect, however, is made dramatic by the wide-tiered branch pattern upon which the flower clusters crowd like a field of filigree mushrooms.

The best forms are 'Lanarth,' 'Rowallane' (which often fruits well, too) and 'Pink Beauty.' Dr. Dirr recommends us to look out for 'Shasta,' a new introduction from the U.S. National Arboretum. This group of viburnums is one of the best of all early summer shrubs, happy in almost full shade. Autumn colour is a gentle purple as a final benison from a plant that has already well earned its keep.

For Fruit

trilobum 8-10 x 10 ft. (2.5-3 x 3 m) It seems sensible to take our native highbush cranberry viburnum as central to a number of invaluable autumn fruiters. An open, often thin bush, it will grow in full shade, but some sun is necessary for decent fruiting — without which there is not much point.

Flower heads are flat plates, pleasant but not outstanding in effect; this comes with the bunches of glistening scarlet berries, weighing down the branches as they ripen among the fall purple-red leaves. The display lasts until well into new year or until the birds or jam-making humans pick them.

V. *opulus* is the nonedible European counterpart that can take wetter conditions. It has fine golden-fruited forms and dwarf types, but the latter, though very tidy for gardeners for whom this is a major attraction regardless of anything else, lacks the species' grace. A sterile mop-head form is the European Guelder rose, easy to grow and effective as a screen; correctly, if confusingly, listed as V. *o.* 'Roseum,' it does in fact pass from green to white and usually stops there.

There are other fine fruiting viburnums, both natives (such as nannyberry) from the Orient, and botanic garden collections should be scoured. Here at Royal Botanical Gardens, for instance, V. *wrightii*, is superb in effect, dripping with blood-red berries. But I do not know if it will maintain this in shade. However, it seems likely, as its close relation *V. dilatatum* and its forms are happy there.

Vinca. Periwinkles are among the most valuable ground-cover shrubs for shade. On banks, difficult otherwise to maintain, they form a perfect layer of foliage and they are equally at home under shrubs and trees. Here in southern Ontario the lesser periwinkle has developed fine colonies in wild woodland through which native plants grow happily.

major. Long evergreen trails are killed above the snow level with us, but the variegated form puts out sufficient spring growth to make it worthwhile.

minor. Lesser periwinkle, though smaller in leaf and flower, is no less vigorous and is quite capable of climbing into and over small shrubs, as does *Lamiastrum*. Under big mature shrubs all is well, and charming variants from the normal blue exist with purple or white flowers, single and double, as well as those with yellow and white variegated leaves.

Weigela. Sprays of foxglovelike flowers in May and June on easily grown eight-foot-high shrubs make this a useful group. Not for densest shade, which causes etiolation and lack of flower, but in north-facing mixed shrub borders they do well. Hybrids based upon *W. florida* are produced mainly in shades of pink and red (though 'Mont Blanc' is a good white). But perhaps the most desirable of all is *W.f.* 'Variegata.' Here the soft pink flowers open with the pink-tinged cream young leaves and combine together in an entirely beautiful way. If the older flowered shoots are then cut away, further strong variegated shoots develop to maintain the foliage effect till autumn. In my own Ontario garden on heavy clay it grows out of a carpet of lily of the valley, whose shining leaves make an admirable foil; in the Chelsea Physic Garden it grew in light sand under an enormous catalpa tree and was also happy. A most adaptable plant. 'Minuet' and 'Rumba' are two new selections from the Dominion Arboretum in Ottawa: the former is dwarf.

Plants for Shady Walls and Fences

It has already been mentioned that walls in shade offer marvellous potential to the adventurous gardener. If shelter as well as shade is provided, a wide range of plants, otherwise frost tender, becomes possible. With this in mind, that common disease, pessimistic zonitis ("Of course I can't grow it — I'm in Zone 5"), can be controlled if not entirely cured — only complete removal to Southern California will do that. Hardiness zones are a valuable aid to choice of plants in general, but they have not been cast in stone, even by the U.S.D.A. Every garden has its own microclimate, which may be warmer or cooler than the norm for the area, that has to be worked with — just as a gardener has to work with his soil — and not fought against.

That having been said yet again, we return to walls. Every aspect has its potential, but there are snares. Early flowers or foliage encouraged by the warmth of an east-facing housefront can get cut by a late frost if the sun gets on to them when the tissues are still frozen. Gardens in frost hollows must beware. (Tree canopy can diffuse that sun, however.) Evergreen plants on south and west walls, in a continental climate, can be subject to leaf burn if fully exposed to the winter sun. The juxtaposition of other plants, deciduous or evergreen, is a help. Plants in isolation or in borders that have been so aggressively tidied and tucked up for the winter suffer most. Surprisingly, north walls are often the most preferable for one's tenderest plants.

Less surprising is the way in which tiny walled town gardens and courtyards can capitalize upon their at first sight unpropitious situations and be turned into exotic bowers of the lushest growth. As with open ground borders, the intention should be to create a combination of colours and textures from flower and foliage for interest throughout the

101

year. Here, as a courtyard is so obviously an extension to the house, its architecture must be considered.

Formality on walls is introduced by rigorously trained fruit trees; apples and pears make the best horizontally branched espaliers, or ornamentals such as pyracantha and japanese quince. All are happy in shade. Informality comes not from unconsidered planting but from a studied combination of plants big and small, each chosen for its particular element. While the clothing of walls and fences is both desirable and irresistible, the lack of one element is unavoidable. This is the valuable effect of visual depth of field. There it is often reduced to an almost flat plane upon which the light, from whichever side the wall faces, must fall.

Planting climbers upon loggias or arbours or pergolas permits one to look *through* these plants: wisteria silhouetted against the light is a different creature from that seen against a wall. Treillage or trelliswork used to be a beautiful but vastly expensive and laboursome aspect of garden "works." Its virtues, however, in combination with a simple pergola, using rot-proof timber (cedar, for example) and rust-free mesh are well worth considering today. Such garden structures are valuable for their immediate effect as well as the support they give to climbers, themselves the quickest of permanent plants to give of their best. The following are the best of those that are centred climatically, in Zone 6. Most will take less-favoured areas: again, each garden is an individual, to be planned and planted as such.

It is worthwhile to discuss briefly the ways in which plants climb, because these affect our methods of cultivation and type of support required. A preliminary question is *why* they climb. The answer is clear: to succeed as organisms in the fight for the necessities of life; to compete, especially for light. Thus numbers of plants have commuted the ability to produce strong strengthening tissue (wood) for speed of growth and reliance on others that have chosen the more conventional way of obtaining a place in the sun.

In doing so, different organs have become adapted as climbing mechanisms. For gardeners the most valuable are those that are able to be self-clinging on vertical surfaces without help. English ivy and climbing hydrangea are typical members of this group that produce a mass of nonfeeding rootlets to hold on with.

Others develop sensitive tendrils. Grapevine and sweet peas are examples: the touch of a developing tendril by a potential support causes rapid cell growth on the side of the tendril opposite from the touch and thus it winds round with whatever it comes into contact. The tendrils of Boston ivy are aided by sucker pads at their tips.

The same sensitivity causes runner beans or honeysuckle stems to twine and for the leaf stalks (petioles) of clematis to twist around a wire or another plant stem.

Finally, certain plants are scramblers rather than true climbers. No rose will get over a high wall by itself unless there is another plant there first. The long rose shoots push themselves through the existing branches, and the downward pointing thorns (doubling as highly effective defence mechanisms) prevent them falling through. Species such as the tender *Rosa gigantea* from the forests of Burma scramble sixty feet (20 m) thus to the tops of trees. By comparison our native shrub roses have straight thorns — defence is still important, but climbing is not.

Now to the plants for shady walls.

Actinidia. Most of the fruit on the shelves in the local market seem to have been a part of our earliest consciousness, and that of our parents and grandparents; traditional foods in every way. It is most unusual for something new to break into that closed shop. But over the past decade the fruits of *Actinidia chinensis* have done so. It is not immediately prepossessing — a brown and bristly hard skinned plum might be a description. But what a revelation when it is cut across. It becomes an elegantly geometric pattern of fresh green and black with an aroma and flavour to match. In no time indeed a slice or two of this has become the cliché to dull desserts — what parsley is to coating cutlets. This is Chinese gooseberry (Chinese, yes, but by no stretch of botanical imagination can it be considered a gooseberry). Nor does the alternate name, kiwi fruit, tell us much; it is a New Zealander only by adoption, for it likes the mild seasons there. With us winter damage is almost inevitable — though it is relatively untried. Seeds from a bought fruit will often germinate. But other species of *Actinidia* are better considered as garden plants. Of the thirty that exist, all Asiatic twiners, three are valuable garden plants for us.

arguta has to be our Chinese gooseberry, as its fruit, olive green when ripe in late September and the size of small pecans, is produced freely on established plants here. It fruits prodigiously at Brooklyn Botanic Garden and at the Arnold Arboretum. The suède-yellow flowers are in clusters, each over an inch across, but are apt to be hidden within the foliage. Incidentally, the "common" names tara vine or yang-tao are less "common" than the botanical one and are best avoided with the confusion they can cause.

kolomikta. This is even less of a flowering ornamental but has the facility of producing brilliantly variegated leaves (a natural attribute that occurs in the wild; it is not a garden mutant). A part of every young leaf near the flower clusters becomes suffused with zones of white and pink. From a distance the effect is entirely floral, but it lasts longer than most flowering periods. In half shade *Actinidia kolomikta* colours well and reaches fifteen feet in height.

polygama. This is the silver vine. As robust as A. *arguta*, it has a similar facility to A. *kolomikta*, but here the leaf suffusion is of white overlaying the green. A cool, mint-julep effect is achieved, enhanced by the creamy cup-shaped flowers. Unfortunately, the fruit is not worth eating raw. It is pickled or salted in Japan, a taste to which sushi bars have yet to accustom us.

Akebia quinata. This and the very similar A. *trifoliata* are sometimes called chocolate vines. It is rather a good name for the strange strings of purplish-brown flowers (even chocolate-scented) that appear with the emergent leaves in spring. The flower clusters are worth closer investigation. The smaller, brighter flowers at the end of the string are male, while the bigger ones — up to an inch across — are the female: an unusual arrangement. But the leaves are really the main attraction of this robust but delicate twiner — fingered foliage like little hands of children, which makes a fine pattern throughout the summer.

In some years fruit is produced, hardly ornamental, yet always causing interest. Each is like a small purple mango, blandly edible.

On a wall *Akebia* is easily kept to the allotted area, but where space is unlimited it can be allowed to romp up trees, tumble over fences or even act as ground cover.

Ampelopsis brevipedunculata. This is the lovely porcelain berry, a relation of the wild grape and even more vigorous, but its bunches of fruit are utterly unique among ornamental plants, being clear kingfisher-blue when ripe. Nothing in detail could be more beautiful. Such an eulogy, however, though it could be continued at some length with complete justification, is of little use in the context of this book because the porcelain berry needs sun fully to live up to its name.

Nonetheless the entry is justified because of a fine variegated variant that exists called 'Elegans.' This is a quick-growing tendril climber whose delicate vine-shaped leaves are irregularly mottled pink and white. Like all variegated plants it helps to light up dark spots. This is a very worthwhile plant, ideal in a town courtyard, even without kingfisher-blue berries.

Aristolochia durior. There are a couple of hundred of these Dutchman's pipes strewn around the tropical world, some of which are grown as greenhouse ornamentals by those who like the bizarre. If floral beauty were the criterion the same derogatory suggestion could be made about this hardy "pipe": dull brownish yellow in colour, rather waxy and mysteriously anatomical in shape. It is pollinated by flies; altogether rather nasty.

Fortunately this inauspicious description does not follow to the foliage, which is no less than magnificent. The neatly circular leaves can be a foot across, delicately netted with milky-white undersides. Against a wall this latter effect is not seen, which makes *Aristolochia* such a fine arbour or pergola plant. When people were still happy to sit in their front porches, this was the plant that invariably shaded them as they watched the local soap opera acted out on the street before them.

While accepting full sun, it will also take shade; a well-drained soil seems to be the only essential to encourage this splendid twiner to reach its twenty- or thirty-foot high potential.

Celastrus scandens is our native bittersweet, a vastly vigorous and aggressive twiner. Like the woodland honeysuckle in Europe, this will clasp young trees so tightly that they turn into living corkscrews. Bittersweet is obviously not a plant for restricted areas or for planting among choice garden plants. But where it can be allowed to scramble about on the edge, even a north-facing edge of woodland, the late-autumn show of fruit is superb.

As a euonymus relation it has a similar pattern of pale yellow pea-sized fruits that split open to show brilliant orange seeds. The display lasts for weeks, usually dispersed by being cut for house decoration and wreath making just before Christmas.

There is no difficulty in cultivation, any site, any soil, but it is essential to buy or propagate from a female plant if fruit is to be enjoyed, and of course a husband will be necessary if other bittersweets are not about.

Clematis. No genus of climbers has been so diversified over the past hundred years or so than this; there are now innumerable hybrids in addition to the couple of hundred wild species from the temperate zones of both hemispheres. Though it is convenient that the choice is heavily reduced by what is on offer, there are many fine *clematis* deserving cultivation that are not yet available from the nursery trade.

Hybrid and species alike are apt to behave in the classic way of shady wall plants — growing like fun but flowering little until they get to the sun at the top. This behaviour must be worked with rather than against. *Clematis* need shade at the root as much as they enjoy sun at the head and hence all but the very vigorous species are admirable for growing up and through other plants. Here they can either complement their support — by being allowed to clamber through a climbing rose, perhaps — or extend the floral interest by being put with something (*Forsythia suspensa*, for instance) that has already given its display. *Clematis* are remarkably adaptable plants and easy to grow, as must be guessed from those enormous old plants of *Clematis* x *jackmanii*, the lovely purple stand-by, tumbling over country porches.

What they will not take is coercion. *Clematis* climb by the twisting of their petioles (leafstalks) around anything they touch. Once there the die is cast and no amount of untwiddling will get them to change their minds. Any training has to be done to each shoot in extreme youth; better to provide both horizontal and vertical wires — a mesh, in fact — or, as has been suggested, another woody plant, as happens naturally in the wild, and let them get on with it.

So long as drainage is adequate or can be made so, any soil seems to suit. Traditionally very acid, rhododendron-growing soils are "improved" by the addition of lime mortar, but this is apt to raise the pH irrevocably as to make subsequent calcifuge planting difficult. It does not seem to matter much to the clematis. Pruning of clematis is a vexed and vexing subject. Left alone, many develop an untidy tangle of shoots all mixed up with last year's growth and a mess of dead leaves — altogether a most unaesthetic heap. Fortunately many clematis are more or less herbaceous: those of the *Jackmanii* and *Viticella* groups can be cut back annually within a foot or two of the ground. This is usually done in spring as the buds are swelling. But if older, woody stems exist they can certainly be left longer to give more immediate height.

The *Lanuginosa* group is most simply treated similarly and the resultant growth will flower from midsummer onward. Those in the *Patens* and *Florida* groups are best left with a framework of strong healthy vines from last year from which the flowering laterals emerge in early summer.

From this web of recommendations, as tangled as an unpruned clematis, one simple rule can be abstracted: in spring cut out anything dead and any top-heavy growth that hangs away from the support. There is, however, the inevitable exception to the rule: *Clematis montana, alpina* and *macropetala* are spring flowering. Nothing should be done to these, if at all, until they have made their marvellous show.

Of the two hundred species few are in general cultivation (keen clematophiles should visit Royal Botanical Gardens, Hamilton, Ontario, where half that number are displayed in a garden devoted to the genus). The following are among the best.

alpina. As its name suggests this comes from the mountains of Europe and eastward through into northern Asia. As the fernlike leaves expand, so do the flowers, delicately nodding bluebells. 'Frances Rivis' is a fine robust form that can reach ten feet in height.

macropetala from Siberia is closely related and even more beautiful. The blue petals (actually sepals — true petals being absent in *Clematis*) enclose a mass of smaller petallike segments that get smaller and paler as they reach the centre. I grow this lovely plant up a young tree of *Magnolia kobus*, whose white flowers fade as the climber comes out. The flowers of both these *clematis* are followed by silky spherical seed heads, beautiful in their own right.

This last attribute is often the most spectacular part of the display made by both *Clematis tangutica* and *C. orientalis*, which in the autumn are covered with feathered seed heads, holding the dewlike diamonds. The former is known as the orange-peel plant from the waxy reflex-tipped petals. This is always noteworthy in flower or seed.

Thick, fleshy petals are also seen in several fine North American species that deserve to be more grown. *C. pitcheri* and *C. glaucophylla* have purplish bells, while *C. texensis* (it seems pretty hardy in spite of its name and origin) is scarlet. These have a long flowering period, with flowers and seed heads together for weeks on end. Any pruning of this group is purely a matter of common sense.

montana is the most spectacular of the latter spring flowers. A big plant may be thirty feet across and draped with ropes of four-petalled flowers, white or pink, according to type. It comes from high in the Himalayas and thus is entirely hardy. Yet is is not so utterly dependable here as in Europe, and one probably needs to experiment with aspect and site. It is certainly worth every effort.

viticella. This delicate, summer and fall-flowering species is among the best for general use, easy to grow and to prune. From southern Europe and western Asia, this has been a well loved garden plant for centuries. John Gerard, the apothecary, grew it in his Holborn garden in the middle of London and recorded the fact in his great *Herbal* of 1597. The typical form has several flowers together, each two or three inches across in soft shades of blue or purple on a 10-foot-high plant. Variants include 'Alba Luxurians,' 'Kermesina' (Vinous red) and 'Royal Velours' (a velvety purple).

The list of big-flowered hybrids is long and it is best to find a local nursery where they can be seen in flower. Any selection now is somewhat arbitrary, but among the best are:

Jackmanii superba (J)   rich purple

Perle d'Azur   (J)   clear blue

Hagley hybrid	(J)	pale pink
Henryi	(L)	huge white flowers with a dark eye of stamens
Nelly Moser	(L)	pale pink with a dark bar down the centre of each petal. The flowers bleach badly in full sun. An ideal clematis for shade.
W. E. Gladstone	(L)	Fine lavender with darker eye
Barbara Jackman	(P)	blue-purple, dark bar
Vyvyan Pennell	(P)	purplish blue, double flowers
Ernest Markham	(V)	velvety red
Huldine	(V)	white with reddish bar on the back of the petals

Clematis are resentful of root disturbance. They should be planted in spring from containers and the new growth gently led the chosen support. A good display can be expected from the second year and for many years beyond.

Euonymus fortunei. Gardeners in northeastern North America are apt to spend much time on lamenting what, by English standards, they cannot grow. It is heartening therefore to be able to eulogize such a valuable plant that does so very much better here (there are plenty of others — flowering dogwood and oxydendron are just two more of my own favourites mentioned in this book).

This relative of the spindle-bushes is now often called wintercreeper, an entirely satisfactory name, as we have no plant that offers more during the coldest months.

As an evergreen for ground cover, a self-clinging climber in the manner of ivy, as a winter-bronze or variegated shrub and a brilliant berrying shrub, it is admirable; when these attributes are combined in a single plant one has met the miraculous.

To be honest, of course, some forms are better for ground covers and climbing ('Dart's Blanket, 'Coloratus'), some for fruit (radicans and 'Vegetus') and others for leaves ('Golden Prince' and 'Silver Queen'), but the combination does occur on some plants in some places.

Summer flowering is not particularly exciting, but the green hanging clusters make an interesting pattern. The fruit, however, as with the shrubby euonymus is highly distinctive, bunches of cream or pinkish capsules that open to display orange seeds. Some forms maintain the show for months.

Wintercreeper is happy in darkest shade in any soil but the ill drained. Again, like ivy, there is a change from juvenile leaves to the adult fruiting form, but the wintercreeper is less dependent on light for the transformation.

Hedera helix. English ivy, as with *Euonymus fortunei*, is a most useful evergreen in our climate for the shade gardener. As ground cover, container plant and self-clinging wall plant, the lustrous leaves always appear fresh and tidy. In the less cold areas large or small leaved forms can be chosen to suit the scale of any site and dark walls are brightened by white-banded or gold-centred variegated cultivars. So easy is ivy to propagate that every gardener can experiment. For the coldest gardens 'Bulgaria' and 'Hebron' are the safest, followed by 'Baltica' and 'Thorndale,' with noticeably smaller and larger leaves respectively. Ivies are easy to obtain and simple to propagate, so everyone can try outside all the forms available. The results may well surprise.

English ivy will make superb ground cover in the densest shade. If the soil is enriched and the area kept well watered for the first year following planting (at two-foot centres) the cover will subsequently accept even tree-root drought with impunity. Plants against walls can be allowed to develop at will or be clipped into formal panels. The suggestion that ivy is injurious to stone or brick work should be discounted; in fact, the leaf canopy sheds water and protects from the elements and the hold-on rootlets are not feeding roots. But the questing shoots *will* get into existing cracks in roof tiles and behind eavestroughs and as they thicken will certainly cause damage. An annual check prevents this with little trouble.

Flowers and fruit are never seen upon the typical climbing or creeping ivy; only when it reaches the sun at the top of the support does the pattern change. Stems become nonclimbing and strongly woody, leaves lose their arrow shape and in autumn spherical heads of greenish flowers are followed by black fruits. In most garden scenes the change is not an improvement and should be pruned out.

Humulus lupulus. For putting the bitter into beer common hops has no equal. As a rapid, but *herbaceous* twiner it is also valuable in the garden. The female plant should be grown that produces clusters of papery, larch-cone-like seed heads. They make a pretty pattern and are a traditional decoration for the pulpit at harvest festival, draping themselves elegantly into charming swags and encouraging unsuitable thoughts during the service.

The bristly leaves are vinelike and a perfectly ordinary green. Unfortunately the golden-leaved form, though excellent in sun, is apt to revert to type in shade; half shade gives half gold.

The Japanese hop is usually grown as an annual and here the white-striped form does maintain its pattern in dappled shade. Hops make a marvellous screen in new gardens where permanent shrubby plants have not had time to build up a framework or where obtrusive chain-link fences spoil the scene. Swimming pools or tennis courts can be transformed into leafy bowers.

Hydrangea petiolaris. We know we should be relegating this species, like a failing football team, to the subspecific league and call it *Hydrangea anomala* spp. *petiolaris*, but it seems unwise to trust our luck too far. Someone might just call it climbing hydrangea and leave it at that — which, of course, a lot of gardeners are happy to do.

Nomenclature apart, this is one of the most valuable of shade-tolerant climbers. It is another plant, like ivy and wintercreeper, that clings by means of rootlets. That it can attain fifty feet or more up a tall tree need not frighten those with only a tithe of that to cover.

While it will also succeed as a rather lumpy ground cover, again in heavy shade, it is seen best on a high wall. Many climbers that put out shoots away from the face of the support develop unsightly tangles. *Hydrangea petiolaris* by comparison puts out nonclinging branches that give a further dimension to the plant — only if these become very large do they drag the plant away from the wall. The situation must be watched and remedied by a little pruning to reduce the weight without diminishing the effect.

Flowering comes in July; huge flat heads of little white scented flowers are encircled by a ring of wide sterile flowers. As with a bush hydrangea, the sterile parts of the inflorescence dry upon the plant and remain attractive for months, even into winter.

Climbing hydrangea, though deciduous, is among the best wall and pergola plants we can grow, and after a year or two to settle in, it is happy in almost any position. It deserves much greater use.

Jasminum nudiflorum. As we all know only too well, the difference between ours and a western European winter is not only the usually low temperatures here but the fact that they are more constant. Often this is an advantage to the world of plants, for what many cannot stand are erratic temperature rises that half break dormancy to be followed by killing frosts. On the other hand we do lack those few encouraging days in January or February that suddenly make it possible to go out into the garden and gather a small bunch of flowers and believe that spring may eventually come.

This plant, winter jasmine, is always the basis of such posies, for its bronze-flushed buds seem to be on the point of opening for several winter months; clear yellow stars are the result. It cannot behave thus here, but deserves consideration for a little flower production in

December and a lot in March. A north or east exposure is best, with some tree canopy for protection.

It is not a true climber but a scrambler with long green wandlike branches. These should be allowed to cascade out from the wall support with only the framework tied back. Winter jasmine can also be used as an admirable cover for steep banks; planted at the top it will tumble down, rooting as it goes and getting the protection of snow cover.

Well-budded branches should be cut just before Christmas for forcing indoors, as we do with forsythia. These are best stood in water in cool place (an earth cellar is ideal) and small amounts brought into the house over the next few weeks.

Lonicera. Honeysuckle or woodbine — the very name evokes cottage gardens with Shakespearian overtones, the sweet scent a part of any "midsummer night's dream." But though not all honeysuckles do possess a scent — our lovely scarlet trumpet honeysuckle depends upon colour to attract pollinators — those that like shade fortunately do.

japonica. This semievergreen Japanese twiner has become such a woodland weed in the mid-Atlantic and southern states of America that merely to mention it in the context of the cultivated garden leaves one open to public doubts of horticultural sanity. But in colder areas where it does not run wild it is a valuable plant. It is not easy to train and is best allowed to tumble over some support or over a wall. From this it puts out trails of foliage that from high summer into autumn hold pairs of cream flowers in the axil of each leaf. This is marvelous material for table decorations. The perfume is especially distinctive at night and suggests that close to a terrace used in the evenings is a sensible spot.

The variety 'Halliana' is commonly offered, not particularly distinct; 'purpurea' has foliage tinged with purple, but this attribute pales in shade and we are back to something like the type. 'Aureo-reticulata' has charming leaves, gold netted, but as it seldom flowers, the point of being a honeysuckle is lost.

periclymenum is the woodbine or honeysuckle of European hedgerows and is delightful on a shady wall or other support. Selections known as Early Dutch and Late Dutch are offered, and together they combine to give heads of flowers, cream flushed purple and ravishingly scented, from June to October. This is a robust twiner best given wires to travel up; its natural supports are apt to find its embrace overfriendly.

x *heckrottii* is the goldflame honeysuckle. It is of hybrid, though rather uncertain, origin. *L. sempervirens* is thought to be one parent and the other *L.* x *americana*. This in itself adds to the confusion because in spite of its name, this latter is the child of two European species of the woodbine type. Thus goldflame seems to get much of its colour, clear pink outside and rich cream within the tube, from America and its grace from Europe; long spikes of flowers are produced throughout summer.

tragophylla. While goldflame is happy in half shade this Chinese species will take more. Its flowers are spectacular; each yellow tube is three inches long and they are carried in heads of two or more. Perhaps it is too much to expect scent, as well. A cross made between this and our scarlet trumpet honeysuckle early this century in Bulgaria is known as *L.* x *tellmanniana*. Here the flowers are just as fine but flushed with bronze or dark red. These superb plants are rare on this side of the Atlantic but are worth every effort to obtain and grow.

Menispermum canadense. The line between weed and wild flower is always a delicate one. Trillium is safe anywhere, goldenrod safe only in Europe. *Menispermum* or moonseed, though native from Quebec down to Georgia and Manitoba to Arkansas, is not well enough known for the judgement to have been made and the line draw. At the Chelsea Physic Garden we grew it in the dryest soil in the shade of a huge willow pattern tree, which indicates the use to which it can be put.

Moonseed is a rampant twiner that will reach a dozen feet if a suitable support is provided. The strings of little, greenish flowers make no show, and though the black fruits are quite attractive, the lustrous leaves, rather like a large limp ivy, are the distinctive feature. Moonseed can be treated as herbaceous and cut down each year, but there seems little reason for this unless the top has become a tangle.

For a rough place or in the mean few inches of soil available between a concrete path and a building we should be grateful for such accommodating plants.

Parthenocissus. The brilliant fall colours of Virginia creeper and Boston ivy are naturally limited in shady situations, yet they grow no less well than in the sun and are unsurpassed for providing a self-clinging cover to the highest wall (tower blocks and skyscrapers only excluded) to eighty feet or so.

Though often confused, the two species are quite distinct.

P. quinquefolia lives up to its name; it has leaves of five distinct parts that are bronze on opening, and as early as September they become a frequent precursor to autumn. Then tops of trees into which it has climbed suddenly seem set alight by its brilliance. On a wall, of course, the effect is in a single plane, but no less fine. This is a native plant with an eastern distribution from southern Canada down to Mexico. It was introduced to

Europe in the 1620s from the centre of its range — much of the rest was still *terra incognita* — and hence *Virginia* creeper.

trisuspidata is Boston ivy. Neither from Boston (in fact an Oriental) nor an ivy, it is nonetheless the plant that provides so many Bostonian halls of academe with an entirely spurious air of extreme antiquity; thus the Ivy League.

As another climber with suckerlike hold fasts on the tips of its tendrils, it is splendidly self-supporting, but both this and the Virginia creeper have to be clawed away from windows if the inhabitants are not to become troglodytic in a couple of years. Leaves of Boston ivy are typically three lobed and vine shaped. Autumn colour again is superb.

henryana from central China is by far the most elegant species; it is also the least hardy. But it is worth every effort to succeed with in a shady courtyard, where the silver bands on its lobed leaves become especially marked. Even at fall the distinction shows as only the green areas turn red. This is a further holdfast climber but much less vigorous than its cousins; a lovely plant.

Polygonum aubertii. The well-known Asiatic silver-lace vine, growing up through the branches of a full-grown tree and foaming with flower like a shaken magnum of champagne, is a magnificent sight in late summer. Grown this way it can be planted in shade to clamber up into the sun. Alternately it still succeeds in full shade.

But this lovely twiner is not a plant for small gardens, except for complete nongardeners, who can put in a single plant and then with relief sit back. Well back.

A closely related species, more often seen in Europe, is known simply as Russian vine. If available, *Polygonum baldschuanicum* is valuable in just the same way and possibly even more vigorous.

Rosa. It would be pleasant if one could recommend a mass of rose species or cultivars for shady walls. Sadly this is not possible. Roses like the sun. But all is not quite lost; sites vary greatly, as has been emphasized again and again. So long as the situation is reasonably open and three or four hours of sun are possible daily, a number of roses will succeed.

Growth will inevitably be more etiolated than in full exposure and plants will flower more at the top of their growth. If planted against one's own, north-facing dividing wall with a neighbour, it must be accepted that they will get most of the benefit. Perhaps they will bring you a bunch of flowers occasionally to encourage good-neighbourly relations. But if one owns both sides of the wall this growth-pattern presents a definite possibility.

Planted still on the shady side, the rose is encouraged to reach the top and tumble down the sunny side. On that side, therefore, the rose can be a conscious part of the flowering scene, associating with summer herbaceous plants below that have no rose roots to compete with. Pruning, too, is made easy from the "back."

The following roses are suitable for at half shade and are also wood hardy. To have the garden draped with wrapped plants for four months seems a visual mistake.

In mild areas it is not difficult to find some fine climbing hybrid roses that will take a lot of shade. In England, for example, I grew the lovely old 'Crimson Glory' twenty feet high in a shady courtyard with *Clematis macropetala* to furnish its inevitably bare base; the numbers of rose cultivars is so great and so easy to obtain that one can do one's own experimentation. In general, however, we are looking for plants of sufficient hardiness that they do not necessarily have to be taken down in autumn and retied in the spring — though keen rosarians will go to endless trouble and be rewarded for their pains.

The hardiness of the bushy *Rosa rugosa* is legendary; almost equally so is the scrambling *R. wichuraiana*. Both species are parents of a group of splendid roses formally known as *Rosa x kordesii*. Raised by the famous German breeder Wilhelm Kordes in the 1950s, they combine hardiness with disease-resistant foliage and repeat flowering. The following is a good group to start with: 'Leverkusen' is pale yellow; 'Parkdirektor Riggers,' blood-red; and 'Dortmund,' red with a white eye. The old white rambler 'Félicité et Perpétue' is also possible; by comparison with this fiercely armed rose, 'Zephyrine Drouhin' is entirely thornless. One of the old Bourbon roses, it is seldom out of flower, cerise pink and fragrant, its colour contrasting with the purple foliage of the young shoots. Here is a rose that at least does not fight back if taken down in autumn.

Schizandra is a small genus of mainly Oriental twiners (though the name was first coined for the one North American species, this seems not to be in cultivation). *S. chinensis* has a wide range. It comes not only from China but Japan and Korea, and hence is reasonably hardy. On a high shady wall, it makes an interesting pattern of smooth oval leaves among which the clusters of pinkish flowers hide, rather like those of a waxy berberis. They make little show. This comes after the leaves fall with the fruit display — bunches of scarlet berries that hang on well into winter. There is a disadvantage: again schizandras have separate sexed plants, like bittersweet, and hence while two plants have to be grown, only one can be seen to earn its keep though. The other ensures that it does so.

Schizophragma is closely related to the climbing hydrangea. It has the same rootlet, climbing adaptation and similar heads of small fertile flowers surrounded by showy sterile flowers. Here, however, the creamy white bracts, one per flower, have a greater substance and make a more definite, if less luxuriant picture. There are only two species.

hydrangeoides comes from Japan, where it scrambles around trees with its climbing hydrangea cousin. It is not easily found in the lists, but is such a good plant that Royal Botanical Gardens, Hamilton, Ontario, is promoting it to the nursery trade and making stock available. A pink-tinged form exists.

integrifolia is a cliff-hanging Chinese counterpart, rather less hardy. But with its enormous bracts, almost as big as those of the handkerchief tree (*Davidia*), it is worth every effort, first to obtain and then to grow.

Vitis. In North America the world "vine" is used generally for all climbers, regardless of their origin or method of travel. Species of *Vitis* can be considered the "true" vines and includes *Vitis vinifera*, the grape. When one refers in English to leaves being vine shaped, or in Latin, for example, to *Anemone vitifolium*, there is a very clear simile being made. We mean resembling the leaves of a grapevine, not to any of the other genera that happen to climb.

However, the *Vitis* species are not much use for shade. They will grow, but neither their fruit nor fall colour is of note with one exception. This is the superb *Vitis coignetiae* from Japan, justifiably known here as the crimson glory vine. Although in shade its normally dramatic autumn tints are toned down, the huge hearted-shaped (not vine-shaped at all) leaves make a dramatic pattern in their own right. It is an extremely vigorous tendril climber that, like one's own wild grapes, will roar up high trees (and look magnificent) but in a small courtyard can also be spur-pruned in winter and pinched back frequently in summer. The effort is well worth the trouble.

The final sentence on *Vitis coignetiae* needs repeating for this whole chapter on climbing plants. Obviously there is added work in providing support wires or trellises on existing walls or in building pergolas or arbours. Yet these are natural parts of garden furnishing and add so much to the scene. And, of course, many of these lovely plants can be grown satisfactorily in no other way.

Herbaceous Perennials for Shade

In ecological terms the role of shade-tolerant herbaceous plants in the wild has already been discussed. For the most part they are species that accept, in adapting their life cycles to what is possible, a ground level position in the stratification of woodlands. Many are such lovely plants that as gardeners we go to great lengths to succeed with them: we try to reproduce their habitats, we reduce competition, we select forms or breed new types that are amenable to cultivation. These are the shade plants par excellence. Many are our native wild flowers.

But in nature there are the habitats that for various reasons of climate or soil cannot or do not support much of a tree or shrub layer. On our own prairies or on the Asiatic steppes (to confine the conversation to areas that produce hardy plants of potential garden merit) the herbaceous habit is king, with spring and summer growth and often autumn flowers before the plant returns to a below-ground resting rootstock for the inclement winters. These are the plants that have been so productive a source for twentieth century flower gardens and (where such a sophisticated concept exists) herbaceous borders.

These are sun lovers; many are daisies and their relations: black-eyed Susans, goldenrods, michaelmas daisies and so on. Yet again, just as gardeners attempt and sometimes succeed in getting shade plants to grow in full sun, so, too, has breeding and selection, in conjunction with careful cultivation, made possible for many sun lovers to take some shade.

One has to be sensible and realize the evolutionary difference implied in the shade-sun divide and not expect the impossible. Flowers that open only in sun, like the South African gazanias, are obviously a nonsense, even were they hardy in shade. Fortunately, even in the wild there are many habitats that hover between forest and prairie. Their plants offer us much, and the following list includes them.

116

An effective garden often combines in a small space a number of regimes that in the wild may not meet for many miles and that we put together for aesthetic reasons. There needs to be, however, a basic "rightness" about our contrived associations that often reflects the original ecological factors, where for instance lush-leaved pond-margin and alpine species are incompatibles whose juxtaposition a gardener can contrive but should abjure.

One question often asked by those who really have little or no sun (and this could be a north-facing town courtyard or apartment balcony) is if herbs can be grown in such a position. The answer is, just a few. There is no point in regretting the impossibility of producing the *bouquet garni* as if straight from a Mediterranean hillside (that would still be impossible if the shady courtyard were in Cannes), so one concentrates on what does succeed. Of culinary annuals or biennials, chervil and parsley do well; of perennials, the mints and golden oregano and sweet cecily. But, then, if the concept of "herb" is extended beyond the culinary, there are many more, woody and otherwise. My *Herbs in the Garden* (Dent 1985) indicates the surprising possibilities. Now follow herbaceous plants for shade.

Acanthus. It might seem perverse to begin this list with a plant whose name and use as the inspiration for the carved capitals of classical Corinthian columns epitomizes hot Mediterranean hillsides in a blaze of full sun. Often there, when most things are starting their summer rest, these great shiny leaves are starting to look their best. Yet paradoxically they will grow in at least half shade: flowering will be restricted, but their splendid clumps of leaves, as architectural in growth as their idealized shapes beneath a pediment, are just as good. With us *Acanthus* is on the borderline of hardiness. It is good therefore against the house with a heap of leaves over its head in winter. If this is impossible, it makes a marvellous tub plant for a shady patio, kept dry in an earth cellar over winter.

mollis 2 x 3 ft. (600 x 900 mm) The plant generally available and in fact the best is *A.m. latifolius*, with great arching leaves. These are so bright and shiny that they pick up flecks of dappled shade and flash it back, and it is one of the few plants to give a dry spot an entirely false air of moist lushness.

spinosus 2 x 2 ft. (600 x 600 mm) A smaller plant, but still of great presence, that flowers more consistently. The flowers are individually rather foxglovelike, in strong spiny spikes. Picked and dried when newly out, they are admirable for winter decoration indoors.

Aconitum. These are the monkshoods, which in shade and generally less sophisticated areas of the garden than formal herbaceous borders satisfactorily take the place of their delphinium relations. Blues or purples are typical colours in tall spikes above elegantly fingered leaves. The roots possess a poison to which there is no known antidote, but as no one is likely to eat them this dread fact need not put off even the most nervous.

napellus 4-5 x 1 ft. (1.2-1.5 m x 300 mm) This is the common European monkshood, cultivated there certainly since the sixteenth century. It is one of those good herbaceous plants that with little help can maintain itself in the shady rough turf of old orchards and help to carry on a flowering meadow feeling long after the spring bulbs are over. The soft pink form 'Carneum' does particularly well in northern gardens, where it enjoys shade. In heat the colour becomes pale and wan.

variegatum 5 x 2 ft. (1.5 m x 600 mm) Where the common monkshood has straight unbranched spikes, this species holds its paler helmets on elegant branching stems. Both these species have been used by breeders to provide a fine range of hybrids of varying colours. They appear in nurserymen's lists under A. x *bicolor*, plus a cultivar. The older types are tall elegant plants for big borders or half-wild places, while the newer Bressingham varieties are typically shorter and sturdier. A. *carmichaelii* is excellent for late-September effect planted with *Cimicifuga* and Japanese anemones.

vulparia 4-5 x 1 ft. (1.2-1.5 m x 300 mm) Here is a yellow species, a sort of horn yellow, on a lax, elegantly leaved plant. Reputedly its root poison is sufficient to have caused its use as a vermin killer and hence the common name of wolf's-bane. A. *lycoctonum* is similar, with more open spikes, still yellow.

Acorus calamus 2 x 1 ft. (600 x 300 mm) The striped variegated form of this pleasant irislike waterside plant is suitable for damp shade in association with primulas, contrasting it vertical emphasis with the broader leaves of hostas. Though a member of the arum family, it lacks a spathe and hence the flowers make no effect. An alternative virtue lies in the aromatic scent from the crushed leaves, which gives its vernacular name — sweet flag; its rhizones provide the calamus of commerce. A. *gramineus* is a thin grassy plant; again the variegated species is the one to grow — if at all.

Actaea. A small group of odd plants, quietly beautiful in leaf, flower and — surprisingly for herbaceous plants — in fruit. The leaves are dissected and rather fernlike, and above these are held the fuzzy flower heads reminiscent of thalictrums (meadow rues), to which *Actaea* is related. The berries are very poisonous. The three species grown all enjoy shade and a leafy soil. We are apt to consider these as simple woodlanders and kept to that sort of site. Brought into the garden and massed, the effect is dramatic. I have seen them planted with white and red auratum lilies at Mr. Frank Cabot's Quebec garden, white with white, red with red. This revelation in August is shown on the jacket of this book.

alba 2½ x 1½ ft. (760 x 450 mm) Although the name applies to the flower colour, it really refers to the glistening white berries, each one enhanced by the swollen scarlet stalk with which it is attached to the spike. This is a real eye stopper in August planted in an area devoted to spring bulbs that at this time are out of sight, or with summer lilies as above described.

rubra 2½ x 1½ ft. (760 x 450 mm) Here the heads of berries, as bright as clustered red currants, become spectacular in August and September. While the plant flourishes in full shade, a gleam of sun at some time of the day enhances its effect, which is good for a couple of months.

spicata 1½ x 1½ ft. (450 x 450 mm) Unlike the above two species, which are native to North America (and were collected early: John Tradescant knew the former in the early seventeenth century), this is the rare Herb Christopher of northern European woods. Smaller but no less eye-catching, the berries are as shining black as those of true deadly nightshade — and equally not to be eaten.

Ajuga reptans 9 x 11 in. (25 x 30 mm) The bugle of moist woodland rides makes a good front-of-bed growth, with leaves nearly flat on the ground and pleasant spikes of dark blue flowers. There are purple-leaved and multicoloured-leaved forms that need sun to colour and are rather pointless in shade, but the charming little 'Variegata,' whose leaves are splashed with white and grey, thrives. It dislikes my own heavy clay, preferring better drainage.

Alchemilla. The lady's mantles are elegantly-leaved plants of woodland edges and upland pastures. Even the smallest or most ordinary are worth growing, but in the context of this list A. *mollis* from Asia Minor is supreme. While it takes full sun in a moist soil (and in the north) it seems particularly right in at least half shade. The pleated silky leaves are of the softest grey-green, and above them the light heads of gold-green flowers are held for weeks in early summer; eighteen inches (450 mm) high, billowing outward like a satin-covered eiderdown.

It makes a lovely edging to a shady path and will seed itself about under shrubs and in the interstices of informal paving, and always looks well. Seldom does it outstay its welcome; deadheading before the seeds are shed will obviously reduce its spread. Usually, however, the seedlings are appreciated in someone else's garden as soon as one's own reaches satiety.

Anaphalis. If one thinks about it, there are very few grey-leaved plants for shade. The reasons are clear enough: the hairy felting that usually gives the effect is a xeromorphic adaptation to protect the plant from excess sun or drying winds. Neither is a problem in woodland, and hence the phenomenon does not exist. Thus one is both surprised and grateful for the following pair of Himalayans, which are invaluable in shady borders.

cinnamomea 2 x 2 ft. (600 x 600 mm) This is more usually seen in the lists as A. (*Gnaphthalium*) *yedoense*. It has white underleaves and felted stalks that carry flat heads of white everlasting flowers. Their papery consistency naturally enables them to last well.

triplinervis 1 x 2 ft. (300 x 600 mm) A shorter plant and perhaps even more desirable for providing the texture and colour of grey Mediterraneans in a shady spot, though not for dry shade. 'Summer Snow' is an admirable and self-descriptive cultivar.

margaritacea 1-3 x 2 ft. (300-900 x 900 mm) Our native pearly everlasting is a similar if less distinguished plant. Happy in dry or moist soil, in shade or sun, it is a most accommodating plant, not to be despised.

Anemone. The windflowers (a direct translation) offer many lovely plants for our shade-garden needs, from little woodland carpeters, epitomized by the European wood anemone, to robust herbaceous plants. All are elegant and light in effect, regardless of size.

x *hybrida* 4-5 x 2 ft. (1.2-1.5 m x 600 mm) It is simpler, if botanically inexact, to put under this name all the so-called Japanese anemones (A. *japonica*, A. *hupehensis*, A. *vitifolia*.) They are easy, common plants and often rather invasive, but provide some of the loveliest sights of the garden year with little effort on the part of the grower.

The fine dark leaves are vine shaped, as might be expected, and through them push the tall, near leafless flower stems. The flowers are like flat single roses, white, pale or dark pink, each with a fine central boss of yellow stamens. Several named cultivars are offered. They associate particularly well in a north-facing herbaceous border with the anaphalises described above. All the cultivars on offer are worth growing, and should be chosen to build up one's intended garden picture.

nemorosa 6 x 6 in. (150 x 150 mm) The exquisite windflower or wood anemone of northern deciduous woodlands can hardly be seen to better advantage than in its natural European habitat of russet-coloured tree leaf-litter, primroses and fresh spears of bluebell leaves. This tells us how they are ideally used, but they succeed equally under shrubs and even in weak orchard grass. The normal type is white, often pinkish in bud, but some fine selections forms are available. 'Allenii' is the biggest and best of the blues.

Other anemones to search out and use in shade are *cylindrica, narcissiflora* and *virginiana*. These North American native species are commonly known as thimbleweeds, referring to the seed heads that elongate after the petals have fallen and before they break up and float off in the wind. A pity, though, about the "weed" suffix: it gives an unfortunate impression, quite unjustified. It is also suitable to include here our very similar *Hepatica*, whose trilobed, bronzy leaves follow the clumps of pink, white or blue windflowers in earliest spring. Lovely, as in the woods, with bloodroot.

Anemonella thalictroides 1 x 1 ft. (300 x 300 mm) An excessive name, though nicely descriptive, of a charming little woodlander also known as rue anemone. It grows wild with us in company with its near cousin *Anemone canadensis*. More delicate in all its parts; exquisite white flowers above meadow-rue leaves. The little tuberous roots are stated as being edible, but it would seem to be as insensitive to do so as consuming larks' tongues on toast.

Anemonopsis macrophylla 2½ x 1½ ft. (760 x 460 mm) This is one of the plants that make any plantsman long for the ideal, deep, leafy-soil woodland. Yet the north border or the shady raised bed make equally good homes for the fernlike leaves and nodding purple flowers. If only one can find the nursery that stocks it.

Angelica archangelica 6 x 3 ft. (2 x 1 m) The great spherical umbels of green flowers above cool green leaves amply embody Marvell's line "a green thought in a green shade." As a statuesque clump in isolation or towering above hostas and smilacina the effect is splendid. But it is biennial and replacements must be kept to hand. Fortunately *Angelica* seeds itself about and any excess can be candied to remind ourselves that many of those green strips on cakes today are plastic. The taste of true *Angelica* is utterly distinct.

Even one crushed leaf is evocative to those of us old enough to know the real thing, which the young have missed.

A stem or two cut as soon as the seeds are formed dries magnificently for winter decoration indoors.

Aquilegia. Most of the modern hybrid long-spurred hybrid columbines, lovely though they are, need at least three-quarters sun, but a couple of species and selections from them are very happy in shade and seed themselves around.

canadensis 2 x 1 ft. (600 x 300 mm) As well as columbine, this charming native also rejoices in the name of meeting houses. Red and yellow spurred flowers nod above the elegant foliage, typical of the whole genus. This grows on dry banks in woodland and hence, bulked up from wild-collected seed, is invaluable for shade after the first flush of spring wild flowers is over.

vulgaris 3 x 1½ ft. (1 m x 460 mm) Granny's bonnet seeds itself around in a range of colours, blue, purple, pink and white above its elegant glaucous leaves. Smaller, with A. *alpina* as its other parent, is the hybrid 'Hensol Harebell,' two and a half by one feet (760 x 300 mm), which also makes itself at home when suited. Early-flowering herbaceous plants of some size like these, in addition to spring bulbs, are always welcome. This is a European and prefers more moisture than our own wild columbine, but is otherwise just as easy. The double-flowered form is not an improvement. Leaf miners can play havoc with the leaves − loathsome but not lethal. Similarly, cabbage butterfly caterpillars seem to love them, and one needs to keep watch.

Arisaema. Here are some lovely arums to associate in a shady border woodland glade with ferns and trilliums. All have typically spathed flowers, but some are oddly hooded.

candidissimum 1 x 1½ ft. (300 x 460 mm) Although a pure white form does exist, as the name suggests, the stiff spathe is usually flushed inside with pink and is green-striped outside. This exquisite flower emerges before the developing leaves, which are themselves noteworthy later; sometimes if one's plant is really happy spikes of red berries follow to give an autumn show, as well as the promise of propagation.

triphyllum 1-2 x 1 ft. (300-600 x 300 mm) This is our own common jack-in-the-pulpit or dragonroot. Here the narrow green-striped spathe is elegantly turned over the spadix, and in the form *zebrinum* has purple and white stripes very much in the fashion of Regency wallpaper. However often seen, this is always an eye-catcher. The autumn spikes of brilliant red (and poisonous) berries are also very decorative. Other arisaemas from the Himalayas and Japan are sometimes on offer and should be snapped up at once. All are fascinating plants for sheltered shady nooks.

Arisarum proboscideum 6 x 6 in. (150 x 150 mm) The "proboscis" of the Latin epithet also provides our own name for this charming little thing — mouse plant. In any cool leafy spot it makes good ground cover with small arrow-shaped leaves through which long tails appear as if a herd of mice were doing hand-stands. Investigation will show them to be the elongated ends of brown and white arum spathes. This comes from Italian woodlands and needs — and deserves — some winter protection.

Arum. Where leaves of arisaemas are lobed or fingered, those of true arums are clearly arrow shaped. The common European lords and ladies (*A. maculatum*) is in no way to be despised for woodland shade — the sight of the unfolding leaves shining in earliest spring is one of the first signs that the year has turned. But better still is its southern relation.

italicum 1½ x 1 ft. (460 x 300 mm) This is the common arum of southern Europe. The flowers are typically araceous with somewhat floppy spathes, usually dull yellow, but purplish to pink forms exist. They are followed by striking spikes of scarlet fruits (not to be taken internally) bright for some weeks from August. But it is the leaves, especially in the lovely marbled form 'Pictum,' that are the prime attraction. They are well up in late November and continue to look fresh throughout winter. If frosted, more come in spring. They make a lovely garden picture with Christmas roses and the earliest snowdrops. Again a heap of dry leaves over the tubers is slight but worthwhile effort to make. Dry shade is acceptable.

Aruncus 6 x 4 ft. (2 x 1.2 m) Goatsbeard is a splendidly robust plant, like a huge astilbe, making a mound of elegant leaves above which come the high plumes of creamy white flowers. It is unusual because it is dioecious (that is, with separately sexed plants; the term monoecious, as in hazel or zucchini, refers to separately sexed flowers on the same plant) with the male flower spikes being marginally the more ornamental. It is happy in almost any position and especially good with rheums and petasites and other grand-leaved plants. 'Knieffii' is a delightful smaller form, only about half the size of the species. Smaller still is the Korean *A. aethusifolius*.

Asarum. The wild ginger of our woods with highly aromatic heart-shaped leaves is one of the joys of summer: however hot the day, the patches of downy leaves hiding their strange waxy urn-shaped flowers look refreshingly cool. This, of course, is *A. canadense*. Easy to grow in moist soil, it associates perfectly, as in the wild, with jack-in-the-pulpit, trilliums and *Anemonella*.

europaeum 6 x 12 in. (150 x 300 mm) This is the once medicinal asarabacca. A smaller, tidier, evergreen species than the above with almost circular leaves of such shininess that they pick up and reflect any gleam of light in the darkest spot. It appears perfectly hardy. Less so but worth trying are related species from the southeastern States. These, such as *A. virginicum*, have marvelous marbled leaves so like those of *Cyclamen hederifolium* that one is apt to be slightly disappointed that cyclamen flowers do not follow.

Asperula odorata 6 in. x 2 ft. (150 x 600 mm) This is the lovely sweet woodruff, and seldom can a name be more descriptive, referring here to its scent, habit and the whorls of little leaves that support the white flowers. Although lovely, it should not be introduced to the choicest shady borders because of its overweening ambition. Anywhere else a gem. Sometimes now included under *Galium*.

Astilbe. There is now a wide range of these elegant moisture lovers. Usually seen lining stream sides or planted in broad swathes with irises and primulas, it might be thought that they offer little to gardens unblessed with water. But this is just where shade is a virtue. So long as the organic content of the soil can be built up to *hold* moisture they are very happy in shady beds, either massed or, when space is limited, restricted to three or four plants of different flowering times, planted with an iris or a hellebore for foliage contrast.

Few plants have both such elegance of foliage and flower; the former is good from its bronzy unfurling to its dried winter state, while the flowers last for weeks and the dead spikes remain ornamental for months. It is necessary to go to the nurserymen's lists to pick out types suitable for one's own needs. *Astilbe* hybrids (usually under the name of *A. x arendsii*) vary from two to four feet in height with a similar spread. The white and pale pink varieties usually have light green leaves, while the darker pinks and red sport suitably dark foliage. Flowering time is from June to early August. Really dwarf forms, no more than a foot high, are now being raised. These are admirable for the front of shady borders and in scale with even the smallest garden.

A. chinensis. 'Pumila' is rightly recommended as the easiest of all astilbes; a strong dark pink, it will take relatively dry sites and still look well.

Astrantia. This is the old masterwort of European woodmargins. A slightly surprising carrot relative (Umbellifer) each of whose typical umbels of flowers is supported by a ring of bracts, providing a spray of little Victorian posies.

major 2 x 1½ ft. (600 x 460 mm) The flowers are white with greenish bracts in the usual form, but pinkish and purplish variants are sometimes offered. The variegated-leaved masterwort can be very striking but loses its brightness in deep shade. An open leafy soil is needed for all of them. Drought is anathema.

maxima 2 x 1 ft. (600 x 300 mm) A rather more distinguished plant, though probably less easy to satisfy, liking a moister soil. The widespreading flower bracts are clear pink.

Begonia grandis 1½ x 1 ft. (450 x 300 mm) It may seem something of a nonsense to be able to list a begonia that survives our winters, but this really does succeed in a protected spot in the shade of a wall shrub. The lovely, typically off-centre leaves are pink underneath and the flowers repeat this colour. If one can get behind and below the leaves from a sunken path, they light up as if with their own internal illumination. Bulbils fall from the leaf axils and extend the group. A white-flowered form is also on offer. Both may be listed as *B. evansiana.*

Bergenia. One of the most valuable genera for ground cover in half shade: splendid great leathery leaves from spreading woody rhizomes and profuse spikes of flowers early spring, pink, purplish or white. They are particularly good in association with building and paving, softening hard edges and enhancing steps and so on. Their ability to survive in the poorest conditions has done them no good; performance and beauty in good conditions are a revelation to anyone having seen them in the former state. Several named forms are now available and others will follow, yet the wild Oriental species remain plants of great beauty.

cordifolia 1½ x 2 ft. (460 x 600 mm) Fine rounded leaves with crinkled edges and tall heads of mauve-pink flowers. The form 'Purpurea' is darker in flower and this colour is reflected in the shining red flower stalks. The leaves often turn purple in winter, but the shadier the spot the less this will occur. *B. crassifolia* is rather similar though distinct; it helps to have the two together to be certain of identification.

purpurascens 1 x 1 ft. (300 x 300 mm) Good in flower but particularly useful for leaf colour in winter. The leaves redden even in shade. 'Sunningdale' inherits this characteristic in a generally better plant.

x *schmidtii* 1½ x 2 ft. (460 x 600 mm) This lovely old hybrid is fine anywhere, but with good cultivation and a warm garden it is possible to pick flowers at Christmas in most years. Then the clear pink flowers are on short stems, but gradually they unfold into graceful sprays above the clear green leaves. The named clones are of mixed parentage and origin. Among the best are 'Abendglut,' the smallest of the group, whose leaves keep close to the ground. The flowers, often double, are deep purplish red. 'Ballawley' by comparison is a monster: two feet high and the same across, but more diffuse and hence lighter in effect than most bergenias and also without much blue in its flowers. A lovely plant. 'Silberlicht' is invaluable as a white bergenia but is cursed with some of the frost tenderness of *B. ciliata*, its lovely but delicate Himalayan parent.

Brunnera macrophylla 2½ x 1½ ft. (460 x 460 mm) Here is a lovely perennial forget-me-not, flowering in April and May with its unfolding leaves. These develop further to provide a good green ground layer in woodland or under shrubs long after most such plants have gone down for their summer rest. The variegated form is much less robust, good as the herbaceous layer of a stratified association in a sheltered courtyard.

Buglossoides rubro-coeruleum (Lithospermum) 1 x 3 ft. (300 x 900 mm) A splendid colonizer under trees in dry soil, with long horizontal growths arching along and rooting the while. Heads of dark-blue borage flowers in June.

Caltha palustris 1 x 1½ ft. (300 x 460 mm) This is the well-known kingcup or marsh marigold of boggy meadows. In a pondless garden a shady corner can be moist enough to accommodate this with an iris or two and some primulas. The charming double form is tighter in habit and better for restricted spots. The intensely double buttonlike flowers have their gold set off by a green eye.

Campanula. By contrast all bellflowers need well-drained soil. Several happily take shade and are good under shrubs and in light tree shade.

glomerata 2 x 1½ ft. (600 x 450 mm) Garden forms of the clustered bellflower, such as 'Superba,' are very useful in borders where a tendency to greed is not a vice. Such a tendency increases to a certainty in *C. rapunculoides* and *C. trachelium*, but their lovely spikes of blue are valuable under trees, in thin orchard grass and big shrub borders, where at ground level only spring bulbs need to try to compete. Clustered bellflower gives colour from June onward.

lactiflora 4-5 x 2 ft. (1.2-1.5 m x 600 mm) This is one of the loveliest of plants, with great sprays of lilac flowers (or pink in the smaller 'Loddon

Anna') in midsummer. Among tall earlier-flowering shrubs or again in orchard grass, it is beautiful with lilies and lupines. It will also do well under trees if the canopy is high: planted behind *Hydrangea arborescens* the effect is stunning.

latifolia 4 x 2 ft. (1.2 m x 600 mm) A British native of northern hedgebanks, and hence is happy to be given some shade farther south. In spite of a dangerous similarity of name to the preceding, in habit it is very different, standing strongly upright. This has a lovely white form at its best in July.

persicifolia 3 x 1 ft. (900 x 300 mm) This old cottage-garden plant is always useful, among shrubs, following bulbs, under roses — especially old-fashioned roses — with its thin-leaved spikes of large open bells. A garden will soon develop colour variants from white to dark blue from self-sown seedlings. All are beautiful and the best should be encouraged. Deadheading extends the show for months.

rotundifolia 1-1½ x 1 ft. (300-450 x 300 mm) English harebell or blue-bells of Scotland offer two geographical names for this lovely little plant that is also native to North America. The exquisite flowers are the invariable pattern for the rather twee hats that pixies wear in 1920s children's books. Happy in part shade and taking up little little space, it gives flower throughout the summer months. The white form is equally charming. The specific epithet is something of a snare; only the most basal leaves are round, and these may well have been chewed off by a passing slug.

Cardamine pratensis 3-4 x ½ ft. (1-1.2 m x 150 mm) The damp water-meadows where this lovely little plant used to be so common in England is less frequently seen. Thus in moist half shade both the species and its double-flowered form are always a gentle pleasure in the garden and are well-worth growing for the gentle violet flowers in May.

Chaerophyllum hirsutum 'Roseum' 2 x 1 ft. (600 x 300 mm) This is the pink form of a common hedgerow cow parsley. If called more grandiloquently "Pink Queen Anne's Lace" it would probably get more takers and once better known get the use it deserves. Good for orchard grass as well as under shrubs, making quite a show of float heads in May and June.

Chelidonium majus 1½ x 1½ ft. (460 x 460 mm) This is the greater celandine (actually a poppy), whose orange sap is reputed to cure warts. The yellow flowers are nothing much, but the glaucous ferny leaves are very attractive. It is happy under shrubs or in open woodland. Root growth appears thin and thus it competes little with other things even when seeding about. The excess seedlings are so easily removed that they cause no problems.

Chelone. The turtleheads (or snakeheads) are not uncommon plants of our moist meadows, with spikes of pink or white flowers in late summer. The effect is something between that of snapdragon and obedient plant.

lyonii 3 x 2 ft. (1 m x 600 mm) The commonest and easiest of all. Not for heavy shade, but in a north border success can be achieved in drier soil than is normally the case.

Chrysanthemum. The conventional autumn-flowering chrysanthemums are not plants for shade, but the genus is a large one and offers several good plants for our needs. I find that the conventional Korean chrysanthemums are happy among shrubs flowering informally but well throughout fall. Growth in half shade is lax, but staking unnecessary.

corymbosum 3½ x 1½ ft. (1.15 m x 460 mm) This has been in European gardens for centuries, but even now is not common. It is a simple plant, easy to grow, and rather resembles a giant feverfew. Even dry shade is acceptable to it and a good late-summer show can be expected.

macrophyllum 4 x 2 ft. (1.2 m x 600 mm) A rather similar but even bigger plant, though with July and August heads of flowers that are a less pure white. The leaves are agreeably aromatic and can be dried to add to potpourri.

parthenium 2 x 1 ft. (600 x 300 mm) This is the old herb feverfew, which has developed something of a reputation lately not as a febrifuge, as its name suggests, but as a migraine cure. While it has undoubtedly helped some sufferers, it has left others with equally unpleasant mouth ulcers, so it is best left as an ornamental garden plant until medical research clarifies the situation. This can be expected in the near future. The species is a pretty thing, with ferny leaves and diffuse heads of white single daisies. A golden-leaved form comes true from seed and so do semi- and fully double types. They need good drainage and seed themselves around. Lovely, easy plants to fill gaps in borders, above spring bulbs or among shrubs. Dry soil is accepted happily.

Cimicifuga. A group of valuable, though still uncommon plants that provide height without bulk. Late summer spikes of creamy white fuzzy flowers are like soft bottlebrushes. Moist half shade is ideal.

racemosa 5 x 2 ft. (1.5 m x 600 mm) The earliest to flower in August and most generally available. Other good species are C. *simplex* and

C. ramosa, which if discovered should be bought at once. These are lovely with Japanese anemones. The flower spikes in seed should be left on to add textural interest to the late-fall scene. Cimicifugas may be found in the lists under a number of names. Black snakeroot, black cohosh and bugbane are but three.

Clintonia. A North American genus for a cool woodland spot or shady bed devoted to choice things. They need lime-free leafy soil. Belonging also to the Liliaceae, foliage is rather like lily of the valley but bigger, and the nodding flowers (pink in *C. andrewsiana* and green-yellowy in the commoner *C. borealis*) are succeeded − if the not very easy plant succeeds at all − by blue berries.

Codonopsis. A group of delicate Asiatic bellflowers, cream, pale or darker blue, and all with extraordinary rings of different colours, orange, near black, greenish, inside the bell. Two are twiners (*C. convolvulacea* and *C. vinciflora*) and others such as *C. clematidea* and *C. ovata* are free-standing but not robust, so all are best among low shrubs where they can scramble or find support. They go down completely in winter to brittle roots (resembling unsuccessful bellbine) so they need careful marking if they are not to be weeded out by mistake. Though probably unavailable from any garden centre, seeds are offered by the more adventurous lists and raising the plants is easy; they flower in a couple of years.

Convallaria. No garden of whatever size can be complete without lily of the valley, though the plant itself may well reject a lot of sites offered to it. Where happy, it will romp about under shrubs and come up in gravel paths. As a natural woodlander, a leafy well-drained soil seems ideal to start with, though where it will move is its own affair. Indeed in some gardens it becomes a noxious weed. It is best to allot a given area under trees or shrubs without other herbaceous plants. The splendid ground-cover effect and even a good show of scarlet (poisonous) berries can then be appreciated after the May-time flowers are over.

majalis 9 x 9 in. (200 x 200 mm) The typical plant with its exquisite scent is varied by 'Fortin's Giant,' bigger in all its parts and flowering a week or so later and thus invaluable for extending the season, and by 'Rosea,' a dusky (some say dirty) pink. *C. m.* 'Variegata' with gold-banded leaves is lovely, for it flowers as well as the type, but the variegation is not always very permanent and even less so in shade. This is in no way aggressive and should be sought out for small gardens.

Corydalis. A group of plants for thin woodland or under shrubs to associate with the smaller spring bulbs. All have lovely lacy leaves and spikes of flowers like minuscule antirrhinums.

bulbosa 9 x 12 in. (230 x 300 mm) This and the even smaller C. *solida* have pale purple flowers and are good mixed with the more conventional small early spring bulbs because they are so different in form. Like them they are out of sight by the end of June. One meets a little corydalis emerging with crocuses from the snow on cretan mountainsides in April. The association is worth copying in the garden.

lutea 1 x 1 ft. (300 x 300 mm) The commonest of the group making a heap of delicate blue-green leaves studded throughout summer with small yellow flowers. It seeds itself into shady rock or paving crevices but never becomes a nuisance; always elegant and fresh-looking.

nobilis 2-3 x 2 ft. (600-900 x 600 mm) From central Asia, this is the grandest of the genus that it is easily possible to grow. Tall spikes of yellow — from a distance the effect is of lupines flowering two months ahead of their time. This is a plant well worth searching out; happy under trees.

Cypripedium. Anyone with a bit of cool woodland or a shady bed of cherished gems will want to try the exquisite hardy lady's slipper orchids. But to obtain them is not easy, even less to be reasonably sure that the stock is a good one and with care will survive. Transplanting from the wild should be utterly resisted unless one can with hand on heart really affirm that the land is under threat from development and that the plants would perish, anyway.

There are several species, all lovely, the flowers made up of a pouch and surrounding petals contrasting in colour.

calceolus 1½ x 1½ ft. (450 x 450 mm) Golden slipper or yellow moccasin flower, this is one of our most beautiful native plants, with fragrant flowers, the purple-brown petals supporting the yellow pouch. There are a number of geographical variants that differ marginally in colour and size; most distinct is that formally known as var. *parviflorum*, where the two longest petals droop and twist like the moustache of a miraculous mandarin. A leafy woodland soil in shade among trilliums and other special plants should bring success.

If other hardy orchids such as *Habenaria* (the fringed orchises) or *Orchis* species are ever offered in the trade they should be snapped up at once. Conditions as for the yellow lady's-slipper.

reginae 2-3 x 1½ ft. (600-900 x 450 mm) This is the showy lady's-slipper, which is one of the great excitements to come across in our boggy woodlands. Nothing can be more beautiful than when the pink and white flowers are seen against the light or are themselves catching a sunbeam against the gloom of the forest floor. Here is a plant that cultivation helps one to appreciate even more, because hopefully in one's own garden one is less prey to the mosquitoes that guard this beauty in the wild. A leafy, always moist position is essential in half shade. Every effort is worth giving.

Delphinium must be mentioned as a lovely genus of herbaceous plants, though all prefer sun and a shady garden must use the best monkshoods for tall blue spikes. Borders that get a bit of sun at some part of the day, however, and are without overhanging branches can offer homes to those species available (though not the red Californians) or to the smaller modern strains such as belladonna hybrids.

Dentaria. A couple of native crucifers like bigger versions of *Cardamine pratensis*, to which they are closely related. The name, or its translation to toothwort, refers to the white tuberous roots. Good for a bit of early colour that is not supplied by bulbs. Both the white *D. diphylla* and pinkish *D. laciniata* are well worth growing and will take the darkest undertree shade, wisely retiring underground when the leaf canopy completely closes in.

Dicentra. These charming little plants enjoy leafy soil in cool shady borders. Above ferny foliage the flower stems arch and carry their flowers dangling below. Edward Lear's famous 'Nonsense Botany' plant, *Manypeeplia upsidedownia*, is a direct crib, unless of course it happened the other way round, with nature yet again copying art.

canadensis 1 x 1 ft. (300 x 300 mm) Our native squirrel corn (from the tiny golden tubers found below ground, as if stored by more than usually tidy squirrels) is an obligate woodlander and so an obvious plant for shade. Little sprays of white, purple-flushed flowers appear in late spring.

cucullaria 1 x 1 ft. (300 x 300 mm) Similar in size, Dutchman's-breeches is well-known for its relatively large, inflated flowers. White with yellow tips, this is another charming native woodlander.

eximia 18 x 18 in. (450 x 450 mm) The eastern bleeding heart is a more robust but no less delightful species. From the wooded mountains of New York State down to Georgia it is one of the best of plants for shady border naturalizing. Delightful foliage and summer-long pink flowers on elongated spikes are always eye-catching. 'Purity' is an exquisite white form. *Dicentra formosa* is the closely related western or Pacific bleeding heart. Where happy, it spreads widely but not invasively. Particularly good named clones or possibly hybrids are 'Adrian Bloom' and 'Pearl Drops'. 'Luxuriant' is a brighter cherry red.

spectabilis 2 x 1½ ft. (600 x 450 mm) One of the classic cottage garden plants that seems to be less happy anywhere else. It needs a cool spot where the fat flowers get a gleam of sun to brighten their rose to crimson. It must have more common names than most other plants, from Japanese bleeding heart and Dutchman's-breeches to lyre flower and lady-in-the-bath (the latter comes clear if an upright flower is gently pulled open, an irresistible annual amusement). A white-flowered form is just as lovely, but less easy to obtain.

Digitalis purpurea. The common foxglove is an invaluable woodland plant varying in colour from the typical rosy purple to white and with strains such as 'Excelsior Hybrids' bringing in pale yellow and near buff. All are beautifully marbled and spotted in the throat. While the hybrid strains are magnificent plants – up to six feet (2 m) high – with flowers all round the stem, it must be said that they lack the grace of the wilding with its one-sided spike. Most are biennial. Thus the first year it is necessary to buy a few plants *and* sow seed to provide flower for year two. Subsequently they will seed themselves about and only need thinning out or moving to where they are most wanted. If the flower spikes are removed the moment flowering is over, a second crop may result; often, too, the plant develops side rosettes that take it into the following year, against the rules. 'Foxy' is a recently developed annual foxglove. Sown in spring, it provides late-summer spikes. This too may overwinter.

There are several perennial species from southern Europe that in general need more sun. But the charming pale-yellow *grandiflora* likes half shade, as does its odd cross with the common foxglove. This is

x *mertonensis*, which has large flowers on squat spikes of a sort of squashed strawberry colour. Although strictly perennial, it needs frequent propagation. Thin dry soil does not suit it. Interesting rather than beautiful.

Diphylleia cymosa 2-3 x 2 ft. (600-900 x 600 mm) Another unusual North American woodlander for the ideal cool leafy spot. The flowers are rather by the way, but a striking late-summer picture is made when the heads of vivid blue berries are held above the great bilobed leaves. The common name of umbrella leaf is well earned; this strange plant is a berberis relation. Moist, leafy soil in even full shade is required.

Disporum. Fairy bells, nodding mandarin and fairy lantern are names that well describe these charming Solomon's seal relatives with pleated leaves and cascading bellflowers in late spring. The foliage maintains textural interest throughout the season. In *Disporum sessile* a fine variegated form is worth searching out. This is about eighteen inches (450 mm) high.

Twice as tall and the best for more sophisticated shady borders is *D. flavum*. There are other western species that if available certainly be tried in the east. Again it is worth remarking the protection offered by woodland sites.

Docecatheon. North Americans related to and enjoying similar conditions to candelabra primulas. They like humus and moisture, with shade in inverse proportion to the other desiderata. Unlike primulas, the petals are sharply reflexed cyclamen-wise to provide the apt name 'Shooting Stars.'

meadia 1½ x 1 ft. (460 x 300 mm) There are several species, of which this is the most robust and generally available. Pink and yellow flowers in May and June. 'Shooting Stars' are easily raised from seed.

Doronicum. In spite of its name, leopard's-bane, it seems to have no reputation of being deadly poisonous, like wolf's-bane. Anyway, it is for looking at. All species have bright yellow daisies early in the year and give nonbulb interest under shrubs, in shady borders or even in open woodland and orchard grassland. With their branching stems above heart-shaped leaves the show lasts for weeks.

'Miss Mason' 1½ x 2 ft. (460 x 600 mm) An old garden plant of unknown origin, it is still one of the best.

pardalianches 3 x 2 ft. (900 x 600 mm) A splendid spreader to put with spring bulbs in woodland, from whose earlier show it takes over; lovely with *Brunnera* and *Mertensia*.

plantagineum 'Harpur Crewe' 2½ x 1 ft. (760 x 300 mm) Another fine old plant, with bigger individual flowers, still of the same rich yellow.

Duchesnea indica. A major disappointment. This plant covers ground looking just like a prolific alpine strawberry with yellow flowers. The fruits look inviting but are disgusting. Much better to plant *Fragaria* proper.

Eomecon chionanthum 1½ x 1½ ft. (460 x 460 mm) The lovely snow poppy from eastern China, for woodland or under shrubs. The smooth round leaves are topped by pure white nodding flowers in May, rather like a big wood anemone. It will certainly need winter protection from a heap of leaves in northern gardens, but is well worth trying if only it can be obtained.

Epimedium. Considering the beauty of this group of plants in flower and foliage and their ease of growth as well as their value as ground cover in shade, it is truly extraordinary that they are not commonly seen in "ordinary gardens." Botanically related to the barberries (a generally shrubby family), their flowers, on wiry spikes, more closely resemble small columbines and have a similar charm. All make tight ground cover and increase rather slowly by shallow-growing rhizomes.

Apart from E. *perralderanum*, which is a valuable evergreen, epimediums have a seasonal growth pattern that is itself a pleasure to observe. If last year's dead leaves are cut away in March (or before in an early season) the flower stems are seen to unfurl. Gradually the leaves follow, initially soft and delicate, yet gradually attaining a wiry strength. Throughout the summer there is solid ground cover toward a foot high. Then in late autumn the leaves take on further colours. Altogether an invaluable group for all shade needs. They divide easily in spring.

To avoid repetition the others can be taken as attaining a foot or so and flowering in April and early May. The best include E. *grandiflorum*, crimson and its variants 'Rose Queen' and 'White Queen.' E. *perralderanum* and E. x *versicolor* 'Sulphureum' are yellow. E. x *rubrum* is the smallest, with pink and white flowers. E. x *warleyense* is one of many fine garden plants that came from the rather terrifying Ellen Willmott's Warley Place. This is glowing terra cotta, a colour unique in epimediums. A particular favourite is E. *youngianum* 'Niveum,' with relatively large white flowers above pale-green foliage. The flower shape recalls those rather extraordinary caps worn by female members of some high-church choirs.

Euphorbia. There can be few genera that exhibit so wide a range of forms, from little annual weeds of our gardens to Christmas-card poinsettias and great cactuslike trees of the African bush. One of the most obvious things that joins the spurges is the poisonous white latex that exudes from any cut surface. As might be expected, all garden situations are needed to encompass a range, and within this are several highly desirable shade plants.

amygdaloides 1½ x 1 ft. (460 x 300 mm) Not a spectacular plant, the European wood spurge nonetheless has a real quiet charm. There are purple-leaved and variegated forms rarely available. Desirable but difficult to get and nowhere near as robust as their parent, which is the most likely to succeed with us. Rather like *Helleborus foetidus* in the way it keeps last year's leafy growth through the winter and succeeds in similar positions and climates.

cyparissias 1 x 2 ft. (300 x 600 mm) An excellent growth cover, even in dry soil and at least half shade. Bright green ferny foliage, yellow-green flower heads all turning bright yellow in fall. Apt to become a weed in good soil.

griffithii 3 x 2 ft. (900 x 600 mm) A Himalayan whose heads of orange-red come as close as we can get to a hardy poinsettia. Usually seen in herbaceous borders, it is also effective under shrubs. With yellow azaleas in half shade this can be one of the most striking sights of the acid-soil shade garden. 'Fire-Glow' is the clone usually offered.

There are other valuable herbaceous spurges that I have not seen in cultivation in this area but fully intend to try. They include

palustris. A robust spurge with fine heads of bitter-yellow and good foliage that turns yellow in the autumn. As its name suggests, as a marsh plant it likes moisture, yet — surprisingly, perhaps — it seems to succeed happily in dry soil in full shade. In such a position its impression of lushness is particularly valuable. The smaller green and yellow *epithymoides* behaves similarly, though too much shade causes etiolated growth and the typical dome of colour is lost.

robbiae is a two-footer and in Britain is one of the best plants for shade. In moist or dry soil it colonizes as much space as it is allowed, with its rosettes of dark green leaves on foot-high stems and clear green flower spikes above.

Finally, *E. sikkimensis* has tall stems of typical greenery-yellery spurge. Flowers are good, but more unusual is the early growth with red stems and white-veined leaves. An interesting and underused genus.

Filipendula. These are the native and exotic meadowsweets. Often confused with *Astilbe* (which has pointed plumes of flowers), these have flat plates of flowers, each equally tiny. The leaves are truly very similar, though on a larger scale, the whole building up very handsome plants.

palmata 4 x 2 ft. (1.2 m x 600 mm) Although a couple of named forms are occasionally offered, the type is fine enough and a good clear pink. *F. purpurea* is similar but flowers a little earlier, the colour a rather fierce cherry red that a shady woodland position helps to cool.

rubra 6 x 4 ft. (2 x 1.2 m) Queen of the prairie is an enormous plant and needs companions in scale if it is not to dominate too aggressively. But it is lovely in a moist position, by a woodland pool with rheums and peltiphyllums, perhaps, and big-leaved rhododendrons behind, to which its summer flowers gives interest after their season is past.

ulmaria 3-4 x 2 ft. (1-1.2 x 5 m) This is the meadowsweet of northern European water meadows, where it grows with rushes and ragged robin.

In spite of its agreeable scent, the species is hardly a worthwhile plant, but a double form has fine fluffy heads in late summer and is splendid in a moist half-shaded spot. Golden and variegated leaves types are for what in the eighteenth century they called "curious gardeners."

Fragaria vesca is the little wild strawberry, happily running about under trees, its starlike flowers out from April to October, followed of course by tiny but delicious fruit. The white-fruited form is the one to get, as the birds sit around waiting for it to ripen and hence give the grower a sporting chance.

Galax urceolata 1½ x 1 ft. (460 x 300 mm) A fine evergreen carpeter from woody hillsides in the Carolinas southward, where it grows with the nearly impossible to cultivate *Epigaea* (trailing Arbutus), fortunately galax is hardy well north of its natural range. Known variously as wandflower, beetleweed and, in a nice adaptation of the Latin, galaxy, it is a most distinctive addition for deep woodland shade. With clumps of round leaves dark green until autumn, when many turn bronze, they are overtopped in June and July with spikes of white flowers like a small *cimicifuga*. The earlier name of *Galax aphylla* still occurs on the lists.

Gentiana. Most gentians — at least those commonly seen — are dwarf plants of high exposed uplands where shade is unknown. Yet one species is among the loveliest of all shade lovers.

asclepiadea 2-3 x 2 ft. (600-900 x 600 mm) The willow gentian has pairs of narrow leaves throughout the length of the gently arching stems and the top dozen pairs carry the flowers in their axils. These are typically mid-blue, but darker and paler forms exist, as well as white. As it is not difficult to grow from seed, it should be sown (as soon as it is ripe and the pots left outside all winter) from one's first bought plants to build up a stock. Worthwhile variants may well appear. While the willow gentian will grow in dry tree shade, it develops its full size and grace in moister leafy soils; lime is no problem. Certainly it is worth every care.

Geranium, with *Bergenia* and *Helleborus* one of the most valuable herbaceous genera for shady places. Those that accept shade — and that is most of them — are also good carpeters, keeping their leaves for much of the year. The floral display is by no means inconsiderable so long as no comparison is made with florists' "geraniums" (actually *Pelargonium*), and then it is a still moot point as to which genus is the more desirable.
   All look best planted in wide swathes as foreground plants to taller things; their foliage always fully furnishes the site. Unless stated, they flower in late spring and early summer.

endressii 1½ x 2 ft. (450 x 600 mm) From the Pyrenees, this is one of the finest geraniums for half shade, with its bright pink flowers held well above the elegant leaves from June through October. If planted under trees in informal areas it will move out into empty places in the sun, but probably prefers and certainly looks better in the cool. Several forms have been selected for further flower colour. 'A. T. Johnson' is silvery pink, while 'Wargrave Pink' is a stronger tint approaching salmon. Both are also bigger in growth than the type, providing vigorous ground cover. 'Claridge Druce' is a hybrid with G. *endressii* in it; here the luxuriant foliage is greyish green, admirably setting off the blue-pink flowers.

'Johnson's Blue' 1 x 2 ft. (300 x 600 mm) Another splendid hybrid. This time the parents are *himalayense* (itself worth growing) and the big European meadow cranesbill. Good ground cover and dark-veined lavender-blue flowers. No more than half shade if it is not to flop unacceptably.

macrorrhizum 1 x 2 ft. (300 x 600 mm) A low ground coverer with near-evergreen aromatic leaves, although they also take on surprising autumn colour. The white form 'Album' and 'Ingwersen's Variety' are to be preferred to the type with its rather dull magenta flowers.

maculatum 2 x 1½ ft. (600 x 460 mm) The only native North American, it has good dissected leaves and rose-pink flowers earlier than most. It needs cool woodland soil. The white form is worth seeking out; pale and delicate, straight out of a pre-Raphaelite painting.

x *magnificum* 2 x 2 ft. (600 x 600 mm) This is often listed as G. *ibericum platypetalum*. It has especially handsome leaves and dark lavender-blue flowers in quantity.

nodosum 1½ x 1½ ft. (450 x 450 mm) Bushy little plant of glossy green leaves with lilac-blue flowers. Here it is possible to add that it thrives in dry shade, not merely accepting it with some reluctance, as is often the case. Flowering goes on for months.

phaeum 2 x 1½ ft. (600 x 450 mm) Opening its first flowers in late April in warm spots, this is perhaps the earliest cranesbill to bloom. The flowers are held well above the foliage and hold their petals reflexed behind a forward-pointing boss of stamens. There are white, mauve and nearly black forms. All are beautiful.

pratense 2 x 2 ft. (600 x 600 mm) The meadow cranesbill is one of the most beautiful wild plants one sees on English holiday, showing off its two-pence-sized (one will have the right currency to hand for comparison) blue flowers particularly well against the lush greenness of those northern hedgebanks. Its preference for the cooler north makes it admirable for open woodland or in orchard grass. In borders the lovely double types spread with less freedom and are thus to be preferred, as are two fine forms from northern India (this species has an enormous geographical distribution) sold as 'Kashmir Purple' and 'Kashmir White.'

psilostemon 3 x 3 ft. (1 x 1 m) In spite of the redoubtable Miss Jekyll's damning phrase "malignant magenta" (she didn't go in for barring holds), this is one plant where the colour is better described, maintaining the alliteration as "magnificent magenta," emphasized as it is by the black eye of every flower. All this above a great heap of fine leaves. In dryish shade it gets less big and looks lovely with yellow and orange Welsh poppies seeding about.

sanguineum 1 x 1 ft. (300 x 300 mm) The bloody cranesbill, an uncommon British native still to be found in the grykes of the limestone pavements on Lancashire hillsides. The lovely pale-pink 'Lancastriense' still grows wild there, too, although in cultivation since the early eighteenth century. A good white form is taller but flops rather.

wallichianum 1 x 2 ft. (300 x 600 mm) In the form 'Buxton's Variety' this is one of the top plants for half or full shade. Clear blue open flowers with white eyes are carried for months above good ground-covering foliage.

Geum. The bigger-flowered *chiloense* hybrids such as 'Lady Stratheden' and 'Mrs. Bradshaw' (orange-yellow and brick-red respectively) are some of the best plants for conventional herbaceous border requirements in shade, flowering from May to October. G. x *borisii*, another old hybrid, is a lovely soft orange.

rivale 1 x 1 ft. (300 x 300 mm) European water avens, known here as Indian chocolate, with pleasant nodding flowers of a purplish, buffish pink, is good in moist shade in an unspectacular way. More noticeable is the hybrid with the wood avens, *Geum* x *intermedium*, if it can be found.

Gillenia trifoliata is one of the several North American native plants that early European colonists saw being used medicinally and thus called Indian physic; bowman's root is another name. It makes a two- to three-foot (600-900 mm) clump covered in summer with starry white flowers. As a plant of open woodlands from Ontario down to Florida, it takes a north border shade very happily.

Glaucidium palmatum 2 x 2 ft. (600 x 600 mm) Usually put in the Ranunculaceae, it is now sometimes accorded a family of its own, no doubt because of its four, not five petals. These are pale lavender in May, the whole effect being rather meconopsislike. Another plant for the shaded corner of gems in moist leafy soil — if ever it is available.

Grasses.

Because the grasses hold together visually, rather as do conifers and ferns, they are grouped here in a similar fashion. Also similarly, the general term includes certain plants that are not true grasses (family Gramineae), but sedges and rushes (*Carex* and *Luzula*), as well. In fact, almost by definition the great majority of true grasses are naturally open-land or prairie plants and hence intolerant of shade. Nonetheless there are several well worth growing. Again as with irises, these are monocotyledonous plants whose narrow leaves and generally vertical emphasis contrast particularly well with the flatter, more solid shape of broad-leaved species.

Carex morrowii is a Japanese plant that, in its variegated form, provides a fine foot-high tussock of gold-striped leaves. Good with small spring bulbs. Softer in texture is our native *C. plantaginea*, green and fresh until Christmas and maintaining its texture even when poking through snow later on. Bigger is

Carex pendula. A most distinguished sedge, a plant of damp woodland making fine two-foot clumps of wide grassy leaves and, above, tall, gracefully arching spikes of flowers that last for months, alive or dead. In cultivation it will take far drier conditions than it inhabits in the wild. A lovely plant for associating with heavier leaved things.

Similar are the wood rushes, *Luzula* spp. with relatively broad, hairy-edged evergreen leaves and spikes of brownish flowers. *L. sylvatica* 'Marginata' has silver-edged leaves. Both make marvellous ground covers even in dry shade once given help to establish themselves.

Some of the fescues are valuable lawn grasses, and *Festuca glauca* makes an attractive grey-blue tussock for no more than half shade. Much more tolerant is *F. scoparia*, which makes a soft carpet in dry shade.

Glyceria maxima is a rumbustious water's edge grass, quite out of place in the garden, but a variegated form is both restrained in habit and accepts dry and shady spots. The white-striped leaves are bright pink as the shoots push up in the spring.

Phalaris arundinacea is another such plant: a wet-land aggressor with a highly garden-worthy variegated variant. This is 'Picta,' ribbon grass or gardener's garters. It makes splendid metre-high white and green clumps, invaluable for indoor decoration. More unusual is *Uniola latifolia*, which resembles a huge quaking grass with hanging corn-dollylike flower clusters.

Several other grasses are possible in at least half shade: the statuesque *Miscanthus*, green or striped; little gold and green *Hakenochloa*, delicate *Deschampsia*. Each should be reviewed for its pattern and powers of contrast not just during summer but throughout the year. Grasses need never be cut down until spring when the new growth appears. They are thus almost continually earning their keep.

Helleborus. Needless to say, Christmas and Lenten roses are not roses at all but buttercup relations. As a marvellous group of plants for shady borders and woodland in almost any soil except the driest and most acid, hellebores cannot be overpraised. Their value is continuous. There are no grander flowers for the open garden in earliest spring with a range of forms and colours that careful breeding and selection is still increasing. Unlike so many other plants, this has in no way upset the natural poise and charm of the genus. Several of the species, notably the Corsican and *H. orientalis*, seed themselves about in shade with gay abandon: the first comes perfectly true, while the second will offer a wide range of colour forms, all worthwhile. Seed germinates quickly when fresh but can go dormant for a couple of years once becoming dry. It is therefore wise to start with a few bought-in plants and sow one's own fresh seed as soon as it is ripe.

atrorubens 1 x 1 ft. (300 x 460 mm) A lovely deciduous Lenten rose that is usually the earliest of its group. It is a warm plum-purple and lasts cut, incidentally, much more certainly than the rest of its group. Each flower stem carries up to five or six typically saucer-shaped flowers. By the time all are over the new leaves have risen up and provided a second picture. This seems not to set seed in captivity. A plant is best lifted in spring, teased apart into a number of crowns, each with thonglike roots. These should be potted. Having got growing, they can then be planted out.

corsicus 2 x 3 ft. (600 x 900 mm) The Corsican hellebore has an oddly biennial subshrubby habit. Spring growth produces strong woody shoots of striking saw-edged leaves. By autumn a fat central bud has developed at the top that bursts into a profuse head of flowers from November to April, depending upon strain, season and site. They are clear pale-green bowls with a boss of stamens enclosed by a ring of nectaries typical of the genus. The display lasts for months. As the seeds' capsules swell their weight causes the shoots to lean outward, leaving the centre open for the next season's growth. It is thus always in beauty. However, it resents searing winter winds and must be given a sheltered shady corner and a heap of leaves before things become too unpleasant.

Botanists now aver that the Corsican hellebore is a geographical sub-species of the Majorcan *H. lividus*. This is less hardy, but hybrids be-tween the two are safer and inherit a pinkish flush to the flowers and, more important, a delightful marbling to the leaves. These make lovely winter plants for the nearly cold greenhouse if they cannot be grown outside.

foetidus 1½ x 1½ ft. (460 x 460 mm) Another evergreen with fingered leaves on a woody stem topped with open heads of purple-edged green bells. The name need put off no one. The smell is not at all obtrusive and the plant is visually striking at all times. Selected forms such as 'Cabbage Stalk' are more vigorous and look splendid with bergenias and hostas. Again some protection is necessary for overwintering stems; though the plant itself is hardy enough, the incipient flowers can get frosted.

niger 1 x 1 ft. (300 x 300 mm) The exquisite Christmas rose is a plant that everybody wants to grow — who can resist the great pure white bowls and their gold stamens appearing in the depths of winter? But few are really good at keeping. It likes shade and moist leafy soil, as well as protection from slugs, which are as fond of it as we are. Important, too, is the form obtained: 'Potters Wheel' is the best of the named kinds. Most, it must be said, are less likely to provide flowers for the Christmas table than *H. atrorubens*; indeed, they are often late for Lent.

Lovely but sterile crosses have been made between the Christmas rose and the Corsican and may be found in one or two specialist catalogues under the name *H. x nigericors*.

orientalis 1½ x 1½ ft. (460 x 460 mm) This and a number of other possibly true species (*abschasicus*, *guttatus*, *kochii*) can be lumped to-gether here as Lenten roses, providing a group of completely beautiful hardy plants. The seasonal growth pattern is like that of the Corsican, but the fine palmate leaves and flower stems arise individually from the rootstock. By flowering time last year's leaves are nearly flat upon the ground. New growth makes a great dome of green.

Flower colour varies from palest primrose-green through white, pink to darkest damson purple. All are variously speckled inside and all are lovely. Once established it seeds itself around with abandon and makes marvellous undertree ground cover.

viridis 1 x 1 ft. (300 x 300 mm) This is the green hellebore native to northern Europe and its habitat of moist woodland on rather heavy alkaline soil indicates its likes. It is deciduous, though on a much smaller scale than the rest, but the bare flower stems of avocado-green flowers are no less lovely. It is the hardiest of all.

Hemerocallis. For shade the Oriental day lilies are almost as important for their foliage as for their flowers, and that effect is certainly longer lasting. The elegant grassy clumps start to grow very early in the year and are brightly pale. The bigger species can be rather invasive, but under trees and big shrubs or in old orchard grass this is no sin. For smaller gardens and choice sites there are also suitable types. Individual flowers are literally ephemeral, of course, but their succession provides colour for a considerable time; a chosen selection could give flower from May onward. The flower buds are edible incidentally, and are sometimes pickled. This does detract from the garden, however.

dumortieri 2 x 1½ ft. (600 x 460 mm) This and the smaller *H. minor* are elegant perennials for early effect, taking over from the spring bulbs and forming tidy compact clumps. Good with *Symphytum grandiflorum* clustering around.

flava 2 x 1½ ft. (600 x 460 mm) This lovely old garden plant has been in cultivation since Elizabethan times and still earns its keep in big gardens. Yellow fragrant flowers are held well above the foliage.

fulva 3½ x 2 ft. (900 x 600 mm) Another old plant that John Gerard (of *Herbal* fame) grew in his garden at Holborn in the late 1500s. They are a sort of orange-suède colour of lovely shape and poise. The spreading clumps of wide grassy leaves will grow in odd half-shady corners and always catch the eye. This is the day lily that has gone wild on so many roadside banks through North America. There is a double form and one with pink flowers that is a parent of so many modern cultivars. Not to be despised, however common.

Day lilies are now available in a wide range of colour — yellows, oranges, pinks and dark reds — often with a different reverse to the petals. One should go to a nursery that offers them or a garden possessing a range of forms to pick out one's favourites. These modern hybrids are generally less vigorous than the types that have stood the test of centuries. Modern hybrid day lilies are not for deep shade but are fine at the woodland edge. Interplanted with daffodils and grown in a range of forms a band of yellow can be obtained from April through to September. It is wise to keep the more sophisticated coral and pink shades to areas close to the house; these are too grand to pretend to be wildlings.

Heracleum mantegazzianum 10 x 5 ft. (3 x 1.5 m) A vast cow parsley from the Caucasus that seeds itself in open woodland with decent moist soil.

Not a plant for small gardens, or where it might compete with smaller things. It should not be meddled with on hot days, when its sap can bring suitably Herculean blisters up on bare skin.

Hesperis matronalis is one of the traditional fragrant flowers of the English cottage garden. As sweet rocket or dames violet it has flowered among the tumble of currant bushes, herbs and simple flowers for centuries. Doubtless it was one of the first garden plants brought to North America by the colonists, for it has certainly made itself at home and has become naturalized in many areas. In the valley below my house the stream sides turn purple in late May and June from solid stands of this lovely plant. While it reaches five feet or so (1.5 m) in such positions it is also happy to colonize dry woodland above the valley, where in all colours from white to purple it adds interest after the true native forest floor plants are mainly over. Easy to raise from seed and obviously it self-sows, but it never becomes a pest. Double-flower forms have to be propagated vegetatively and are both desirable and rare.

Heuchera. Cottage garden plants resembling London pride with good foliage and spires of small flowers for the front of shady borders. *H. americana* is grown especially for its satiny hummocks of ivy-shaped leaves. This is a better woodland plant than the hybrids; concentration upon flower size and colour invariably leads to neglect of foliage. *Heuchera* has also been crossed with *Tiarella* to give the attractive little bigeneric hybrid x *Heucherella.*

sanguinea 1 x 1 ft. (300 x 300 mm) Known as coral bells, this pretty plant has been given the "Bressingham Bloom Treatment" in Norfolk, England, and produced some excellent garden plants for early summer effect. It can be taken as axiomatic that clonal names on herbaceous plants prefixed by "Bloom" or "Bressingham" are safe bets.

Hosta. A shady garden without hostas is inconceivable. Their lustrous broad leaves provide marvellous garden contrast with other shade lovers — ferns or hemerocallis — and are also invaluable cut for the house. Leaf colour varies through shades of green and near blue, while others offer astonishing variegated forms. Flower spikes, which may be over three feet (1 m) high, carry lilylike trumpets in shades of purple and pale lavender paling to white; it should be noted, however, that the best flowering hosta, *H. plantaginea*, is not a plant for deep shade, nor is its lovely form 'Royal Standard.'
    All the others, however, flourish in shady borders and even under trees if the soil is not too dry. Here, however, smooth-leaved types such as *H. lancifolia*, *crispula* and *ventricosa* are best. Profusion of flower is

likely to be in inverse proportion to depth of shade, but leaves may well be bigger and finer. Those with puckered leaves (the ones to avoid under trees) are known aptly as seersucker plantain lilies.

A great virtue of hostas is their ease of cultivation and increase. Chopping bits out of established clumps in spring as one would cut a slice of a round cake is as easy a method as any; the slice is transplanted and its hole filled in with good compost and no harm done. Seeds of those that are fertile can be used to produce quantities of plants for mass plantings. Three years are needed, however, before their ground cover is effective, and they will of course be extremely variable. Good stock may produce something really remarkable.

Hostas have been a part of the Japanese garden scene for centuries and it was from Japanese gardens that the original early-nineteenth-century introductions came, which explains the unusual situation of variegated forms having full specific status. As all hostas are good, it is probably sufficient here to group the few readily available according to size.

Small hostas 1½ x 1½ ft. (460 x 460 mm)

albomarginata. Good glossy oval leaves with pronounced white edge. Spikes of purple flowers. There is a green-leaved white-flowered type. 'Louisa' is a lovely seedling whose narrow leaf has a distinct white edge; white flowers.

lancifolia. A dark-flowered green-leaved plant that puts up a good late display even under trees in dry soil. One of the very best for small gardens. Lovely with autumn cyclamen.

undulata. Another variegated plant, but here the creamy nonphotosynthetic area is the leaf centre. Leaves are noticeably twisted. *univittata* is an all-green garden form, bigger and quicker of increase.

venusta is the most available of the real dollhouse-sized hostas. Only six inches (150 mm) in height, with violet flowers.

Mid-size 2 x 2 ft. (600 x 600 mm)

Fine white-edged plants include H. *crispula* and H. *decorata.* H. *fortunei* has a range of forms both green and variegated, but the finest (some would say of all hostas) is H. *f. albopicta.* Its rolled leaves open to a clear yellow that gradually fades while a green edge darkens. As the season advances the leaves become soft green all over. Above this the flowers are palest purple. 'Mount Royal' has blue-green leaves with white flowers on tall stems making a fine clump.

Big Hostas. 2½-3 x 3 ft. (760 mm-1 m x 760 mm)

H. sieboldiana in foliage is the grandest of all, with huge heart-shaped leaves a foot across and a marvellous glaucous blue. 'Frances Williams' is a fine selection with a gold edge, flower almost white. Gardens that cannot give room to such a vast plant should try to obtain the lovely *H. tokudama* half the size and just as blue. But it is rare and probably expensive.

'Krossa Regal' is remarkable in that the flower spikes can reach six feet (2 m) in height. The plant is vase shaped, altogether noteworthy.

Houttoynia cordata 1 x 1 ft. (300 x 300 mm) The dark heart-shaped leaves topped by pure white flowers are effective in moist shady spots. A double form is even better, but both can be rather invasive. Less so is an extraordinary variegated version with pink, bronze and white-flashed foliage. This is listed as 'Quadricolor.'

Hylomecon japonicum 1 x 1 ft. (300 x 300 mm) A Japanese woodlander for a shady spot that is rather like a taller yellow wood anemone. It slowly makes a good clump and flowers for some time.

Iris. The vertical emphasis that monocotyledons supply to the garden scene and that is so important for contrast is provided admirably by many irises. While the majority are sun lovers, a few can be included here. Of the tall bearded irises only a couple of the original species or near species accept shade with any equanimity.

cristata 9 x 9 in. (150 x 150 mm) This is a beautiful little East Coast native with fans of leaves and large yellow-crested flowers in a wide range of colours from white and mist blue to deep purple. Though needing a reasonably moist spot, it often does very well right against the boles of forest trees. *Iris tectorum* is very similar but twice the size. A light, well-drained soil is essential; poor drainage is anathema. These small irises are extremely useful in the shade garden to maintain lush leafiness when the majority of our native herbaceous plants are taking their well-earned late-summer rest.

germanica 2½ x 1 ft. (760 x 900 mm) The old purple flag iris is the easiest of plants and will take dry half shade under trees here just as one sees it in its southern European home. *I. florentina*, orrisroot, with white flowers, is equally accommodating. Similar in habit but a more desirable plant is *Iris pallida dalmatica*, whose leaves have a grey-blue cast. This has produced a couple of variegated forms that are in the very front rank of striped-leaved plants; white or golden bands etch the spearlike leaves, making a marvelous pattern lovely for building up cool garden pictures in shade. All of this group flower in late spring or early summer.

pseudacorus 4 x 1 ft. (1-2 m x 300 mm) The European yellow riverside flag has naturalized here in a number of areas and is good if space is available in moist half shade, but is too big and coarse for most garden scenes. Its golden variegated form is perfectly acceptable in a moist north-facing border, however, where its vertical spears light up their spot; inevitably reduced flowering is no great loss.

Kirengeshoma palmata 3½ x 2 ft. (1 m x 600 mm) Here is one of the plants that, admired in another garden, makes one insist on a shady border. Elegant black stems carry rather vinelike leaves and diffuse sprays of bantam-egg-sized-and-shaped flowers of clear buttermilk yellow. Coming up through hostas the effect is superb, particularly if the flowers can catch a gleam of late-evening sun. This is one of the best of all late-flowering herbaceous shade lovers and is now becoming more readily available.

Lamiastrum galeobdolon 1 ft. (300 mm) x infinity The variegated yellow archangel is one of the most marvellous plants for ground cover under trees, with marbled leaves and spikes of yellow flowers in May. But it is not for small gardens without constant cutting back, or for putting with small shrubs, over which it will climb to give the effect of a muster of moles behaving badly under a down quilt.

Lamium. The closely related dead nettles are admirable ground cover in shade with hellebores and summer snowflake, for example. They are too strong for small spring bulbs.

maculatum 3-4 x 2 ft. (1-1.2 m x 600 mm) The wild type with marbled leaves and mauve flowers seems rather more vigorous than its pink- and white-flowered forms and much more than the golden one. Particularly striking is the fully silver type called 'Beacon Silver.' 'Chequers' is also good. These are easily raised from soft tip cuttings, and a wide carpet can quickly be built up.

Ligularia. A genus that used to be amalgamated with *Senecio.* They are all great strong plants with fine heads of yellow or orange daisies in summer; much moisture is required, and as its availability declines, so progressively does the need for shade increase. For with such lush leaves to maintain, summer drought is understandably unacceptable. A wilting *Ligularia* is a sorry sight.

dentata 4 x 2 ft. (1.2 m x 600 mm) In the shade of shrubs near water this is one of the most striking of summer flowers, with its great flat heads of orange daisies. It will survive neglect and still appear with all the typically invasive waterside plants. For north-facing borders in more sophisticated surroundings the rather smaller purple-leaved cultivars 'Othello' and his inamorata 'Desdemona' are more suitable. The purple-and-orange colour combination is both bold and successful in high summer. Immediate deadheading extends the show considerably.

'Gregynog Gold' is a remarkable hybrid between L. *dentata* and L. *veitchiana* (itself well worth growing for its tall narrow spikes of flowers). The hybrid is intermediate in shape of inflorescence. These are like orange pyramids above the strong round leaves.

przewalskii 6 x 3 ft. (2 x 1 m) 'The Rocket' is the best form of this elegant daisy. Tall black stems with narrow-fingered leaves and thin spikes of yellow flowers in July and August. A position close to where Japanese primulas have finished their display is perfect.

tussilaginea is an evergreen species looking like a shiny coltsfoot and without much in the way of flowers. It is often grown as a house plant, and one consolation of living in cold areas is the probability that this nasty plant will be killed the first winter it is left outside. The spotted leaved forms merely compounds the problem.

Liriope. A group of grassy-leaved perennials from the Far East with tight spikes of beadlike, usually bluish flowers in September and October. They flower poorly in deepest shade but nonetheless manage to make reasonable ground cover even there. L. *muscari* is the best, with the smaller L. *graminifolia* most accepting of poor conditions.

Thus where toward half sun is available, *Liriope* makes some of the best grassy ground cover possible. The white forms are an attractive addition to the commoner blues and purple. Variegated types are fine in warm spots but in general seem less hardy, as is the closely related and very similar *Ophiopogon*. Good cultivars to look for are 'Lilac Beauty' and 'Majestic'; 'Gold Banded' and 'Silvery Midget' are obviously variegated.

Lobelia. The tall perennial lobelias could hardly be more different from the flat conventional blue part of patriotic red, white and blue bedding schemes. We are fortunate that one, cardinal flower, is a native plant of wooded stream sides, usually on acid soils. Such a habitat indicates cultivational needs.

cardinalis 3-4 x 1 ft. (1-1.2 x 2 m) From a purplish rosette of leaves, narrow spires of dramatic scarlet arise in high summer. While the moist woodland floor is an ideal site, *cardinalis* is one of the best plants for a north-facing border in rich soil. Lovely with hostas.

syphilitica 2-3 x 1 ft. (600-900 x 300 mm) Also a native, this is a clear-blue version, rather sturdier in habit and happy in somewhat drier positions. A cross between the two and royal purple in colour is *L*. x *vedrariensis (gerardii)*, and other hybrid selections are in the pipeline. They should be tried whenever found.

Lupinus polyphyllus. Mr. Russell's splendid selections (Russell lupins have been a byword for decades) are generally considered plants for sunny borders, but the old blue species succeeds in thin orchard grass on well-drained soils and seeds itself around. Cut down after flowering in May and June, a second crop will appear. I am agreeably surprised to find how well a mixed batch of Russell lupins are doing in my garden in at least half shade among shrubs and fighting it out with *Pachysandra* at ground level. In such company they appear quite different plants.

Lysimachia nummularia is the creeping Jenny of our moist woods. It makes good ground-level cover with the bonus of shining yellow flowers. A gold-leaved form is very striking for deep moist shade.

clethroides 2½ x 1½ ft. (760 x 460 mm) For late flower in a north border this is a favourite perennial. On an established clump the spikes of white flowers are shaped like croziers carried by a bevy of bishops on church parade.

ephemerum 2½ x 1 ft. (760 x 300 mm) Spikes of white flowers above grey foliage. Like anaphalis this is one of the few grey plants for shade. An excellent white garden plant and happy in half shade. Rather earlier than the preceeding.

punctata 4 x 2 ft. (1.2 m x 600 mm) Strong yellow heads (each flower like that of creeping Jenny) in high summer above an invasive pinkish rootstock. Another good plant for moist semishade in wild places. It is apt to be defoliated by a sawfly caterpillar and this must be watched for and dealt with before one is left with bare stems.

Lythrum salicaria 4 x 2 ft. (1.2 m x 600 mm) Purple loosestrife is one of the most decorative waterside plants, with great July spikes of brilliant pink. It has become naturalized in wet spots through the Northeast. The colour is softened in half shade and 'Rose Queen' and 'Morden Pink' have less of magenta about them. Planted by water, the reflective effect is superb and is repeated in October, when the foliage turns bright orange. If only someone would find a white form... In the garden almost any soil suits.

Macleaya. It is scarcely believable that the name plume poppy really does state the botanical relationship of these tall plants with their feathery spikes of petalless flowers in July and August. But the orange sap immediately recalls that of Chelidonium. The lovely milk-white and grey-green leaves are also similar in shape. While not taking heavy shade, they are fine among tall shrubs in light soil and will take their tops into the sun. They resent wet feet and grow miserably.

cordata 6-7 x 2 ft. (2-2.2 m x 600 mm) Even in smaller gardens the height is not overpowering because of the light effect; nor does the plant run about aggressively, as does the commoner and bigger

microcarpa 7 + x 3 ft. (2.2 + x 1 m) Here the plumes are an unusual buff tone. 'Coral Plume' is even better. Still often listed as *Bocconia*.

Maianthemum bifolium ½ x 1 ft. (150 x 300 mm) Like a smaller lily of the valley with upright leaves, this is a worthwhile woodlander for cool spots under shrubs with trilliums and erythroniums. Scentless spikes of little white flowers open in May. Often difficult to establish, but when really suited it fairly roars away. Then it will make solid ground cover right up to the boles of trees.

Malva moschata is musk mallow, one of the loveliest of old-fashioned perennials. It makes a bush of finely divided leaves covered in satiny pink or white flowers in July, and if deadheaded, onward. Not for deep shade or wet soils.

Meconopsis. Anyone who sees for the first time the fabled Himalayan blue poppies really succeeding will rush back home to see if a suitable site can be found or contrived. This is the typical place that so much of this book is concerned with: shade, moisture, protection from wind and a leafy lime-free soil. The best-known species is the following

betonicifolia (baileyi) 3-4 x 1½ ft. (1-1.2 m x 460 mm) When not really happy this beauty behaves monocarpically and dies after flowering. But where suited it is a perfectly good perennial with its yellow-centred clear-blue flowers in late June and July. Fresh seed germinates with abandon, but it is less simple to grow the plants on. Worth every effort and every care. The 'Branklyn Form' selected at the famous Scottish National Trust garden of Branklyn in Perth is the best.

cambrica 1½ x 1 ft. (460 x 300 mm) The Welsh poppy is a favourite easy seeder in shade or sun. Above a clump of elegant divided leaves the flowers are either soft orange or clear yellow. Both exist in double forms. It is lovely appearing in the cracks of paving, softening hard edges and blending with any colour but the hardest pinks. Dramatic with *Geranium psilostemon*.

grandis 4-5 x 2 ft. (1.2-1.5 m x 600 mm) Even if it never flowered the handsome clumps of hairy leaves would be worth growing. As it does, with tall stems of blue, purple or white bowls veined like Tiffany lamps, it is one of the joys of any garden that can offer the right conditions. The plant has a wide distribution in the upper Himalayan valleys of Sikkim, Nepal and Tibet, and now that these areas are open again to botanists further collections may well offer still more forms.

Hybrids between this and M. *betonicifolia* are usually grouped under M. x *sheldonii* and are splendid plants. It is recommended that the clumps be divided after flowering and carefully looked after until reestablished.

Meconopses have a reputation for being difficult-to-grow, specialists-only plants. Certainly they require care, but no more than what is required for many less beautiful things.

Melissa officinalis 2 x 2 ft. (600 x 600 mm) The golden variegated form of lemon balm is invaluable for brightening a shady border and providing leaves to crush in the hand as one passes. In seeding it reverts to green and can become a nuisance, especially on heavy soils. Therefore flowers spikes should be removed as soon as they have reached their full height. Nothing much is lost in floral display; the foliage is what is important.

Mentha. Mints, with Angelica and lemon balm, are of the few culinary herbs that accept shade. The ornamental-leaved mints can equally be used in the kitchen, so they are the ones to grow; they are also less susceptible to the unsightly mint rust disease. While revelling in moisture, mints grow quite well in drier conditions but do not grow as tall.

x *gentilis* 1½ x 1½ ft. (460 x 460 mm) This is ginger mint, the name referring not to its scent but foliar colour. Wide spreading above ground, it takes drought quite well and is the brightest in leaf of them all.

piperita var. *citrata* 2 x 1½ ft. (600 x 400 mm) The dark purple leaves and delicious scent of eau de cologne mint makes it as distinctive in the hand as in the border. Not for casting into mint sauce, however, unless you want lamb to taste like Esteé Lauder smells.

requienii ½ x 6 in. (5 x 60 mm) By far the smallest plant described in this book, Corsican mint is a minuscule carpeter for filling cracks between paving in shady courtyards. Often only a sudden whiff of mint indicates its presence as one treads upon it. Then those with keen sight may notice the pinhead purple flowers. Great fun to grow and surprise visitors with.

x *rotundifolia* 'Variegata' 2 x 2 ft. (600 x 600 mm) By comparison with the robust type the softly downy leaves of this plant are pale green and white, with palest lavender flower spikes in summer. Pinching these out gives better foliage.

Mertensia virginica 1½ x 1 ft. (460 x 300 mm) This is the Virginian cowslip — the sort of name expatriates take from favourite plants of their homeland — even when resemblance is more than a little tenuous, as here. *Mertensia* is that unusual creature a smooth-leaved borage, with elegant drooping sprays of blue flowers in May. It associates well with late-spring bulbs and deciduous ferns in particular, whose developing fronds take the area that *Mertensia* soon vacates. The white form has charm, but the blue is better.

Mitella. Little white-flowered colonizers from North America that revel in cool woodland soil. M. *diphylla* from Minnesota down to Virginia is most likely to be available. This is known as coolwort;: others are called mitrewort or bishop's cap, referring to the ecclesiastical pattern of the flowers.

Monarda. Of the wild bergamots, lovely aromatic natives, only one can take a bit of shade. Fortunately it is the best.

didyma 3 x 2 ft. (700 x 600 mm) Bee balm, or Oswego tea, enjoys good food and drink in a well-drained border where a north exposure is very acceptable. The hooded flowers are carried in whorls up the spike and come in a range of colours. Named forms include 'Cambridge Scarlet,' 'Croftway Pink' and 'Snow Queen,' all perfectly self-descriptive. They are among the brightest of summer border plants.

Myosotis. Though not good perennials, any forget-me-not is worth encouraging to seed itself about with Welsh poppies and suchlike around shrubs in full or half shade. A couple of plants potted up and brought inside as soon as the ground thaws out in spring are a joy on a windowsill a month before they open outside. But watch for aphids, which find myosotis as bees proverbially do the honey pot.

Myrrhis odorata 2½ x 2 ft. (760 x 600 mm) This elegant, aromatic cow parsley shares northern English hedgebanks with *Geranium pratense* and spires of *Campanula latifolia*, and such an inspired association could be repeated in a shady spot here with advantage. Sweet Cicely has finely cut leaves and good heads of creamy flowers. There is then a choice:

either the plant may be left to produce its surprisingly large black fruits or, as Miss Jekyll recommended, cut the whole thing to the ground, when a second crop of fresh green leaves will appear to enliven the late summer scene. Crushed leaves smell strongly of aniseed.

Omphalodes. Two venus's-navelworts (the name refers to the distinctive shape of the seeds) are admirable for the front of shady borders, the north side of rock gardens and similar spots. Both have broad leaves and clear-blue forget-me-not flowers in spring. *O. verna* precedes *O. cappadocica* in flowering time and also the speed at which it will do a bit of gentle carpet laying.

Paeonia. The gorgeous genus of peonies offers little to the woodland garden proper but much to half-shady shrub borders, where their early leaf growth and flowers enliven ground around deciduous shrubs. Some slight frost protection is also afforded thereby. Peonies in dry soil particularly appreciate some shade, which helps to retain the otherwise rather fleeting flowers. But flower is not all: developing leaves and swelling buds can be ravishing and scarlet seed pods and blue seeds dramatic with the late-summer colouring foliage. These remarks apply particularly to the species and old hybrids. The modern hybrids enjoy more specialist treatment and positioning; deadheading is necessary and ample water is desirable throughout the growing season, but waterlogging spells death.

The following list includes most of the wild species that have a distribution from western Europe to eastern Asia. Few, it must be admitted, are generally available, but seed sometimes is. A three-year-old plant has begun to develop a good flowering clump and it will increase in size and beauty from year to year, needing no division for a dozen years or more unless it is required for propagation. Then great care must be taken not to damage the tuberous roots more than is inevitable. The species generally flower earlier than the hybrids, whose season with us in southern Ontario is late May and the first half of June.

daurica 2½ x 2½ ft. (750 x 750 mm) This is light in effect, with elegantly borne yellow-centred pinkish-white flowers above good green-fingered leaves with wavy edges.

lactiflora 3 x 2 ft. (900 x 600 mm) A parent of most of the big Chinese hybrid peonies, yet it is as good as any. Foliage emerges and maintains a strong red tint against which the great white bowls of flowers are admirably set. Sometimes listed as *P. albiflora* and *P. whitleyi major. P. obovata alba* is another good white, smaller in stature with lovely dusky-pink young growth. These are all elegantly aristocratic plants.

mlokosewitschii 2½ x 2½ ft. (760 x 760 mm) Such a splendid tongue twister makes everyone remember this plant. And so we should. As the pale primrose flowers open in early May (or earlier in the South) to show the gold stamens, we experience one of the exquisite moments of the garden year. Foliage is rounded, with pink stems, and has an overall air of softness. The mid-August seed display is often dramatic but can seldom be allowed to remain. Such a beauty is too valuable not to increase.

officinalis 2 x 2 ft. (600 x 600 mm) The old herbalists' peony is less fleeting in flower than some of the foregoing and hence can take more sun. But it is still good under shrubs, in cottage-garden orchard conditions or mixed up with gooseberries and currants. The great double red is in the memory of everyone who has enjoyed a country garden childhood. There are pink and white forms, double and single.

suffruticosa 6 x 9 ft. (2 x 3 m) The moutan, or tree peony, ought to perhaps be included among the shrubs for limy soils, but to split up a genus is confusing. Hence its position here. Not normally considered a plant for shade, a magnificent specimen under the spreading boughs of a great tree at Wave Hill, New York, prompts this entry. Obviously sufficient moisture is essential; beyond that there is no doubt that shade helps to prolong the otherwise short, if glorious season.

For such a site the older types appear best, such as 'Bijou de Chusan' and 'Rock's Variety.' Both have great peony flowers six inches across above the waved blue-green leaves, a Chinese screen painting come to life.

tenuifolia 1½ x 1½ ft. (460 x 460 mm) One of the latest to flower in mid-June. Dark red flowers glisten above fernlike foliage; this is the tidiest of peonies.

veitchii 1½ x 1½ ft. (460 x 460 mm) Slow to leaf, which could be an advantage in chilly areas, but develops quickly to show off its hanging flowers. These are a clean, unaggressive magenta.

wittmanniana 2½ x 2½ ft. (760 x 760 mm) The biggest herbaceous species, in effect, with huge pale rounded leaves and cool yellow-cream flowers. Inside, the boss of stamens is green, lit up by the pink eyes of the stigmas. These lovely flowers are only at their best for a week, but the buildup to flowering, the mature foliage and the seed pods combine to give interest for months.

Pentaglottis sempervirens 1½ x 2 ft. (460 x 600 mm) The evergreen alkanet is a typically bristly borage with bright-blue flowers in June, specking the spreading foliage. Rather aggressive but worth having in a neglected spot; good with *Symphytum orientale*. Even dry shade under trees is acceptable.

Petasites. Dangerous plants to introduce into small gardens because of their speed of increase, but in moist soil under trees they are valuable and can look superb.

hybridus is the European butterbur, with low cones of purple flowers (that are in fact rayless daisies) in spring, followed by huge two- to three-foot (600-900 mm) wide leaves.

japonicus 3 x 5 ft. (1 x 1.5 m) is more ornamental in spring, when the flower heads emerge from the bare soil. Each is perfect for a dinner-table decoration (talking from experience) when the host is in a hurry, resembling a carefully arranged posy of white apetalous daisies surrounded by green leaves (bracts, in fact). The monstrous ground-covering leaves follow, carried like umbrellas on thick petioles that are in Japan eaten as a vegetable — a method of keeping it under control that might well be adopted in the West.

Phlox. The big garden phloxes, forms of *P. paniculata*, in their splendid range of colour are not for overhead shade, though open north-facing borders suit them admirably, especially in less moisture-retentive soils. The delicious dusky scent is particularly evocative of warm evenings in old gardens. More suited to our needs are the elegant *P. maculata* types with longer, narrower heads of flowers; if only they can be found. 'Omega' is a fine old cultivar and even the species, known as wild sweet william in its North Carolina home, is worth growing.

divaricata 1 x 2 ft. (300 or 600 mm) Another native "wild sweet william," so that blue phlox is a less confusing name. A wide spreading plant, rooting at the nodes as it goes with spring heads of blue (of course), white and pink. A splendid and underused plant to put with bulbs, around shrubs and under trees.

The well-known hybrid 'Chattahoochee' unfortunately insists upon sun.

stolonifera 1 x 2 ft. (300 x 600 mm) Rather smaller than the last species, creeping phlox is just as valuable for woodland and shady shrub borders' ground cover. The hairy leaves are rather leathery and lay flat upon the ground as the shoots trail outward. Fine flowering heads come up from leaf axils, pink, blue and violet in late spring. A mountain plant from Pennsylvania southward.

Physalis. Chinese lanterns are surely less often seen than formerly. Perhaps the trend to smaller gardens has reduced their use. Certainly a big clump is needed to produce cutting material for winter decoration and the plant does look rather miserable in summer, with coarse leaves and mean little potato flowers. But when the leaves drop and the inflated capsules turn bright orange all is forgiven.

franchetii 2 x 3 ft. (600 x 900 mm) This is the stronger species, with one or two selected forms sometimes available. July flowers of no virtue.

Physostegia virginiana is the obedient plant whose pink salvialike flowers can all be pushed to one side of the spike — where they unaccountably remain. The species is rather tall and coarse, but a two and a half foot (750 mm) white form called 'Summer Snow' is excellent and flowers earlier than the type. 'Vivid,' smaller still, is lovely with Japanese anemones in the front of a half-shady border in moist soil in autumn.

Podophyllum. These unusual-looking plants have a family to themselves, related to the *Berberidaceae*, which includes the epimediums. Unfolding *Podophyllum* foliage has a similar texture and colouring, yet a beauty that is entirely its own.

peltatum 1 x 1 ft. (300 x 300 mm) This is May-apple, surely one of our most distinctive and beautiful native plants. As the shoots emerge in spring each appears like a rosy parasol mushroom whose "cap," the circular leaf pair, does not become horizontal until the stem has attained its full height. Then, hanging coyly beneath the umbrella, a simple white roselike flower opens, fleeting but exquisite. Unlike many of our woodlanders May-apple keeps its leaf pattern throughout summer until, as it withers in fall, the "apple" (actually more like a yellow-egg plum) is seen hanging upon the bare stem — to be collected for jam or allowed to drop its seeds.

Its Asiatic relative *P. emodi* is a similar plant of scrubby hillsides, pink in flower and fruit, equally beautiful and easy to grow. Seed is sometimes available from specialist seedsmen. It takes three years to flower.

Polygonatum. True Solomon's seal is one of the treasurers of European woods, arching over the flowering bluebells with perfect complementary grace. This is *P. multiflorum* with its row of white bells hanging beneath an elegantly arching stem of paired leaves.

x *hybridum* 3 x 1 ft.. (900 x 300 mm) The produce of two very similar species is the one usually seen in gardens and it exhibits suitably hybrid vigour. Although preferring moist shade, it will flourish even beneath evergreen trees if the humus content of the soil can be built up. Lovely under early rhododendrons, which by this time are looking a bit *déjà vu*, with hostas, ferns and *Smilacina*.

There are rare variegated and double-flowered forms well worth searching out. A monster, *P. commutatum*, reputed to get twice the size, suitably in scale with large-leaved rhododendrons, comes from New Hampshire south toward Mexico. Northern collections must be used for northern gardens. Its flowers have a more yellowish cast.

Other, less spectacular species exist, native and exotic. All are typical woodlanders and useful for texture and form if of little dramatic flowering effect.

Polygonum. It is comforting that in addition to knotgrass and other noxious weeds the genus offers some good garden plants, as well. It also includes those vast broad-leaved plants with bamboolike stalks that were so often rashly planted by water gardens in the past. Nonetheless they look lovely, and the dead stalks are admirable for children's bonfires, when every node explodes like a pistol shot. Though it is wise not to plant *P. cuspidatum* and its friends unless your acres are broader than most, I must admit that having inherited a couple of clumps, I find them too attractive to remove (if this be possible, which I doubt). Snowdrops nestle among the roots without coming to harm.

amplexicaule 4 x 4 ft. (1.2 x 1.2 m) A fine leafy plant with tight sprays of tiny flowers that in 'Atrosangineum' are a definite crimson. A good wild-garden plant with August flowers under shrubs, though mean in growth in dry soils.

bistorta 'Superbum' 2 x 2 ft. (600 x 600 mm) A selected form of the common bistort is a good north-border plant for moist soils. Undersides of the foliage have an attractive milky cast.

campanulatum 3½ x 3 ft. (1 x 1 m) A very elegant, though rather rampageous plant for moist spots. Grey-green foliage and lovely sprays of soft heather-bell flowers in cool pink late in summer.

polystachyum 5 x 5 ft. (1.5 x 1.5 m) A bigger and even more invasive plant with almost spiraealike heads of white flowers in the fall. For woodland glades and big wild garden areas, where it makes a marvellous late effect.

Primula. One of the groups that makes every gardener covet water and, failing that, shady spots in which to encourage a range of these beauties to grow. Primroses are of course woodland plants par excellence (open hillsides in the Outer Hebredean Isles, equally covered with them, never cease to surprise; in such maritime remoteness their need for moisture at the root and humidity around the leaves is presumably equally met). In cool northern gardens they can be encouraged around the boles of trees, and the introduction of a few of the soft-pink P. *sibthorpii* will gradually develop into a range of pale shades that may colonize thin grass. Also there are lovely named forms such as 'Garryarde Guinevere.' While growing the double primroses can develop into something of a cult, few are easy to grow. Another annual primula pleasure is polyanthus time; these are taller then primroses and have cowslip and oxlip blood (or sap) to produce a loose head of flowers. There are now vastly bigger and brighter forms, but for general garden effect, especially in informal situations, it is better to renounce these or at least keep to definite colour strains. The old 'Munstead' type in a range of yellows is difficult to beat, though the 'Barnhavens' are close to it and should be sought out. They are produced in the Lake District of England.

Once established, polyanthus produces seed that germinates quickly when fresh, and a new batch can always be kept coming along. They are plants one has to work at, but are well worth the trouble.

For small borders or north-facing rock beds there are numbers of esoteric Himalayans as well as well-known little garden primulas such as 'Wanda' (easy and dependable).

Bigger, and relishing shade if sunnier borders lack moisture, is P. *denticulata*, the drumstick primula, available from white through the soft lavender of the type to dark crimson and purples — another easy plant.

The pleasures (and let it be said labours) of pond- or stream-margin gardening where swathes of primulas dominate the June scene are bound to be for relatively few gardeners. Nonetheless any leafy soil in the least half shade that can be kept moist can offer homes to the more robust for floral association with meconopses, and later perhaps certain lilies such as *Lilium michiganense* continue the show.

The candelabra section offers some lovely plants. These carry their flowers in five or six distinct whorls up two to three feet (600 — 900 mm) high stems that are often mealy and white. The most robust and hence safest species for positions that would not be their first choice include:

bulleyana, a strong orange yellow.

japonica, naturally a purplish red, but careful selection has produced among other named forms 'Miller's Crimson' and 'Postford White.' These seed themselves around in my garden in a boggy spot that has an ominous connection with an old septic tile bed. I am happy to accept the primulas without asking questions.

prolifera is a fine clear yellow, its whorls of flowers borne on particularly elegant scapes.

pulverulenta is another elegant plant, with near purple flowers. The lovely 'Bartley Strain' is pale pink, a perfect colour to blend with its mealy-white stems. The 'Bartley Strain' breeds true.

Another section takes its name from *P. sikkimensis*, a strong grower with yellow flowers in an umbel. The leaves of the robust *P. florindae*, unlike all those so far mentioned, are nearly heart shaped on long stems and from the rosette mealy stems arise two feet (600 mm) or more high, each topped with a cascade of pale-yellow scented flowers. Smaller, in a range of pinks, is the delicate *P. sieboldii*. Moist but not boggy soil is needed here.

Success with any of these will inevitably encourage the growing of other candelabra primula species. They are easily raised from fresh seed, preferably sown as soon as ripe in August. Overwintered in boxes as cool as possible without actually freezing hard in boxes, one or two might flower the next year, but the real display is expected the following year. They are generally not long lived, and it is wise to have a few coming on each year.

Most of us, lacking the perfect waterside conditions, will not have many of each. Colours, however, must be carefully considered and the fiercer reds or magentas cooled with the foliage of other things.

Prunella vulgaris is the naturalized self-heal, once considered invaluable for staunching hemorrhages. As low ground cover for moist places its blue spikes in summer are welcome. Better and bigger is *P. grandiflora* 'Loveliness,' a pink variant.

Pulmonaria. The lungworts are useful cottage garden plants for early flower and later foliage whose spotted leaves have given both the vernacular and Latin names. Early herbalists saw in spots and leaf shape a certain guide to pulmonary disorders that, according to the doctrine of signatures, this plant was bound to cure. There are a half-dozen of these borage relations sharing with other members the odd, yet charming habit of opening flowers one colour, usually pink, and turning them blue before falling. This has led to the other common name of soldiers and sailors. The following are usually available, but any on offer are worth collecting for building up stock sufficient to use for ground cover under spring flowering shrubs such as corylopsis and forsythia. Most flower in March and April, depending on site and area.

angustifolia 1 x 1½ ft. (300 x 450 mm) An immaculate (literally) lungwort with good blue flowers from pink buds. There are one or two named forms such as 'Munstead Variety' and 'Sissinghurst White,' selections from two of the most significant gardens of this century.

officinalis 1 x 1½ ft. (300 x 450 mm) This is lungwort proper, the species with medicinal overtones. Spotted leaves and flowers of conventional colour. For garden use it is less distinctive than the others but still of value. 'Mrs. Moon' is the best form.

rubra 1 x 2 ft. (300 x 600 mm) Eventually quite a robust plant, but the earliest unfolding February or March flowers appear on very short stalks. Their clear coral red, however, is unique at that season of the year.

saccharata 1 x 2 ft. (300 x 600 mm) Perhaps the most vigorous (except *mollis*, seldom available), with greyish spotted leaves and a fine sequence of colour from opening flowers.

Ranunculus. Most garden-worthy members of this genus are sun lovers, but three common meadow buttercups — all lovely plants in the right place — have old-established double forms worth searching out. *R. acris* can reach three feet (1 m), but *R. bulbosus* and *R. repens* are only a third of that size. The latter runs about somewhat, especially in moist soil.

aconitifolius 3 x 5 ft. (1 x 1 m) A lovely white buttercup with generous foliage. The double form is known as 'Fair Maids of France' and is worth every effort to obtain. For half shade.

Rheum palmatum. Ordinary culinary rhubarb would be a striking enough plant if brought into the border and encouraged to flower, but this is better, especially in its 'Atrosanguineum' or 'Bowles's forms. The deeply divided leaves have purplish reverse and the six-foot (2 m) high flower heads are brightly crimson. Not for deep shade, but in dryish soil some is essential. Excellent and in scale with ligularias, the biggest hostas and Solomon's seal.

Rodgersia. Fine strong plants of a scale to fit with the *Rheum* described above its friends. They all enjoy leafy moist soil. While only the first makes the claim to its name, other Rodgersias also have leaves like those of big horse chestnuts (Aesculus), each emerging on its own hairy stalk from the ground. The cream or pinkish flowers are rather like scaled-up meadowsweet.

aesculifolia 4 x 2 ft. (1.2 m x 600 mm) The grandest, with purplish-bronze leaves, horse-chestnut-like and heads of flowers a froth of cream in July.

pinnata 3 x 2 ft. (1 m x 600 mm) Here the chestnut leaves are paired back to back, with strawberries-and-cream-coloured flowers. 'Superba' is a form that lives up to its name, with bigger, shiny leaves and bright pink flowers at the same time of year.

podophylla 3 x 3 ft. (1 x 1 m) On top of their stem the leaflets more resemble a whorl of oak leaves or, if one is to believe the name, ducksfeet. Unfurling bronze, they green in the fullness of summer but turn dark again in autumn if in sufficient light.

tabularis 3 x 2½ ft. (900 x 750 mm) The leaf shape here takes on quite another form, being circular, almost three feet (1 m) across and held up centrally by its stalk, resembling an inflated *Peltiphyllum* (a West Coast plant that could well be tried in warm spots of the Northeast. Above these trays of pale green the pale-cream flowers are held in spikes up to five feet (1.5 m) rather later than the others. A plant of great architectural value in its season.

Saxifraga. Many of this huge genus are rosette-forming alpine or subalpine plants that have no place here, but two groups offer valuable shade plants for the front of borders. First the "mossy" saxifrages. As the name suggests, wide clumps of tight green growth develop and bear thin stalks with relatively large flowers, pink or white. Species included here are *Ss. geranioides, hypnoides* and *trifurcata.*

A second group is based upon that old favourite London pride (*S. umbrosa*), whose evergreen rosettes of flat leaves put up such fairy stems of pink-spotted white flowers. Excellent ground cover and a May-June display. One clump pulled apart in early autumn will furnish quite an area.

Saxifraga stolonifera is often seen as a hanging basket plant and the diversity of its common names, strawberry geranium, strawberry begonia, creeping sailor, etc. indicates its popularity. Running about just like a strawberry, its stolons root, form a new plant and then rush on, covering the ground the while. It may not be as fully hardy as one would like (and the variegated 'Tricolor' even less so), but it is so easy to keep a bit indoors and then put it out that such simple insurance is well worth the effort.

Scopolia carniolica ½ x 1½ ft. (150 x 460 mm) Not often seen, this odd potato relation puts up its stems hung with orange-brown bells very early in the season, when it exhibits a definite charm. But it becomes dull later, so plant with other, later, bigger things.

Scrophularia aquatica 'Variegata' 3 x 1 ft. (900 x 300 mm) No beauty of flower, but the creamy variegated leaves on tall square stems light up a shady border in moist soil most effectively.

Smilacina racemosa. The false Solomon's seal or false spikenard. A favourite plant throughout its growth. Arching stems of apple-green leaves produce creamy heads rather like a drooping astilbe (though related to lilies). It resents much lime and in good leafy soil it will make a wide clump two feet (600 mm) high. Like hostas the foliage turns a clear yellow with autumn frosts, and it is enlivened by sprays of red-currant-like berries, often colourful into November. One of the most valuable and lovely woodland plants. How fortunate that it should be a native.

Solidago. North Americans are apt to fall about with hoots of derision when they discover their goldenrod "weeds" used in sophisticated herbaceous borders in Britain. Useful though they be there, these big, open-ground plants are not for shade, as anyone knows from seeing them in the wild. But we have a couple of splendid shade-loving goldenrods that are valuable woodlanders.

caesia 1½ x 2 ft. (450-600 mm) This appears adapted not only for shade, but for shady banks, where it arches outward, holding its flowers horizontally along the length. Wreath or blue-stem goldenrod are names that are sometimes used. A most beautiful September plant. Another for complete shade is *Solidago flexicaulis*, the broad leaved or zigzag goldenrod. These are well worth bringing into the shady garden.

Stylophorum diphyllum. A charming North American woodlander attaining eighteen inches (460 mm) or so. It resembles a smaller-leaved, but bigger-flowered greater celandine — just the attributes needed by the latter plant, which is apt to be rather weedy. Thus good-sized yellow poppy flowers in early summer. When happy in woodsy soil it seeds itself around, but never unwelcomely.

Symphytum. Bristly perennial borages, the comfreys are easily grown and useful plants, but the bigger the coarser.

grandiflorum 1 x 2 ft. (300 x 600 mm) The best for low ground cover, with croziers of nodding pale-yellow flowers in spring. Wide swathes of ground even in dryish shade will be colonized. Erupting clumps of day lilies look well as changes in emphasis. This is a valuable shade plant that should be used more — if it can be found.

orientale 2 x 2 ft. (600 x 600 mm) Surprisingly soft for a comfrey, with pale-green leaves and profuse white flowers. This and other clump-forming species such as *caucasicum* (blue) and x *uplandicum* (pink changing to blue rather like the lungworts), four feet high (1.2 m), should be cut down after flowering, when fresh new leaves will appear to enliven the rest of the season.

Tellima grandiflora 2 x 1½ ft. (600 x 460 mm) Clumps of rounded leaves put up thin spikes of little fringed green bells in May and June.

Ground-cover ability under shrubs is good, with the leaves turning bronze in winter. This pleasant trait is emphasized in the form 'Purpurea.' An easily grown plant, attractive in all seasons.

Tiarella. Admirable ground cover under shrubs or for the front of shady borders. As with *Tellima*, the leaves turn bronze in winter. White foamy spikes about nine inches high in *cordifolia* and rather more in *wherryi* hide the foliage in May. The former is tufted and needs division to build up a colony; the latter runs about of its own accord.

Tolmiea menziesii. 'Pick-a-back' or piggyback plant, with old leaves carrying a developing young plant. Rather *Tellima*-like in leaf, but the little flowers on eighteen-inch (460 mm) spikes are brown and rather dull. May get killed without snow protection, but can often be grown indoors and hence is obtainable from house-plant stock.

Tricyrtis. The oriental toad lilies make no dramatic show but always fascinate on closer inspection. For the ideal moist and leafy woodland soil or a suitable synthetic alternative. There are several species, all rather similar, two to three feet with (600-900 mm) high spikes of smallish purple-spotted flowers. Elegant and distinctive. *T. hirta* is perhaps the hardiest.

Trientalis borealis is the starflower of our northern pinewoods. This charming little plant is well worth introducing into similar garden situations — cool leafy soil in full shade, where if suited it will run about in an unaggressive way. Whorled leaves support white flowers in early summer.

Trillium. There are about thirty of these exquisite wake-robins, with leaves and floral parts, as the name suggest, in threes. All are worth growing. They appreciate a deep moist leafy soil. While they are admirable in woodland as in their natural habitats, they are ideal for that special shady bed where other treasurers are nurtured. The species likely to be available include:

cernuum 1 x 1 ft. (300 x 300 mm) Nodding trillium is a typically delicate member of the genus. The white flowers with their reflexed petals are carried from the centre of their leafy triad on thin stalks and hence appear to be baling out over the side.

erectum 1½ x 1 ft. (450 x 300 mm) Brownish purple is the colour usually given for the flowers; old dried blood is about right, but greenish white forms are also common. All have the fetid, fly-pollinating odour that promotes the name stinking Benjamin. Not, in fact, a problem or a reason for not growing it.

grandiflorum 1-1½ x 1 ft. (300-460 x 300 mm) No plant is more beautiful when seen, or more evocative of our local woodlands when described. Fortunately it is probably the best "doer" in our gardens. The flowers are about three inches (80 mm) across, of perfect whiteness that pinkens as they age. It makes a happy, graceful clump. A favourite plant for dappled shade in leafy soil. A fine double form is sometimes offered. Though a lovely plant in its own right and longer lasting, it does lack some of the wildling's grace. The strange types sometimes seen among an extensive wild stand, with varying amounts of green on the petals, are seldom constant when bought into cultivation and are best left where they are. As indeed are all wild plants, unless they are in some danger from "development."

sessile 1 x 1 ft. (300 x 300 mm) Standing directly upon the triple leaves are the three yellowish petals, long, narrow and held vertically; the effect is rather that of an art nouveau candlestick. *T. chloropetalum* is a monstrous West Coast variant of this, still with the marvellously mottled leaves of the type.

undulatum 6-18 x 6 in. (100-300 x 100 mm) The painted trillium is a characteristic species of the Appalachians and parts of the Canadian Shield. It is a plant of highly acid soil; whereas the others accept it, this one insists upon it in the garden. Certainly it is worth some effort to make it happy; the narrow waved white petals, each with a scarlet sunburst at its base, are most distinctive.

Trollius. The globeflowers are plants of moist meadows and hence, in suitable water-retentive soils, enjoy the sun. On light sands, however, full sun makes them wilt piteously; a north-facing border is ideal.

acaulis 6 x 9 in. (150 x 230 mm) One of the dwarf species from the Himalayas, with two-inch-wide double buttercup flowers in June, deep orange and big for the plant. *T. pumilus* is related.

europaeus 2 x 1 ft. (600 x 300 mm) Native, though not common to much of upland northern Europe, this globeflower is well worth growing with yellow primulas and ferns. Hybrids with Oriental species are more robust and can take more sun. They are usually listed under *T. x cultorum.*

ledebourii 2-3 x 1½ ft. (600-900 x 460 mm) There is some doubt as to the true name of the plant usually offered under this name. Nonetheless it is a good robust globeflower, with anemone-centred blooms of soft orange. A good named clone is 'Imperial Orange.'

Uvularia. A small group of charming Solomon's seal relations from North America enjoying similar conditions.

grandiflora 2 x 1 ft. (600 x 300 mm) Is the only one likely to be available. It has pale-yellow bells in late May with twisted petals hanging from its arched growth. Fleeting in flower, it is known as merrybells; haybells, cowbells and bellwort are often names that clearly agree upon its appearance. *U. perfoliata* is paler and hence called strawbell.

Vancouveria. The three species are like smaller versions of *Epimedium*, with which they were once botanically joined. Under shrubs they offer similar virtues of elegant leaves that unfold in shades of pink and above which the tiny yellow or white flowers hover like a cloud of flies.

V. hexandra is deciduous, while *Vv. chrysantha* and *planipetala* are evergreens. As westerners (as the dedicatory name suggests) they are on the borderline of hardiness with us and thus the deciduous species is safest.

Veratrum. One of the most striking herbaceous perennials for shade. Above broad, deeply ribbed leaves that make an almost bromeliadlike rosette, great spikes of starry flowers shoot up. They last long in flower and maintain their statuesque effect for several months, when this passes, in the green species almost imperceptibly, into seedpods. Moist shade is enjoyed. While they are probably not in commercial circulation, seed is sometimes offered by specialists' firms; it should be snapped up at once. Plants will take three years to flower, but the wait is worth it.

album 5 x 2 ft. (1.5 m x 600 mm) Just to confuse this is known as false helleborine, but related neither to hellebore (a buttercup) or to helleborine (an orchid), it is in fact a member of the Liliaceae. The great spikes of flower are of palest avocado green in late July and August, the season for all these fine plants.

nigrum 5 x 2 ft. (1.5 m x 600 mm) Here the flowers are of an extraordinary burnished maroon. Each spike carries hundreds of them and makes a remarkable sight for some weeks. Worth every effort to secure.

viride 4 x 2 ft. (1.2 m x 600 mm) This is a native plant (the other two are European), once used as an arrow poison and also in trial-by-ordeal by the Indians. The highly poisonous alkaloids of all veratrums slow down the heart, eventually to the point at which it stops. *V. viride*, as its name suggests, is green flowered and is another good garden plant of character.

Viola. Many violets are plants of woodland or hedgebanks and remain charming for just those roles in the garden. Those needing division are good for the front of shady borders, where they can have an eye kept on them (out of sight is apt to be out of mind until it is too late), while others can be left to seed about under shrubs. Those listed below are a tiny sample of the species that exist. All are charming and should be encouraged; some have colonized patches of my backyard lawn, which we mow round with care until flowering is over — then they don't mind the grass-cutting regime.

cornuta 9 in. x 1½ ft. (230 x 460 mm) Long spurred flowers of true deep-violet colour (as they should be) are produced in quantity. This is a parent of the tufted pansies. Clipping over the plants after flowering encourages the production of a second, early-autumn crop. The ever-green leaves make good ground cover if the plant survives in one's area.

labradorica 6 in. x 1 ft. (150 x 300 mm) Particularly valuable for its deep purple leaves, which a modicum of sun will darken further. The flowers are a good light blue. Seeds itself around happily, never becoming a pest.

papilionacea 9 in. x 1 ft. (230 x 300 mm) A robust violet from eastern North America, where it is our commonest native species. Various colour forms exist in the wild and in cultivation. It succeeds happily at the boles of trees and is ideal to give interest to the base of a lawn specimen to follow snowdrops or aconites. Botanically this should now be called *V. sororia*, but the butterfly name is more descriptive. The greyish-flowered Confederate violet is a well-known form.

septentrionalis 6 x 6 in. (150 x 150 mm) A small plant with outsize flowers, pale blue in the type, but the white form available is particularly attractive, having a green "eye" from which purple veining feathers down into the lower petals. This is another North American woodlander, this time from Maine down to the Appalachian Mountains.

Bulbs in the Shade

This chapter is concerned not just with plants whose resting organs are literally bulbs — that is, a collection of swollen and compressed leaf bases upon a flattened basal stem-disc — but other species that disappear below ground to some other sort of resting organ for some of the year and reemerge for their relatively short flowering and leafing season. It has already been shown that such a pattern of growth is typical of many plants directly adapted to woodland conditions and that it has developed in response to light and moisture availablility beneath deciduous trees. It provides the main layer of woodland beauty in the spring.

The plants described in this section therefore include, with the true bulbs such as *Narcissus* and *Endymion*, tubers such as *Cyclamen* and *Eranthis*. Where the plant is relatively large, however, it is listed under herbaceous plants, as are some smaller species grouped under their generic headings, as in *Anemone*. All are native to woodland areas in North America, Europe and the Himalayan foothills. The range is potentially tremendous, but there are the normal problems if availability. Those keen to extend their plant collections in this field should be willing to spend time and patience in growing the plants from seed, which may be offered more frequently than flowering-sized specimens. There is enormous pleasure in home-raised stock. It may include interesting variants and one starts with a useful number at a not exorbitant cost.

As perennials, which they are, one's hope is that bulbous (using the word in its nonbotanical, broadest sense) plants will behave perenially, going from strength to strength and colonizing shady areas under shrubs or in woodland as they do (or are presumed to do) in their native habitats. An impression of at least apparent naturalism is often important.

Nonetheless it must be agreed that even a woodland garden is not natural, but a highly sophisticated combination of units carefully

166

arranged to develop something of an ecological equilibrium, the balance being maintained, if one is to be honest, by effective gardening. This no doubt is one reason that it is possible to consider gardening an art form.

It permits and even encourages the inclusion here, in all but the most purist circles, of plants that do not really "belong." There must of course still be some direct connection for the association to be acceptable, for it to look right even when, if deep thought is given to it, it is an ecological impossibility. (Perhaps, indeed, that phrase is itself one definition of a garden. Certainly it sounds like an examination question of daunting complexity.)

Thus one can add to the scene nonshade lovers such as tulips and crocuses. The latter in particular must have a reasonable light concentration or the flowers will fail to open (and one of the great pleasures to say *Crocus chrysanthus* and its selections is the dusky feathering of colours on the outside of the petals seen when they are closed, compared to the brilliance of their open stars and contrasting stigmata and stamens). These plants are fine under *deciduous* shrubs so that light concentration is high when they are in flower. In my garden *Tulipa tarda* is deep inside an old clump of bottlebrush buckeye and has been there for years.

Such plants succeed in visual association because they are, with all bulbs and corms, botanically monocotyledons. Relations — in the plant world, at least — usually get on well together. Some are likely, however, to lack that desirable character of permanence, and they often decline to a useless nonflowering state in two or three years. Everyone who grows the lovely little yellow *Iris danfordiae* understands this. The bulbs always break down after flowering, but we still buy the plant. Used with restraint this may not matter; the cost is not vast to add annually a few clumps of this or that to brighten a particular spot or to build up an especially felicitous combination at an important focal position. Deep planting may be an answer, even nine inches deep.

One further point. Bulbous plants are usually above ground for only four to five months of the year and for the first and last of these are visually no great shakes. What to do about that? Some combination with ground cover is obviously desirable, unless the garden is big enough for the area virtually to be avoided for half the year or unless in woodland proper the leaf-litter is of such quality as to be attractive in its own right.

Both the herbaceous and shrub lists in this book include suitable ground-cover plants for shade, but unless they are used only in their own right they should come into their full growth at a time when they are not in serious competition with the bulbs beneath. Winter aconite, flowering in February and March and virtually out of sight by May, when lily of the valley is at its first flush, is the sort of pairing to accomplish. Practice and observation will develop others. Now to the bulbs themselves.

Allium. The culinary arts would be utterly at a loss without onions, leeks, shallots, chives and garlic (some people might add "so much the better" to the last). In the garden, while not so vital, there are some highly ornamental species. Of these, without doubt the best are sun lovers. For our needs we must use those that flower the earliest, and as this is never before June, they can only be seen as being on the fringe of shady gardens. One of the very best in any site is A. *christopheri* (*albopilosum*) sometimes called stars of Persia.

   A six-inch sphere of pale-purple stars suddenly explodes eighteen inches (450 mm) above ground. After ten days of colour — lovely with grey leaves — the head, holding its shape and texture, begins to dry off, at which time it is fit to be cut and hung up for winter decorations months later. Do buy a half-dozen each year if it fails to be a perennial with you.

moly, the lily leek, is perfectly happy in a light shade and stays above ground longer. Its foot-high (300 mm) heads of yellow bells open in June above mid-blue-green leaves.

giganteum is another irresistible. Purple-headed drumsticks for the big bass drum tower up through lower things, five feet (1.5 m) high. Planted at the base of late-leafing subshrubs such as *Hibiscus palustris* and its new varieties, it gives interest to an area otherwise empty for much of the year. A. *aflatunense* is rather smaller and earlier but similar in effect. Another very lovely plant.

Anemone — See herbaceous list.

Arisaema — See herbaceous list.

Arisarum — See herbaceous list.

Arum — See herbaceous list.

Chionodoxa is aptly called glory of the snow, brilliant blue stars each with a white eye of which half-dozen are carried on each stem. The best is C. *luciliae*, another fine plant from Asia Minor, that epicentre of garden bulbs. Its pink forms are not as good. Similar are the scillas, of which S. *siberica* is the commonest and best. In dark woodland gardens of the Niagara Escarpment in Hamilton, Ontario, this little bulb spreads a deep-blue mantle across the leaf-litter in earliest spring.

(Spanish bluebell, incidentally, is still sometimes listed under scilla; see here *Endymion*.

Crocuses are among the most beloved of early spring bulbs. Not for evergreen shade, they must have sun for their flowers to expand, which they do each day (and close at night) in response to what they consider to be suitable pollinating weather. Why bother to open shop if the bees are not out with their pollen baskets?

But in grass under orchard fruit trees or lawn specimens the big Dutch hybrids are splendid, white, yellow and mauve, planted in sheets. Among the usual woodlanders or in shrub borders the small species are best, forms of *C. chrysanthus* and *C. tomasinianus*, which when suited spread both by seed and division of the corms in a most heartening fashion. All are lovely with the early-flowering heathers.

Cyclamen. Hardy cyclamen are one of the joys of the garden. It is impossible to have too many, and with a collection of the dozen or so species available, helped by a cool greenhouse, flowers are possible for most of the year. For shade we can try *C. coum* and its forms, in a carefully selected spot under a choice shrub — *Corylopsis*, perhaps, or *Corylus avellana* 'Contorta.' The cowslip yellow waves above the chubby pink and purple cyclamen flowers. When happy this little plant will seed itself around and appear in a surprising range of places.

hederifolium (neapolitanum). An extraordinarily nonchalant species from southern Europe. It produces its exquisite shuttlecock flowers, pink or white, from rock-hard ground in August and continues into October. The swelling seed capsules wind down to soil level on springlike stalks, and in mild areas the developing leaves, marbled green and grey, start to provide a winter-long carpet of quiet colour; attractive until May. Generally leafing has to wait till spring with us.

This is one of the few plants that one might put, with a clump or two of *Galanthus elwesii* and *Carex morrowii*, at the base of an important specimen lawn tree — just enough apart from each other to supply a few weeks of added interest where the bole meets the soil.

repandum. A woodland species with good marbled leaves and deep rose-pink flowers in May. Less easy to establish than the others.

All cyclamen, if bought as dry corms, should be planted in pots with a bit of peat or leaf-litter and the smooth side down to get them moving. Better still is to obtain pot-grown plants in leaf, or indeed grow one's own from seed. Flowering takes two to three years.

Endymion hispanicus is the Spanish bluebell. Like a hyacinth with widely spaced bells it can attain a couple of feet in height (600 mm). White and pink forms as well as the blue are common, and a dozen or two brought in will probably include them. All are lovely and easy in normal leafy soil. Real florists' hyacinths, though not for woodland (the proportion is all wrong) are the best bulbs for early colour in dark courtyards or in a little town front yard where no sun at all appears. They will be rather late but will still develop perfectly, form and scent unimpaired by an unprepossessing position. They will, however, need annual replacement – an entirely justifiable extravagance. Once flowered, bulbs can be replanted in rougher spots to recover gradually. Bulbs from pots indoors, having been kept frost-free while in leaf, should also not be rejected. An aid to garden furnishing.

Eranthis. The winter aconite, each golden buttercuplike flower surrounded by a choirboy's ruff of green, is one of the most heartening signs of earliest spring. In moist limy or lime-free woodland it carpets the ground, spreading out into grass. But it is resentful of cultivation above it and difficult to establish from dry tubers, as usually offered, unless bought in quantity with the expectation of a fifty percent failure rate. To beg a clump or two from a generous friend as it finishes flowering is the best way to get one's own winter aconite going. Lovely coming through an ivy or periwinkle ground cover under tall deciduous trees.

E. hyemalis is the usual, naturalized aconite. *E. cilicica* and the bispecific hybrid between the two (x *tubergenii*) have rather bigger flowers of greater substance.

Erythonium americanum is our exquisite trout lily, a joy in late April, when its marbled leaves unfold and the little stems push up their yellow lily flowers through the leaf-litter. Just below my house the valley sides are covered with this lovely plant, happy in the hideously heavy clay. In the garden similar shaded conditions are needed, but flowering can be erratic. The fine West Coast erythoniums flower more regularly but lack complete hardiness and like more sun. But they are worth trying, at least the pink *E. revolutum* and its robust form 'White Beauty.' The yellow Californian *E. tuolumnense* is also available, but for no more than half shade.

Galanthus. A woodland garden, or indeed any garden, without snowdrops hardly deserves the name. In mild areas flower is possible from October through to March, but the pre-Christmas species from Greece need more sun than woodland gives them and need not be considered here. Of the rest *G. nivalis* is *the* snowdrop, which has produced a range of variants whose most minuscule differences have been pounced upon with glad cries by galanthomaniacs. These often kind people are apt to pass on the disease with generous gifts of the plants that spread it. There is no known antidote.

The common snowdrop increases freely in both its double and single forms in moist woodland or under shrubs where excessive cultivations are eschewed. Where the broad effect is impossible, clumps of the bigger selected types are better: 'Magnet,' 'Atkinsii,' or 'Sam Arnott,' for instance. Their cost, if ever offered, may surprise the unprepared; catalogues should be read sitting down.

Other good species from southeast Europe prefer drier soil but still enjoy shade; they include G. *caucasicus* and the bright green-leaved G. *platyphyllus* (*ikariae latifolius*). Of these bigger species G. *elwesii* is perhaps the easiest, with wide greyish leaves and strong flowers six inches up.

Like aconites and cyclamen, snowdrops are best obtained growing "in the green," as it is described, and any moving done at home should be carried out *as soon as flowering is over.* Feeding snowdrops with bonemeal at this time and division of tight clumps every three or four years pays dividends.

Iris. The exquisite dwarf irises are plants of rocky hillsides in southern Europe and Asia Minor, where they often grow in the shade of thorny scrub — often the only place they are not chewed off by passing goats. While the latter hazard is fortunately not common in our gardens, the habitat can be copied. First to flower is the yellow *I. danfordiae*, only three or four inches high. Invariably the bulb breaks up after flowering, which deep planting in the early fall — at least eight inches — helps to prevent. This seems an extravagant depth for such a little bulb, but it does work. Hardly bigger is the clear blue *I. histrioides*, followed the *I. reticulata* group. All are around nine inches high and are deliciously scented of violets, whose colour also appears in the range in addition to pale blue ('Cantab') and deep purple ('J. S. Dijt').

The grassy leaves extend after flowering and the whole plant goes to rest by mid-June. Again deep planting encourages good bulb growth and keeps them out of the way of subsequent cultivation if, for example, some summer annuals are to be planted on top.

Leucojum. The snowflakes are less well-known than snowdrops, though the individual flowers are similar.

aestivum. The so-called summer snowflake in fact flowers in late May and early June, but its lush clumps of daffodillike leaves make it conspicuous much sooner. It is native to willow-shaded damp meadows in Europe but seems remarkably amenable to drier spots so long as it is protected from the sun. 'Gravetye' is a superior form. The much smaller species

L. vernum enjoys moist shade and flowers with the snowdrops, which it resembles. Here all six perianth segments are the same size, making a regular bell form, white with yellow tips.

Lilium. Most lilies are rather like *Clematis* in that they appreciate shade at the roots but enjoy bringing their heads into the sun. That, too, is how they look best. Sun, especially dappled sun, adds brilliance and a crystalline dimension to the petals.

It is not surprising that like roses certain lilies have been cultivated as objects of beauty, and also for use in religious celebrations, since earliest times. The Madonna lily shares with the rose the role of beauty's epitome.

There are some eighty wild species of lilies spread around the Northern Hemisphere. They differ so greatly in form and in cultivational requirements that it is not easy to devise any useful groupings. To some extent perhaps a simple geographical classification is a help, if only as an aide-mémoire. Unlike daffodils, hyacinths or tulips, the bulbs of lilies are without an enclosing tunic, being made up of overlapping scales like a loose globe artichoke. They thus desiccate quickly when out of the soil; also, roots never fully dry up at resting time. "Shelf-life" at a plant centre is thus distinctly limited. If ordered by post they must be planted as soon as received in the fall, usually October, but so long as a fork can be got into the ground anything is better than trying to overwinter them indoors. The bulbs are rock hardy.

For moist dappled shade several of our eastern North American lilies are the best. Again, in our Royal Botanical Gardens' valleys grow fine stands of *Lilium canadense* ssp. *michiganense*, marvelous, seven foot high (2 m) stems holding a dozen or more orange-scarlet turkscaps in July. The Canada lily itself is yellow, while *L. superbum*, the North American turkscap, is a further variation on the theme.

European lilies include several small flowered turkscaps, of which *L. martagon*, deep purple or white, is the easiest, very happy in deciduous woodland. Similar but only half the height is the yellow *L. pyrenaicum*.

Of the Oriental species both *L. auratum* (the golden-rayed lily of Japan) and *L. speciosum* offer late-season pleasures. Both like half shade and prefer acid soil.

While this mentions only a small proportion of wild species lilies, there are even more hybrids available in a vast range of colours, sizes and shapes. In general they are happier in sun. All are beautiful and one must go to the gardens with collections to pick out one's favourite and then hope the nursery lists stock them. With careful choice, sufficient space and a deep enough pocket lilies may be had in flower from June to October inclusive.

One final plant must be mentioned. The lovely Madonna lily, L. *candidum*, is a mysterious plant of highly erratic preferences. Often seen best in old farm gardens in full sun in a row in the vegetable garden, at Highdown near Worthing in England it succeeded best in shade — perhaps slightly embarrassed by the grand company it kept there. Usually, like the other Europeans, it prefers lime, but then one will suddenly see successful groups in acid soil in Scotland. It is all very confusing. If good stock can be obtained one must just experiment. It is worth every effort. One thing is certain, it is not like other lilies. Coming into growth in late summer and with overwintering leaves it must be planted in August at the latest.

The Cascade strain is now available with bigger, longer-lasting flowers and seems less prone to the debilitating virus that is the scourge of lilies.

Muscari. Even the commonest grape hyacinth is not a plant for deep shade. There the already long leaves become etiolated and the flower spikes reduce proportionately. Yet on the edge of shrub plantings they can be a great success. Leafing begins as early as September, while the clear-blue flowers do not follow until April. They increase easily. M. *armeniacum* is still one of the best, not improved in double forms.

Narcissus. If there is one plant that needs no description it is *Narcissus.* Daffodils, beloved by all, flower in every garden from window box to country estates and are grown by the acre as cut flowers for several months on end. Only their diversity and use need comment here.

There are between twenty and thirty wild species of *Narcissus*, spread about Europe and extending into North Africa. Several interbreed in the wild and in cultivation the genus has been the subject of intense hybridization. Many hundreds of resultant cultivars have been named.

With such a wide natural distribution it is obvious that not all are suitable for our general needs in the shady garden; some of the oldest are. *Narcissus pseudonarcissus* is the lovely little Lent lily of deciduous woodlands of southern England and France. It is the typical daffodil and a parent of the majority of later forms. Several closely related species and primary hybrids such as the old N. x *incomparabilis* (with N. *poeticus*), named by Philip Miller in the mid-eighteenth century, are entirely suitable.

Following these, over the past two centuries diversity of shape, length of trumpet (or none — the old cottage garden double yellow is illustrated in Gerard's *Herbal* of 1597 and with a whole page of distinct forms in Parkinson's *Paradisus* thirty years later) colour and size have been sought. In general all are happy in the part shade of shrubs and deciduous trees and in old orchard grass. Benefiting noticeably from application of a foliar feed to the leaves after flowering, they go from strength to strength year after year. There are few more beautiful sights than long-established daffodils under the soft pink and white of apple trees in flower. The effect appears utterly uncontrived and natural, as indeed it should.

In spite of this, choice of cultivar needs a moment's thought. In the search for further diversity hybridists have brought in colours that, though exquisite in themselves, no longer associate so easily in the woodland garden. Those with vivid orange and scarlet cups should be kept away from the blue-pink of early rhododendrons and heathers flowering at the same time; palest yellows and creams are the choice here. Similarly in small gardens the biggest trumpet cultivars are best replaced by smaller, lighter forms, which usually have a bit of N. cyclamineus or N. triandrus in them. 'February Gold,' 'Peeping Tom' and 'Thalia' are fine examples. For garden effect it is always better to plant numbers, relative to the area concerned, of few types rather than a kaleidoscopic mixture of many.

It might just be mentioned in passing that bargain offers for "naturalizing" of daffodil bulbs that have been forced for flower are just those least able to cope with the competition of orchard grass. If they are to be bought, and bargains are as irresistible as temptations, they should be planted in nursery rows for a year or two to build up strength and size.

Daffodils do not take kindly to annual lifting, drying off and replanting. It is an onerous chore about which many people complain − yet still they do it. It should be emphasized that if left alone, daffodil bulbs are dormant for a very short time in summer. A bulb lifted in August will already have started to push out roots, and this indicates that they need a long season for proper growth if the plants are to be considered true perennials.

Thus one should plant early (certainly in September), deep (the top of the bulb at least six inches below soil surface) and for permanence; ground-cover plants or even summer annuals can grow on top of them. One further point if the latter activity is followed: the young annuals can be planted between the declining daffodil foliage, which should not be removed until yellow or be either tied or plaited into tidy knots. There must be better ways to spend one's gardening time.

These last rather tetchy remarks can be taken also to apply to tulips. Planting can be later − up to November − but depths ideally need to be more, the tips of the bulb eight inches down, if they are to be left in situ, building up strength and beauty form year to year. Only when tulips are a consciously sequential part of seasonal bedding do they need the labour-some plant − and − lift syndrome. And certainly in the informality of the woodland garden this can be avoided.

The big hybrid tulips, the Darwins, Parrots and Triumphs, are of course not for us; they are already too tall and generally too late to benefit from light preleafing conditions under deciduous trees. But several low wild tulip species are ideal.

The earliest to flower have a starry flower pattern almost like those of crocuses and indeed are not much bigger. But the petals have a brilliance and sheen that is all their own. *Tulipa tarda* has already been mentioned. *T. urumiensis*, yellow with bronze backs to the petals, is similar. Several are brilliant scarlet, such as *T. linifolia, batalinii* and *praestans*, the latter with several flowers to each stem. For sheer size of flower nothing compares with the eye-stopping *T. fosterana* 'Red Emperor.' Best kept away from the small spring bulbs that might well refuse to open in the presence of such flamboyance. I grow a big bed of these with lambs-ears under an old yellowwood tree, an association that has gone on happily for years.

Other early dwarfs are the waterlily tulip *T. kaufmanniana* and *T. greigii* (with marvellously striped leaves), both of which come from high inhospitable hillsides in Turketstan. Both are delightful in their own right, and in recent years a dazzling range of colours has been produced. Some are a bit fierce to associate with the gentler woodlanders, but cultivationally they accept the conditions because the early-spring sun gets to them when they need it. This is the secret, though an open secret, to successful woodland gardening.

Ferns for Shade

It is no exaggeration to add a word to "Ferns for Shade" and write "Ferns Are for Shade." This is quite true, mainly because ferns are, by comparison with all the other plants discussed in this book, evolutionarily more primitive. They are nearer the beginning of that classic struggle in which, starting with simple algae in water hundreds of millions of years ago, the plant kingdom began to colonize dry land. Gradually more highly developed plants evolved; ancestors of mosses and liverworts first and eventually the flowering plants as we know them, each group and each species perfectly adapted, as we have seen with regard to shade, to a particular ecological niche.

Evolutionarily it seems that ferns take a place between the Thallophytes (mosses and liverworts) and the Spermatophytes, the seed-bearing plants, their closest relationships perhaps being with conifers and cycads, the simplest Spermatophytes. The full group is known as pteridophytes, and includes not just recognizable ferns but fern allies — the selaginellas, club mosses and equisetums. None of these are likely to be chosen as garden plants. The last named are the horsetails, often extremely persistent noxious weeds. (This is a pity: *E. telmateia*, the greater horsetail, is an extremely beautiful plant for moist shade but runs for miles underground and is apt to get completely out of control. Fortunately Roundup has been invented.)

The point that is being made about the relatively primitive origin of ferns is that in becoming able to succeed in drier and drier conditions, plants have had to develop organs and techniques to avoid desiccation. One such development is a cuticle, a "skin," of varying thickness on the surfaces of leaves, which prevents or helps to reduce water loss. This is of course especially necessary for plants growing in full sun.

176

Although in evolutionary terms they have come a long way from algae and, with their highly effective conducting tissues not far short of conifers, have gone a long way toward the seed-bearing plants, they are still very dependent upon moisture availability.

This dependence is double-edged. Lack of a fully effective cuticle means that even mature fern plants dry up and die more quickly if sufficient moisture is not available from the soil; it also means that atmospheric humidity is important, and that in turn means shade as a desideratum of successful cultivation for most of them.

There is another aspect in which ferns are utterly moisture-dependent and this is in their reproduction. In the garden we are usually happy to increase ferns by division, which is just as well, because their sexual method is a decidedly complicated one.

Ferns, we observe, do not flower but bear, usually under their fronds (leaves), bars or spots of darker tissue that eventually produce dustlike spores (lay a mature fern frond on white paper overnight and a perfect pattern of the spore-producing sori is reproduced by next morning). If spores are sown a new fern plant does not develop, for these are not seeds, product of sexual fusion. Germination of a spore in moisture and shade produces a tiny liverwortlike plate of green tissue, the prothallus. This in turn eventually develops male and female sexual organs, and motile spermatozoids from the former swim to fertilize the latter. Only now does a first little recognizable fern frond develop as a start toward the plant we know and wish to grow. This pattern of a leafy asexual plant and tiny sexual prothallus is known as the "alternation of generations."

The significance of all this is obvious: ferns are very moisture-dependent. Ferns are for shade. Throughout the world there are around ten thousand different species of ferns, with their greatest concentration in the forested montane areas of the humid tropics. Here they are often epiphytic. In temperate areas wild ferns are usually terrestrial, but still almost always woodland plants. (Bracken is a fine open-ground exception, but no one is likely to recommend it for garden cultivation!) The visual range is considerable: some are deciduous, others evergreen; all are elegant in pattern — 'ferny,' 'fernlike' are frequent and very clear complimentary adjectives that we use about many other plants. It should be emphasized that "asparagus fern" is certainly not a true fern but a lily relation.

In spite of this obvious emphasis upon moisture, a few worthwhile species can succeed in dry shade. (The smallest ferns like lip-fern, wall-rue and rusty-back, however, which colonize rock crevices and can retire into a state of semiquiescence in dry periods, are not listed here, though they are charming for rock gardens.) Both the lady fern and male fern will take dry shade during summer, but it is important that they have had adequate moisture in spring, when their fronds are developing. Without this, though the plants survive, growth is apt to be stunted and the plants lack that essential air of green well-being that is so important a part of their beauty.

In the following select list only those ferns likely to be available from the trade are included, though there is no doubt that many good plants, especially from Japan and possibly New Zealand's South Island, have yet to be introduced to our gardens and there are more good natives un-used. Similarly, though a few are still offered, mention is made here only in passing of the mutant forms with cristate or differently divided fronds that were once so keenly collected. The phrase "the Victorian fern craze" (using David Allen's book title) admirably sums up the intense interest in fern growing in the middle years of the last century, when the search for variants became an avid occupation especially, it seems, in England for reverend gentlemen and ladies of gentle birth. Moore and Lindley's great folio tome of British ferns (1854) describes in detail seventeen distinct forms of common polypody and the fourteen male fern types and exquisitely illustrates most of them. The majority of these are now lost to us, yet no doubt a renaissance in pteridomania would find replacements.

Meanwhile here are some basic species. All are lovely plants to give that lushness that is an expected part of the shady garden.

Adiantum. Of two hundred lovely maidenhair ferns strewn around the world only one is native to our area and hence definitely hardy; it comes from moist May-apple and trillium woods. But it would also be worth attempting the European maidenhair. This is

capillus-veneris 1 x 1 ft. (300 x 300 mm) A typically delicate plant for the sort of sheltered shady nook that suits *Begonia grandis* (*evansiana*). Such a combination in a courtyard corner gives the impression of a Wardian case with the lid off.

pedatum 1½ x 1 ft. (450 x 300 mm) Our wildling has longer, narrower pinnae, pink when young, on wiry black stems. Another lovely plant for a sheltered spot. The adiantums are delicate plants both in appearance and in constitution and cannot take much competition from more robust things.

Asplenium scolopendrium. The European Hart's tongue fern is one of the most striking foliage plants for shade. To see it lining the steep banks of a sunken Devon lane is to realize its ornamental value. The long evergreen leaves growing in a shuttlecock are barred with sori on the reverse like a mackerel's back. Sufficiently vigorous in most shade to compete and contrast with hostas and astilbes, yet unlike them also offering good winter effect in mild areas. Where this is not permitted, fine new fronds appear in spring. Forms with fingered tips are not an improvement.

Athyrium filix-foemina. The lady fern of our woodlands is a distinguished plant. Not unlike the male fern but, as its pre-women's lib name suggests, more elegant, lacelike and altogether more desirable. Geographical forms vary in size and not surprisingly in hardiness.

goeringianum pictum, the Japanese painted fern, is a related species of extraordinary beauty; though capable of attaining the lady fern's two feet (600 mm) or so, it is apt to be less. The delicate fronds are truly silver, flushed with the dark-pink colour of the midribs. This is a plant to build a small garden picture around, arranging that it gets a gleam of late sun, though in moist shade for the rest of the day.

Cystopteris bulbifera. A pretty little running fern with pale fronds. Good under small rhododendrons with purple prunella and other small ground huggers. Known also from Newfoundland southward as berry bladderfern, this name refers to the little golden bulbils carried on the underside of the fronds. These drop off to form new plants. For moist soil only.

Dryopteris. A big genus of confusing origins and nomenclature offering several lovely garden plants.

austriaca. Dark in colour and spreading in habit, the shield fern has usually two-foot-long fronds, though geographical variants (it is native to most of the Northern Hemisphere) and frond forms exist in a range of sizes. There is lots of nomenclatural synonymy here.

erythrosora is the Japanese shield fern. The doubly divided fronds are about one and a half feet (450 mm) long with distinctive crimson sori (the spore-bearing organs) on the undersides. This charming Oriental is evergreen in most areas.

felix-mas. Here is a species that seems to accept what for ferns is the generally unacceptable: dry shade. Certainly the fronds are finer in good conditions, but so long as a reasonable start is given in spring to the first flush of growth, it will maintain itself in remarkably good heart throughout the summer. A common but very worthwhile plant, lovely with foxgloves in a woodland glade. Native here as well as in European woods, it can make a great starfish of fronds five feet (1.5 m) across.

Matteucia struthiopteris. The ostrich plume fern is native to Europe and Asia (our native M. *pensylvanica* is very similar but possibly more up-right in growth). It is one of the most lovely ferns for moist shade, with its fresh green shuttlecocks in spring. These darken with the summer, browning pleasantly in autumn and leaving, for winter effect, the dark antler-velvet fertile fronds standing stiffly erect until the following spring starts the cycle again. These are apt not to last if flowers arrangers are let loose. Height with us is usually toward three feet (1 m) or so, but it may exceed this if happy.

Onoclea sensibilis. The name sensitive fern leads the hopeful to expect the waved pale-green fronds to collapse at the touch of a finger like the leaves of *Mimosa pudica.* Sadly the only fingers to be effective are those of Jack Frost, whose lightest breath is enough to send the plant to rest for the winter. When really happy in moist woodland *Onoclea* reaches two and a half feet and can be quite invasive, but beautifully so. Often it shares woodland bogs with skunk cabbage, turning a dark glade to an emerald carpet in high summer. The effect is strangely tropical.

Osmunda offers three native ferns of great garden presence; though de-ciduous, the fronds are often sufficiently stiff and vertically held when dead that winter texture remains, changing with frost and snow.

cinnamomea known by gardeners as cinnamon fern (referring to the colour of the fronds in fall) but by cooks as fiddleheads. A fine upright plant is produced (if not eaten to death) with spires of brown fertile fronds in the centre, giving a most statuesque effect. A group of cinna-mon fern erupting from a carpet of lily of the valley in moist shade is a dramatic sight.

claytoniana is the interrupted fern native here (and also consumed). I have also found the same plant at twelve thousand feet (4,000 m), in the western Himalayas. A fine four-footer, the pinnae (leaflets) near the base of the frond can be either sterile or spore producing, the latter brown, and hence the interruption to the normally architectural exactness of most fern fronds.

regalis. Royal fern is the grandest of all and a marvellous moist shade plant, even with its feet in water. It makes a five-foot-high clump, like a huge maidenhair, some of whose fronds produce warm rust-brown sporing heads. The fibrous rootstock chopped fine used to be essential part of composts for growing tropical orchids. It is still valuable, just difficult to get, and one is loath to dig up one's own garden plant to grow something no more beautiful.

Polystichum. In this genus are some of the loveliest ferns we can grow and certainly the best of the evergreen species.

acrosticoides and *munitum* are from eastern and western North America respectively, and known as Christmas ferns or sword ferns. The latter is bigger — lovely with snowdrops clustering around its base — and some selections are just as hardy.

However, if our East Coast native is the only one available, snap it up and plant extravagantly to maintain some summer green amid the winter snow. Fronds can be a couple of feet in length.

Europe's shield ferns are hardly less beautiful and as easily grown. *P. setiferum* survives in old cottage gardens there when almost everything else, often the cottage itself, has been overwhelmed with willowherb and brambles. Wide-spreading, soft-scale-covered fronds are beautiful from the moment they unfold until the following year's growth replaces them; lovely against steps. But like *Epimedium* this moment of seasonal change should be watched for and the old fronds cut away to give the new ones their day. Some ferns bear bulbils and a pegged-down frond roots along its length to make increase easy; often the bulbil types are even more divided in the leaf and are particularly fine. They should be sought out. They are wider than high, two by three feet (600 x 900 mm) perhaps.

Thelypteris palustris is the marsh fern. Bright yet pale-green fronds appear from a running (but not aggressive — well, not very) rootstock; it is good in moist soil under calcifuge shrubs. Downy wood fern, snuffbox fern and meadow fern all come into this group. Charming plants all.

Annuals for Shade

There is no doubt that for those whose idea of gardening is limited in the Northeast to May-to-September activities, the shady garden leaves much to be desired. It lacks sun and therefore it lacks the annual bedding-plant binge to which so many people seem indissolvably wedded. Shady gardens may make one think a bit harder, but at least they prevent the all too common dreary syndrome that rejects as if it did not exist rather more than half the year.

And for those who spend much of their summers at a country cottage, it is even more of a nonsense; one is not around to enjoy the best of the colour and just worries from a distance whether the arrangements made for watering the wretched plants are working according to plan. In this context there is much to be said for a garden in sun or shade that concentrates on spring and early-summer perennials and shrubs with others to light up the autumn. Gay high-summer annuals (which even the most purist plantsman would not entirely reject) are then used in two or three important focal points — in the ground or in containers — for which trickle irrigation can be arranged. But this is not to promote such a rigid alternative that, just because in our native woodlands floral display ends as summer begins, the same should apply in wooded gardens.

On the contrary, if we are at home we want colour. And it is entirely possible so long as it is realized that the majority of summer annuals are inveterate sun worshippers. Marigolds from Mexico, South African geraniums and most of the garden-centre favourites will just not perform: leaf is produced at the expense of flower. The effect is not worth the effort. Obviously success can only be achieved by using those species that are evolutionarily programmed to complete their life cycles without full sun.

Even then care must be given to providing adequate summer moisture. Under the canopy of trees, rain is deflected and what reaches the ground is eagerly sought for by their questing roots, though the typical woodland perennials and bulbs are going to rest and are no longer competitors. Left by itself, the top few inches of soil can be dust dry: however, water applied beneath the canopy is at least not immediately evaporated by a burning sun and the young plants begin to benefit. In the shade of uncompetitive buildings, of course, they do even better.

There is still the decision to make as to how best supplement the permanent plants. Many, such as the ferns, maintain summer foliage, and indeed their cool greenness is a major pleasure when days are hot and humid. It must be accepted that a blaze of colour is neither possible nor even desirable. Spots need to be chosen where the effect is most noticed — from windows of the house, around a patio or sitting area — and there it must be concentrated.

The list, then, of bright summer annuals for shade is very short (as has been explained, the pattern of our deciduous woodland canopy development is such that there are no native annuals in these sites) and depends upon a mere half-dozen species and their hybrids. Of these three are tropical perennials that, started early enough from seed under glass, are happy enough in a hot summer outside. Begonia, impatiens and *Vinca rosea* are the staple fare for summer shade. Fortunately the prodigious efforts of plant breeders over the years have so extended their range in size, flower and leaf colour and habit that it is difficult to accept that so few original wild species are involved.

Begonia semperflorens — *cultorum* is the fibrous-rooted or wax begonia; the middle part of its botanical name describes its value to us — literally ever flowering. This is true; once started, so long as water and heat are adequate the plants are never without flowers, a wonderful attribute. The original wild species that makes up this group come from the eastern side of South America, from Colombia down to Argentina, with Brazil being central to their distribution.

Begonia has among the smallest seeds known, with about two million seeds to the ounce: a much better plant for the parable of the mustard seed, had it been known in first century Palestine.

Wax begonias cannot be planted out until all danger of frost is passed; this of course is a variable feast depending upon one's own area and microclimate. It also depends upon the ground being available and warm enough to ensure ongoing growth. A late, wet spring is anathema to these topicals.

For late-May planting, seed has to be sown in January. Raising begonias from seed is not difficult so long as minimum temperatures of 70°F (21°C) until germination and 65°F (18°C) can be maintained. A light peaty compost is used and the dustlike seed is barely covered with gritty sand. When they emerge the seedlings more resemble moss or liverwort than a flowering plant and need to be pricked out into trays as soon as they are big enough to handle. Half-strength, then full-strength soluble fertilizer is given weekly to keep them moving. Once they start to meet in the trays they are then best transferred into single pots. In this way they can be kept growing for weeks until the weather is fit or their place ready.

Clearly the whole process is a laboursome one and not without snags unless greenhouse or light-bench conditions are good. A good alternative is to come in at the penultimate act, to buy a flat or two of young plants and then pot them up. Individual care even on windowsills ensures good strong plants that are put out without root damage. These will give the quickest and longest effect in the garden.

Colours in fibrous-rooted begonias range from pure white through all shades of pink to bright scarlet. Every flower, made up of two large and two small petals, has a central boss of yellow stamens. This shows up best in the paler shades, which also display a crystalline sheen that the reds seem to lack.

The bigger seed firms list over thirty different cultivars varying not only in flower but leaf colour, which can be pale green or deepest bronze; mature plants can be six inches (16 cm) to almost twice that in height.

When using begonias to give summer colour to shaded areas in which spring bulbs or woodland perennials are permanently planted it is usually best to keep to the green-leaved forms with white or pale-pink flowers. Pockets of soil can be loosened among the declining foliage of the early things and the young begonias can go in to take over the space as it becomes available. In this way there is little obvious gap between the seasons and between the very different plant regimes.

The brighter and bronze-leaved forms are more suited to conscious bedding schemes closer to the house, where their visual sophistication seems more at home. These are the spots, too, for big-flowered tuberous-rooted begonias. Here several Andean species have been used, by hybridization and selection, to produce an extraordinary range of colours. Only the blues and purples are missing from the otherwise complete spectrum.

Though the tuberous begonias are often grown as annuals from seeds as described above for their fibrous-rooted cousins, it is also convenient to obtain dried tubers. These are started into growth in flats of peaty compost. Warmth and moisture are of course mandatory, but as the tuber is essentially a mature plant at rest, it is not necessary to begin the process until well into spring, when suitable temperatures are easier to maintain.

The usual types, with their heavy camellialike flowers, are easily knocked down by summer rains and although widely used as open groundbedding plants seem to me better employed in containers. These and the cascade types of tuberous begonias for hanging baskets are splendid on shady patios and under vine-wreathed loggias and give a wonderfully concentrated floral effect for four summer months.

Begonias are only excelled as annuals for shade by the brilliance of Zanzibar balsam, *Impatiens wallerana*. Under the old name of busy Lizzie this fleshy-stemmed two-footer has been a front-room window plant for a couple of centuries, but suddenly, in the past twenty years the plant breeders have changed it out of all recognition to the plant grown by the acre today. Again, like begonia, here is a perennial treated as an annual. Seed is sown, uncovered, during the second half of February in a temperature of 21°C (70°F), and ensuring that sudden sunshine does not burn these shade lovers, the plants are grown on until frost-free nights are certain outside. To ensure good plants for planting out, they are best potted individually for the last two or three weeks of their indoor life, as with begonias, and kept as described above. This is a critical time that affects the first month or more of the garden display.

If moisture is provided, *Impatiens* (or patience plant, patient Lucy or sultana) will flower throughout the summer in the darkest situations. At Royal Botanical Gardens we grow great ribbons of impatiens under high dark trees and swathes of it around the architectural trunks of old mugo pines. The effect is magical. Some years colours are kept separate; in others we use one of the mixtures, bright as confetti, in these difficult spots.

In my own garden I prefer, as with begonias, to keep the brilliant colours close to the house and plant white and pale-pink types with their fresh green foliage among the declining bulbs and woodlanders under the distant trees.

Here they happily associate with ferns and astilbes to maintain the cool effect that we crave in the steamy July days.

Each seed house has its own range and the choice is enormous, with a dozen or so colour variants being offered within each "series," the latter word indicating parental origins with constant habit and height. It is best not to mix plants of different series. Obviously one's local garden centre will not offer every type, but still, colours should range from white through all the pinks to orange and pale purple; bicolors also exist, as do doubles and those with variegated foliage.

It must be emphasized that begonias and impatiens planted in the shade of trees must be given adequate moisture and feeding if this season-through potential is to be fulfilled. It is a waste of the initial investment of time and money not to. One further point: as both genera are perennial, they can be propagated easily by cuttings. If plants get leggy in their pots before being planted out they must have their tips pinched out. These will root easily in water and bought-in stock is quickly doubled. Similarly at the end of summer cuttings can be rooted and a nucleus stock overwintered indoors. These are the most adaptable of plants.

Mimulus is the monkey flower or musk flower. Sadly, for nearly three-quarters of a century the latter name has been without justification: *Mimulus moschatus* is a West Coast foxglove relation that became a favourite Victorian house plant because of its wide-mouthed mottled yellow flowers and musklike scent. Then, around 1914, the scent was lost in cultivated forms, and in spite of searching, no wild musky mimulus could be found. We are left with monkey flower, which fortunately has enough visual attraction to maintain its garden place. Breeding new selections has give us what is usually listed as *Mimulus hybridus* (M. *tigrinus* is the same thing), a splendid little annual for moist shady positions. Mixtures only are offered; flowers in shades of yellow, bronze and red, striped and spotted like so many barred butterflies.

Seed is sown at the beginning of February at a temperature of 21°C (70°F); the usual greenhouse treatment gives fine plants to put out in May. Later sowings can take place under glass or even directly outside in May, so long as moist soil conditions are maintained. A packet of seed can be scattered very thinly among the dying foliage of spring bulbs with a little mixed peat and sand sieved over the top and watered. This gives a late-summer show.

Torenia fournieri is an attractive annual from tropical Vietnam, sometimes called wishbone flower or bluewings. Another foxglove relation, it was for ages a somewhat esoteric pot plant for botanical gardens. However, it has been shown to perform well outside from a March sowing indoors where summers are warm.

It makes a bushy upright plant a foot or so high and is admirable in clumps in a shady border. Unlike the spreading annuals so far described, *Torenia* has more leaf and "weight" and is thus better placed in its own right rather than as a filler. The pale-blue, purple-cheeked flowers are rather like snapdragons of the most unlikely colour. The white form is not an improvement.

The last player in this quartet of annuals for shade is another tropical perennial, this time from Madagascar and southern India. It came nameless to England in the 1750s from the Paris *Jardin des Plantes* (Madagascar then being a French possession). It was recognized as a periwinkle, and the great Swedish botanist Linnaeus called it *Vinca rosea*, or pink periwinkle; it is still under this name that it is generally found in the seed lists (encyclopedias use the now botanically correct *Catharanthus*).

Seed is sown from mid-February in a temperature of 27°C (80°F) and the seedlings moved on as growth permits. Madagascar periwinkle is very slow growing when young and seedlings are apt to just sit and sulk, particularly if the compost gets overwet. Planting out takes place only after all chance of frost is passed. Half shade is the most satisfactory in well-drained soil, where a season-long display will be maintained.

The original wild plant is an open two-foot bush with flat pink flowers, but recent selective breeding has given dwarfer, bushier forms with a number of colour forms. Clear rose-pink and white exist, with or without a contrasting eye of the other colour. What remains constant is the glossy foliage and the rotate corolla, typical of all periwinkles. A couple of plants may be lifted toward the end of the season to continue their role as house plants. Cuttings from these may then be taken the following spring instead of starting anew from seed.

While the above make up the main quartet of annuals for shade, other fine plants are happy not to have a full place in the sun. The pink and purple forms of sweet alyssum and the clear-blue lobelias are old-fashioned plants that have been used for a century or more in cottage gardens. There the typical tumble of plants accepted these little carpeters, just as we can today.

It will be noticed that no annual daisy plants have been recommended for shade. Indeed they are typical sun lovers, and those that open and close their flowers like gazanias just shut up shop completely. Nothing could be less useful. One exception is the little Mexican *Sanvitalia procumbens*. Like a dwarf, spreading zinnia it is covered with dime-sized daisies, light or dark yellow, each with a black eye. Here is a plant that is new to all but the most specialist seed lists and one that is demonstrating that it can move into shadier areas without loss of quality.

This will undoubtedly be the case with other summer annuals. And, it must be repeated, each garden and each site within the garden is different. The question must be continually asked, then answered by observation: How dark, how light is this spot? Does it get some sun in the morning or later on? Only then can the diversity of plants be suitably exploited.

One further dimension exists in shade-accepting annuals, and this is with foliage plants. In Royal Botanical Gardens' famous display rock garden a lot of coleus are used under trees to replace May-flowering tulips. Although the mixed forms grow happily enough, the best effect comes from golden or other pale-leaved types, which lighten up dark corners wonderfully. With a rich soil and copious watering great leafy clumps of foliage are quickly built up.

Many of our conventional house plants are happy with poor light conditions — they have to be, indeed. But few are so easily propagated and quickly growing as to make their use outside very feasible. A splendid exception is *Caladium*, an aroid. Another is the spider plant, *Chlorophytum*, which produces young tufts of leaves on its flowering branches.

These root readily and one can quickly build up a couple of dozen young plants. The tussocks of white-and-green-striped leaves are equally effective as edging in formal bedding schemes or used to bulk up permanent planting in a shady border. But their best effect is in urns or tubs, where by midsummer a cascade of leaves and young plantlets tumbles forward, dramatic in their own right and superb as a foil to the bigger impatiens or begonias.

In this context of container plants in the shade it is worth emphasizing that in our climate there is nothing that many of our house plants enjoy more than spending the summer outdoors. We, most of us, know the feeling. Having spent something of a troglodytic winter, they cannot take full sunlight or fierce winds — they burn and scorch at once — but this is where the shady courtyard, the room outside, is invaluable. Fine groups, therefore, of *Ficus benjamina* and *Dieffenbachia* can be put together to give the visual tropical effect that our July and August temperatures and humidity can warrant.

The foliage specimens can be enlivened around their bases with begonias and other brilliant annuals that would be impossible indoors. As gardeners, too, we are bound (rather like the fashion designers) to be planning for a future season. This is the moment to buy house plants "on special offer" and grow them on until, as true tropicals, they have to move indoors in late September.

Other house plants need a summer holiday for another reason; potted azaleas and clivias are building up their flower buds for next winter's display and the convenience of watering and feeding in the shaded courtyard is a major aid to their success. These should be left out until the last possible minute — a degree or two of frost will not hurt — until the very last day of an Indian summer.

This is the time, too, before it is all just a memory beneath the winter snow, to take stock of the shady garden. What, this year, was the greatest success? We must do it again. What disappointed? Why? Now is the time to plan, to order new plants, to read books. In spite of all appearances to the contrary, spring and another year of garden pleasures will come.

Bibliography

Gardening in the Shade, H. K. Morse, Scribners, 1962

Herbs in the Garden, Allen Paterson, Dent, 1985

Hortus III, Bailey Hortorium staff, Macmillan, 1976

Manual of Woody Landscape Material, M. Dirr, Stipes Publishing Co., revised ed. 1977

Perennials, P. Harper and F. M. McGowthy, HP Books, 1985

R.H.S. Dictionary, Royal Horticultural Society, Ed. P. M. Synge, 2nd Edition, Oxford, 1956

Successful Gardening in the Shade, H. van P. Wilson, Doubleday, 1974

Trilliums of Ontario, J. S. Pringle, Royal Botanical Gardens, 1984

The Victorian Fern Craze, David Allen, Hutchinson, 1969

Index

191